THE DEAD SEA SCROLLS

*This book is
dedicated to the
Army Chaplains
who ran on
Exercise
Millennium
Pilgrim in the
Holy Land.*

THE

DEAD SEA SCROLLS

and the Jewish Origins of

CHRISTIANITY

Carsten Peter Thiede

palgrave

for St. Martin's Press

First published 2001 by
PALGRAVE™
175 Fifth Avenue, New York, N.Y. 10010
Companies and representatives throughout the world.

PALGRAVE is the new global publishing imprint of St. Martin's Press LLC
Scholarly and Reference Division and Palgrave Publishers Ltd.
(formerly Macmillan Press Ltd.).

Acknowledgments
The scripture quotations contained herein are from The Revised Standard Version of the Bible, copyright © 1946, 1952, 1971 by the Division of Christian Education of the National Council of the Churches of Christ in the United States of America, and are used by permission. All rights reserved. The scripture quotations contained herein are from The New Revised Standard Version of the Bible, Anglicized Edition, copyright © 1989, 1995 by the Division of Christian Education of the National Council of the Churches of Christ in the United States of America, and are used by permission. All rights reserved.

New English Bible copyright © 1961, 1970 by Oxford University Press and Cambridge University Press.
Scripture quotations taken from the New Jerusalem Bible, published and copyright © 1985 by Darton, Longman and Todd Ltd and les Editions du Cerf, and by Doubleday, a division of Bantam Doubleday Dell Publishing Group, Inc. Used by permission of Darton, Longman and Todd Ltd, and Doubleday, a division of Random House, Inc.

Scripture quotations taken from the *Holy Bible: New International Version*, copyright © 1973, 1978, 1984 by International Bible Society. Used by permission of Hodder & Stoghton Limited. All rights reserved. 'NIV' is a registered trademark of International Bible Society. UK trademark number 1448790.

ISBN 0-312-29361-5

Library of Congress Cataloging-in-Publication Data available at the Library of Congress.

First published in Great Britain by Lion Publishing plc

First PALGRAVE edition: September 2001
10 9 8 7 6 5 4 3 2 1

Printed in the United States of America.

Contents

Acknowledgments

A book on the Dead Sea Scrolls cannot be written without support and advice from many quarters. Tens of thousands of learned and less learned articles and hundreds of books have been published on the scrolls since 1947, and no single scholar can keep abreast of them all. I am deeply grateful to colleagues and friends who have encouraged and challenged me in my pursuit of fresh insights – Joe Zias in Jerusalem, Jim Charlesworth in Princeton and Chaim Noll in Beer-Sheva above all. At the Israel Antiquities Authority in Jerusalem, Pnina Shor and Ruta Peled have supported my confocal laser scanning research of the scrolls from the beginning, a fruitful cooperation which will continue with a new microscope just installed at the John Rockefeller Museum. Jan Gunneweg of the Hebrew University, Jerusalem, has generously helped with unpublished information on his Neutron Activation Analysis of Qumran pottery. In the still highly controversial area of the fragments from Cave 7, constant encouragement has come from Shemaryahu Talmon of the Hebrew University, Jerusalem, and I am particularly grateful to scholars who have recently corroborated José O'Callaghan's and my own work on 7Q4 and 7Q5 – above all Karl Jaroš and Herbert Hunger in Vienna, Heiki Koskenniemi in Turku, Orsolina Montevecchi in Milan, Ory Mazar in Jerusalem, Joan M. Vernet at Cremisan, Bethlehem, and Ferdinand Rohrhirsch in Eichstätt. This book would not have seen the light of day without the patient perseverance of Maurice Lyon at Lion Publishing, Oxford. It is dedicated to the Army Chaplains whom I joined on Exercise Millennium Pilgrim in the Holy Land, in November and December 1999, remembering the time we spent in the places where the scrolls were written, read and studied 2,000 years ago.

CARSTEN PETER THIEDE

Introduction

The Dead Sea Scrolls are famous. But what are they famous for? For the alleged attempts of the churches to hide the truth about them from the general public? For the so-called insights they provide into the origins of Christianity as a far-from-original copycat movement split from the Essenes – as certain authors and their eager followers have tried to tell a gullible public? For their secret messages about people from the early church, like James and Paul, as conspiracy theorists want us to believe? For the fact that they are the only surviving Jewish manuscript library of the late Second Temple period – the years between 150 BC and AD 68? For the fact that the eleven caves discovered with the texts, and the ancient settlement nearby, are among the greatest archaeological excavations of the twentieth century, even though the original find was made by the Bedouins, not by archaeologists? Or for the manifold links they provide between Jewish thought and the teaching of Jesus, between the Hebrew and the Greek versions of the Bible, between religion and politics in a multicultural area of the Roman empire, at a time when most Jews were eagerly expecting their Saviour, the prophesied Messiah?

One could go on. It is practically impossible for either Jews or Christians who are studying their roots to escape the Dead Sea Scrolls. Books about the Bible and its environment, about Jewish history and early Christianity in a real world populated by real people refer to them incessantly. And yet, what do we really know about the scrolls, their writers and readers, their fascination and importance? Can we penetrate the smokescreen of rumours and legends, conflicting theories and wishful thinking?

The myths about the machinations of secret agencies hiding controversial scrolls have long been exposed as tendentious nonsense.[1] Claims about simple, and perhaps simple-minded, Christian imitations of Essene models have been unmasked as the wishful thinking of those who cannot accept the novelty value of Christian theology within and beyond traditional Judaism. This book will provide many examples, not by means of an apologetic counter-attack, but by the patient study of the scrolls themselves and, above all, their cultural, political and religious context. From time to time, state-of-the-art technology has proved invaluable and will be referred to. This is the case, for example, when the radiocarbon (^{14}C) analysis of some Dead Sea Scrolls confirms the solid dating achieved by traditional comparative palaeography,[2] proving beyond reasonable doubt that the Hebrew and Aramaic scrolls which are supposed to contain 'coded' information about James, Paul and the early church were in fact written in the first century BC.

It has been said that two Dead Sea Scrolls scholars have at least three different opinions. The entrenched positions about the relationship between early Christianity and the scrolls, or about the identification of the Jewish-Christian papyrus fragments from Cave 7, remind one of the old joke about an observant Jew stranded on a remote island. When his rescuers arrive, they find him sitting near two synagogues. Why did you build two synagogues? they ask. Well, he says, this one here is the one I go to, and the other one over there is the one I do not go to. Fragmentary as they are, many of the scrolls are open to conflicting interpretation – and it is this apparent uncertainty which may open new, and surprising, vistas. We shall encounter one such example in a controversial fragment of the famous War Scroll, and another one in the fascinating quest for the true identity of a papyrus from Cave 7: is it from Enoch – a non-biblical writing alluded to by Jesus (Mark 12:25) and quoted in a letter traditionally attributed to his half-brother Jude (Jude 13–16) – or is it a fragment of 1 Timothy, a 'pastoral epistle' preserved among the letters written by a Jew called Paul (1 Timothy 3:16 – 4:3)? What if the writings of the very first Christians, Jews all of them, were indeed collected, read and studied by fellow Jews in the Qumran library?

Following the trail of the scrolls, from their traces in the writings of ancient authors such as Origen, a man who knew about caves with jars and scrolls in the early third century and used at least one of these scrolls 1,700 years before the Bedouins rediscovered the caves, to the letters of a proud Jewish woman called Babata, we encounter forgotten people and unexpected connections.

We even happen upon a non-existent scroll, the book of Esther, which appears to be the only biblical text absent from the writings discovered at Qumran. But the scrolls from the Dead Sea caves are more than documents from a time warp. They help us to understand Judaism and its development during the centuries between the completion of the Hebrew Bible and the origins of Christianity. Peculiarities of the biblical scrolls found between Masada and Qumran shed light on the use of the Old Testament in New Testament writings. And the exciting – and excited – eschatology which we find in the scrolls, a fervent mood of hope and expectation, explains the background to the message proclaimed by the first followers of Jesus. They, like Jesus himself, were orthodox Jews. It has been said, tautologically perhaps, that Christianity is Jewish. We tend to forget this truism, after 2,000 years of mainly anti-Jewish church history. The scrolls invite us to develop a new awareness of our roots, and step by step, the following pages attempt to contribute to this process.

What the Ancients Knew

THE CASE OF A STRANGE SECT AT THE DEAD SEA

Long before the caves of the Dead Sea Scrolls and the ruins of Qumran were discovered and connected with a Jewish group commonly called 'Essenes', it was known that a certain Jewish orthodox movement had settled near the Dead Sea, somewhere between Jericho and En Gedi. There was Pliny the Elder, the Roman statesman and natural historian who died during the eruption of Vesuvius in AD 79. He mentions the general region of their settlement and calls them 'Essenes'. In Alexandria, there was Philo, an influential Jewish philosopher and diplomat, who died in c. AD 50. He knew at least some of their teachings – a fact which seems to show the contents of the Dead Sea Scrolls were anything but secret documents for a small Jewish group of hidden desert 'monks'. And there was Josephus, a former Pharisee and priest, a Jewish general in the revolt against the Romans, and finally, an adviser and historian at the court of the Roman emperor Vespasian. He knew 'Essenes' personally, knew their teachings, and had very distinct ideas about this movement and their influence on religion and society.

This chapter quotes, describes and analyses their statements. And it goes on to ask why these 'Essenes' are not mentioned in the New Testament, that other collection of contemporary Jewish, messianic documents. Or are they there, somewhere, after all?

From Pliny to Josephus

Everyone who visits the ruins of Qumran for the first time is struck by a surprising impression: the rediscovered settlement is not an isolated place of refuge in the middle of nowhere, out of reach to the ordinary traveller, surrounded by an arid desert with nothing but the Dead Sea to enliven the eye. On the contrary, it is situated on a plateau, clearly visible even from a distance on the road which links Jericho with Masada, En Gedi, Sodom and Eilat. Virtually next door, a couple of hundred yards away, there is a flourishing oasis called En Feshkha. Cattle, plants, trees and fresh water in abundance are the hallmarks of this oasis. Neither the road nor the oasis are new; they existed when those who settled at Qumran first came to this site. In fact, the habitation of this region by people who did not intend to live in excessive poverty is documented as early as the neolithicum. Qumran was not called Qumran in those days – that is a modern Arabic name given to the place when it was re-excavated near the caves as late as 1953–56, during the Jordanian occupation of the region.[1] From Joshua 15:61–62, at the end of a list of the cities belonging to the tribe of Judah, we may gather that its ancient biblical name probably was Secacah: 'And in the desert were Beth-Arabah, Middin, Secacah, Nibshan, the City of Salt and En Gedi. These are six towns with their farmsteads.' In other words, En Feshkha would have been the 'farmstead' of Secacah. And Secacah is singled out as a Dead Sea settlement in the famous Copper Scroll from Cave 3 (3Q 15). This is an inventory of priestly and community treasures clearly linked with a particular community – the one which we call Essenes – who apparently hid them from the approaching Romans before they finally occupied the area in AD 68.[2]

The oldest non-Jewish source is provided by Pliny the Elder. He was an uncle of that other Pliny, conveniently called the Younger. The younger Pliny was a Roman governor in Pontus and Bithynia (the area addressed in Peter's first letter) between c. AD 111 and 113 and became famous for his published correspondence with Emperor Trajan about the legal niceties of anti-Christian trials. Uncle Gaius, the Elder, was an army commander and procurator in several provinces,

Secacah was inhabited at least from the eighth century BC. After an interruption, probably in the early sixth century BC, it was reinhabited by new settlers – commonly called Essenes – during the reign of John Hyrcanus (135–104 BC). The settlement may have been destroyed by an earthquake and an ensuing fire in 31 BC, or by the Parthians in c. 39 BC, or during the skirmishes between Herod the Great and the Hasmonean Antigonos (c. 37 BC). Whatever the cause may have been, we are talking about the same period, and about the fact that Qumran *was* destroyed. It was rebuilt, apparently by the same people who had lived there before, during the reign of Archelaus (4 BC–AD 6), a ruler also mentioned in the New Testament (Matthew 2:22). If Herod did favour the Essenes, as Josephus claims (*Antiquities* 15, 373–78), it is certainly noteworthy that they did not live at Qumran during his reign. It seems this period coincides with the Essene establishment of a major centre in Jerusalem, supported by Herod the Great, on the south-west hill which today is called Mount Zion. And it should not be overlooked that some of the literature which was used by the Essenes (like the Book of Jubilees which was found in Caves 1, 2, 3, 4 and 11) existed long before the movement which we may identify as the Essenes of Pliny, Philo and Josephus, split from the Sadducean temple priesthood and went into 'exile' as the faithful few of Israel. According to the chronology of a very central text, the so-called Damascus Document, this happened in 196 BC. Twenty years later, in 176 BC, the 'Teacher of Righteousness', whom we shall encounter again in this book, rose from among the group as their charismatic leader. The Damascus Document was written, it seems, not long after the Teacher's death in c. 150 BC, during the reign of the High Priest Jonathan (160–142 BC) who may or may not have been the 'Wicked Priest' attacked in the scrolls. It looks as though the Teacher guided the movement before it settled in Qumran, and perhaps the decision to move to Qumran, probably from the 'Land of Damascus' in the Yarmuk region – closer to Jerusalem but still in the 'wilderness' – was inspired by his death. In any case, all we can say at this stage is this: a kind of Essenism taken on and developed by the Qumran/Jerusalem centres may have existed a considerable time prior to the rise of the movement which lived in Qumran and Jerusalem until these places were destroyed by the Romans in AD 68 and 70 respectively. This does not give us 'thousands of years', but a considerable period of development before Pliny set pen to paper.[6]

But what are we supposed to make of those masses (*turba*) of newcomers who flocked to the site and adopted the Essene lifestyle? Taken in its narrowest sense, Pliny's statement is plainly wrong. The size of the settlement did not allow for more than 60–100 inhabitants. But the archaeology of the area has shown many more settlers were living nearby, on the outskirts, and particularly at the oasis of En Feshkha which was (and is) literally only a stone's throw away. Judging by remains found at graveyards, whole families with children may have lived there, people who – in the terminology of Christian communities – might be called 'tertiaries'. Pliny's description could therefore be an accurate reflection of this evidence: single people and families, fed up with their previous lives, 'escaped' to Qumran and settled in the vicinity of the main settlement. But even so, we are not given any details. Whatever source Pliny used for his information, he did not quote from Essene literature, nor did he explain why so many people felt attracted to their lifestyle. Celibacy alone does not sound sufficiently persuasive for multitudes including men with wives and children. Philo and Josephus will provide us with further information. As for the centre at the Dead Sea, there is one other early author who confirmed Pliny's description of the site and its inhabitants. He was a man called 'Gold-Mouth' (Greek *Chrysostomos*) by his contemporaries: Dion, born in Prusa (modern Bursa), a city in the district of Bithynia which is mentioned in 1 Peter 1:1. He lived from c. 40 to c. 115 AD, opposed Emperor Domitian, was sent into exile, but was eventually rehabilitated and appreciated as an outstanding philosopher and orator by Domitian's successors Nerva and Trajan. During his years in exile, in the 90s of the first century, Dion travelled widely throughout the empire and met other travellers whose impressions he used at leisure. Since Qumran was occupied by the Romans in AD 68, it is doubtful whether he saw the site himself when it was an Essene settlement, but it is quite possible that his knowledge was derived from first-hand information. Synesius of Cyrene, who preserved Dion's statement in his biography of the gold-mouthed one, had this to say:

> *Elsewhere, he [Dion] praises the Essenes who have their own*
> *prosperous city [polin] near the Dead Sea, in the middle of*
> *Palestine, not very far from Sodom.*[7]

We are not told what Dion praised them for. Like Pliny, he situates them near the Dead Sea. The reference to Sodom is neither here nor there; in those days, some people thought it was at the southern tip of the Dead Sea, where the modern town of S(o)dom is situated, and others located it in the north. If Dion was one of those who preferred the northern site – like Philo, for example,[8] – his description would agree with that of Pliny. And like Pliny, who presupposes it indirectly, he seems to have known about the relative affluence of the Essenes. If the oasis of En Feshkha was seen as part of the Essene settlement, or, as Dion calls it, their 'polis', then indeed there is no reason to suppose the hallmark of life down there was poverty, attrition, hunger and thirst in a less-than-splendid isolation. A consciously frugal lifestyle may be all the more convincing if it is exercised within eyesight of fish, flesh and fowl in abundance. In any case, the fame of the Essenes must have spread to distant regions of the Roman empire – where men such as Pliny and Dion lived and wrote – to such an extent that their praiseworthiness was recorded even after they had ceased to exist.

Pliny and Dion were non-Jewish compilers. They focused on the

Dead Sea. Others painted a broader canvas and emphasized that this habitation at the Dead Sea was the centre, but not the only settlement, village, town or city associated with the Essenes. This, in any case, is presumed by two contemporary authors – and unlike Pliny and Dion, Jewish ones at that – Philo of Alexandria and Josephus. Philo, perhaps the greatest Jewish philosopher of the late Second Temple period, a diplomat who led a delegation to Emperor Gaius (Caligula) and protested against anti-Jewish events in his city (and wrote a moving essay about it), saw Judaism in Galilee, Judea and Samaria from a distance – geographically and also, to a certain extent, culturally. It seems that he, like many Jews in the diaspora, did not know Hebrew and depended entirely on the Greek translation of the Bible, the so-called Septuagint.[9] He duly cut the Gordian knot of Hebrew versus Greek scripture by calling the Septuagint equally inspired by God.[10] Thus, we may safely assume the only Essene writings of which he could have had first-hand knowledge were those written in Greek. And there were indeed a few, some of them rediscovered in Caves 4 and 7; those from Cave 4 may even have been known outside Qumran before the death of Philo, in c. 50 AD. Indeed Philo wrote about Essene community settlements all over the Jewish homeland:

> Certain among them [the Jews in Syrian Palestine], to the number
> of over four thousand, are called Essaeans [Essaîoi]. Although this
> word is not, strictly speaking, Greek, I think it may be related to
> the word 'holiness'. Indeed these men are utterly dedicated to the
> service of God; they do not offer animal sacrifice, judging it more
> fitting to render their minds truly holy. For it should be explained
> that, fleeing the cities because of the ungodliness customary among
> town-dwellers, they live in villages; for they know that, as noxious
> air breeds epidemics there, so does the social life afflict the soul
> with incurable ills. Some Essaeans work in the fields, and others

19

practise various crafts contributing to peace; and in this way they are useful to themselves and to their neighbours. They do not hoard silver or gold, and do not acquire vast domains with the intention of drawing revenue from them, but they procure for themselves only what is necessary to life. Almost alone among mankind, they live without goods and without property; and this by preference, and not as a result of a reverse of fortune. They think themselves thus very rich, rightly considering frugality and contentment to be real superabundance.[11] In vain would one look among them for makers of arrows, or javelins, or swords, or helmets, or armour, or shields; in short, for makers of arms, or military machines, or any instrument of war, or even of peaceful objects which might be turned to evil purpose. They have not the smallest idea, not even a dream, of wholesale, retail, or marine commerce, rejecting everything that might excite them to cupidity.[12] There are no slaves among them, not a single one, but being all free they help one another.[13]

Philo goes on for several more pages, but they are about the 'philosophy' and other aspects of Essenism, and to this we shall return later. In another writing, a kind of 'apology' of Judaism written for non-Jewish readers, he takes up the thread and sheds some additional light on their lifestyle. Towards the end, he offers a curious and lengthy diatribe against the dangerous and subversive flattery of women which we have preferred to omit from the following quote:

They live in a number of towns in Judea, and also in many villages and large groups. Their enlistment is not due to race (the word race is unsuitable where volunteers are concerned), but is due to zeal for the cause of virtue and an ardent love of men… There are farmers among them expert in the art of sowing and cultivation of plants, shepherds leading every sort of flock, and bee-keepers. So

20

they have to suffer no privation of what is indispensable to essential
needs, and they never defer until the morrow whatever serves
to procure them blameless revenue. When each man receives his
salary for these different trades, he hands it over to one person,
the steward elected by them, and as soon as the steward receives
his money, he immediately buys what is necessary and provides
ample food, as well as whatever else is necessary to human life.
Daily they share the same way of life, the same table, and even
the same tastes, all of them loving frugality and hating luxury
as a plague for body and soul... Shrewdly preparing themselves
against the principal obstacle threatening to dissolve the bonds of
communal life, they banned marriage at the same time as they
ordered the practice of perfect continence. Indeed no Essaean takes
a woman because women are selfish, excessively jealous, skilful in
ensnaring the morals of a spouse and in seducing him by endless
charms... The life of the Essaeans is indeed so enviable that not
only individuals but even great kings are seized with admiration
before such men, and are glad to pay homage to their honourable
character by heaping favours and honours upon them.[14]

A slightly younger observer of the scene was Josephus. He has been
described as one of the most fascinating characters of his time. Born
in c. AD 37, he was a trained Pharisee and priest, went to Rome with
a Jewish delegation in c. 64, secured the release of some priests who
had been sent to the capital on a false charge by procurator Felix (the
same Felix who held Paul captive at Caesarea), was persuaded to join
the zealots who revolted against the Romans between 66 and 74,
became a commander of their forces in Galilee, fought on horseback
in battles near Bethsaida, was captured and was a candidate for
execution when he had a brilliant idea: he predicted that his captor,
the Roman general, Vespasian, would become emperor. It was a fair
chance, fifty-fifty. Without this wager, the likelihood of his survival

would have been zero. To almost everyone's surprise, Vespasian did become emperor in AD 69 and left his son Titus to finish the job of destroying Jerusalem and the Temple and of mopping up the Jewish insurgents. Josephus become the emperor's adviser on Judaism, a pampered courtier who lived mainly in Rome until his death in c. AD 98. Josephus, who assumed the name of the imperial family of the Flavians and was henceforth called Josephus Flavius, wrote a series of historical and semi-autobiographical books, among them the *Jewish War* and the *Jewish Antiquities*. Both these writings contain innumerable details about Jewish life, culture, politics and religion from ancient days to his own time. Even people from the pages of the New Testament play a role in the *Antiquities*: John the Baptist, Caiaphas, Pontius Pilate, the Herodians, Jesus, and his brother James.[15] Josephus, it seems, knew the Essenes quite well – in any case, he claimed he had spent some time with them before he decided to join the Pharisees instead:

> When I was about sixteen, I wanted to gain first-hand experience
> of our different movements. There are three: first the Pharisees,
> second the Sadducees, and third the Essenes – as I have noted
> frequently. I thought that I would be able to choose the best, by
> learning about all these schools. Thus I steeled myself for the task
> and studied the three courses with some effort.[16]

In spite of this personal acquaintance – and Josephus is the only contemporary author who claims to have spent time with the Essenes – his portrayal of their theology is tinted by his own position in the religio-political power game before and during the Jewish revolt. Like Philo, he mentions a number of approximately 4,000 male Essenes, and says their dwelling places were to be found in the whole country.[17] Such camps and quarters are mentioned in the Damascus Document,[18] and a Qumran text which has only survived as a fragment, 4Q 159 ('Ordinances', fragments 2–4), refers to at least one settlement outside Qumran for which it provides legal advice. A movement called the 'Therapeutae', active mainly in Egypt, is also linked with the Essenes, and there were commercial and cultural links between both parts of the Roman empire.[19] In fact, Essene or near-Essene groups or offshoots may have continued to exist in Egypt long after their disappearance from the Holy Land. It may not be an accident that an early medieval copy of the archetypally Essene Damascus Document was found in the *genizah*, the storage room for damaged or discarded manuscripts, at the Ben Ezra synagogue of Old Cairo in 1897. There is no reason why individual Essenes should not have reached other centres of the empire, Athens and Rome among them, and why they should not have developed nuances within the framework of Essene rules and regulations, which were reflected in different scrolls.[20] But this question, tantalizing as it may be, is beyond the scope of this chapter. If the number of 'mainland' Essenes given by Josephus is even remotely correct, it follows that these people simply had to settle in other places outside Qumran as well; the number of houses and the size of the dining hall at Qumran did not allow for more than 60 to 100 – some scholars would say up to 150 – inhabitants at a time.[21] Here is one of the relevant passages from Josephus:

> *The Essenes renounce pleasure as an evil, and regard continence and resistance to the passions as a virtue. They disdain marriage for themselves, but adopt the children of others at a tender age in order to instruct them; they regard them as belonging to them by kinship, and condition them to conform to their own customs. It is not that they abolish marriage, or the propagation of the species resulting from it, but that they are on their guard against the licentiousness of women and are convinced that none of them is faithful to one man. They despise riches and their communal life*

is admirable. In vain would one search among them for one man with a greater fortune than another. Indeed, it is a law that those who enter the sect shall surrender their property to the order; so neither the humiliation of poverty nor the pride of wealth is to be seen anywhere among them. Since their possessions are mingled, there exists for them all, as for brothers, one single property... They are not in one town only, but in every town several of them form a colony. Also, everything they have is at the disposal of members of the group arriving from elsewhere as though it were their own, and they enter into the house of people whom they have never seen before as though they were intimate friends. For this reason also, they carry nothing with them when they travel: they are, however, armed against brigands. In every town a quaestor of the order, specially responsible for guests, is appointed steward of clothing and other necessaries.[22]

These four then, Pliny the Elder, Dion of Prusa, Philo and Josephus are informants who lived while the Essenes were flourishing and whose writings are based on contemporary information. This remains true in spite of the fact that with one exception (Philo), they all wrote after the destruction of Qumran and the dispersion of the Essenes in AD 68. Even without the complexities of Essene discipline, theology and Messianism, it seems we already have a miniature painting with a few basic colours: the Essenes had their headquarters near the Dead Sea, south of Jericho and north of En Gedi; they possessed a second centre in Jerusalem between the reign of Herod the Great and the destruction of the city in AD 70; they counted roughly 4,000 members most of whom lived in towns and settlements all over the country; they were a closely knit, well-organized, communitarian movement with separate branches, some of which were frightened of women and celibate at least at the priestly core of the movement, but not necessarily elsewhere. And, strikingly, they were admired for their lifestyle by other Jews and even by non-Jews. Whatever the Dead Sea Scrolls and archaeology were to add to this picture after their rediscovery between 1947 and 1956, this, at any rate, is a nucleus of information which was already available for outsiders in the diaspora before AD 50 (Philo of Alexandria), after the Roman occupation of Qumran in AD 68 and until 1947, when the first cave and its scrolls was rediscovered.

Later authors procured details of less certain origin. One of them is worth quoting, however, for he was a famous collector of source material which has not been preserved elsewhere. His name is Hippolytus, a Christian who lived from c. 170 to c. 236. He was a presbyter in Rome and may even have been an anti-bishop or 'pope' to Callistus from AD 217 to 222. His most important writing, a *Refutation Against All Heresies* in ten books, was lost until Books 4 to 10 were rediscovered in a manuscript on Mount Athos, in the nineteenth century. It seems that Hippolytus knew the works of Josephus, since long passages look like a paraphrase of descriptions in the *War* and in the *Antiquities*; but he obviously had access to other sources about the Essenes which are no longer extant. Here is an example of the picture he draws:

> They come together in one place, girding themselves with linen
> girdles to conceal their private parts. In this manner, they perform
> ablutions in cold water, and after being thus cleansed, they repair
> together into one apartment – no one who entertains a different
> opinion from themselves being with them in the house – and
> proceed to partake of breakfast. When they have taken their
> seats in order and in silence, the loaves are set out, and next some
> sort of food to eat along with it, and each receives from these a
> sufficient portion. No one, however, will taste these before the
> priest utters a prayer and blessing over them. After breakfast,
> he again says a prayer: as at the beginning, so at the conclusion

of their meal they hymn God.[23] *Next, after they have laid aside
as sacred the garments in which they have been clothed while
together taking their repast within – now these garments are linen
– and having resumed the clothes in the vestibule, they hasten to
agreeable occupations until evening. They partake of supper, doing
all things in like manner to those already mentioned. No one will
at any time cry aloud, nor will any other tumultuous voice be
heard, but they each converse quietly, and with decorum one
concedes the conversation to the other, so that the stillness of
those within appears a sort of mystery to those outside. They are
invariably sober, both eating and drinking all things by measure.*[24]

Towards the end of his depiction, he suddenly highlights an Essene teaching which the non-Jewish authors Pliny and Dion preferred to ignore (if they were aware of it, which we do not know for certain). Philo does not mention it either (for whatever reason), and Josephus, glancing at Greek mythology, plays it down with a certain sleight of hand: the Essenes' belief in a bodily resurrection. Hippolytus writes,

*The doctrine of the Resurrection has also derived support among
them, for they acknowledge both that the flesh will rise again,
and that it will be immortal, in the same manner as the soul is
already imperishable. They maintain that when the soul has been
separated from the body, it is now borne into one place, which is
well ventilated and full of light, and there it rests until judgment.
This locality the Greeks were acquainted with by hearsay, calling
it Isles of the Blessed. But there are many other tenets of these
men which the wise of the Greeks have appropriated and thus
have from time to time formed their own opinions. For the
discipline of these men in regard to the Divinity is of greater
antiquity than that of all nations.*[25]

Hippolytus goes on to argue that the Greeks and indeed everyone else derived their concept of God and creation from Jewish thought. To him, the Essenes were a kind of theological avant-garde, but at the same time firmly based on ancestral teachings. More than 100 years after their disappearance from the stage of history, Hippolytus is the first Christian to regard them explicitly as kindred spirits at least in some of the central areas of the Jewish heritage which Christians and Essenes had in common. We shall see in Chapter VIII how a Qumran fragment, found in Cave 4 and numbered 4Q 521, does indeed deal with the question of the bodily resurrection, proving Hippolytus to be a trustworthy late classical source. It is one of those fascinating cases where similarities between Essene theology and the teaching of Jesus are visible, going back to the same Old Testament passages, against the tenets of the priestly Sadducees who rejected it (Mark 12:18–27).

And there were still others who took notice of the Essenes. The fanatic followers of the messianic revolutionary Bar Kokhba, whose revolt led to an even more devastating destruction of Jerusalem by the Romans in AD 135, had hideouts in the wadis and caves near Qumran. Looking at the ruins of the Essene settlement, they called it the 'Castle of the Pious Ones', or, in the original, *Mezad Chasidim*. As in modern Hebrew, a 'hasid' or 'chasid' (the initial letter is pronounced like the *ch* in Scottish 'loch') is quite literally a 'pious one'. The reference was found in one of the Bar Kokhba letters of c. AD 133–35 from the Wadi Murabba'at.[26] The Romans, who had occupied Qumran in AD 68,[27] left this minor 'outpost' in the mid-70s of the first century, after the fall of Masada, and about sixty years later, some of the Essenes found refuge in their former barracks – previously the living quarters of the Essenes. The writer of the Wadi Murabba'at letter tells his addressee he intends to go to this place and stay put. Most of his companions, he writes, had already been killed by the Romans. Seven Bar Kokhba coins were found in the settlement; but there is no trace of any attempt to reopen and use the caves.

The implicit admiration for the Essenes which can be detected in the attribute *Chasidim* – given the fact that Bar Kokhba himself was an orthodox, pious Jew – may have been caused by an enduring memory: the Essenes had fought valiantly against the Romans during the first revolt which ended with the destruction of their living quarters at Qumran in AD 68 and in Jerusalem in AD 70. One of them, called John the Essene, was a general in charge of the district of Thamna during that revolt – a fact which indicates that the Essenes had an accepted role to play in Jewish society, and they were no ultra-orthodox fanatics who refused to have anything to do with the real world outside. John died in a failed attack on Askalon, held by the Romans, in AD 67. Josephus tells us how other Essenes suffered torture and death rather than giving in to Roman pressure to 'blaspheme their legislator [God] or to eat what was forbidden to them [i.e. non-*kosher* food]'.[28]

An interlude: celibacy or marriage?

If we want to understand the life and lifestyle of a movement, it always helps to listen to the people concerned themselves. We shall encounter many examples in further chapters. At this stage, let us look at one of the most important and oldest community writings, the Damascus Document (CD),[29] which mentions 'camps' in the plural and refers to 'cities' inhabited by members.[30] The first of these references, CD 7:6–7, introduces another interesting aspect: Apparently, Essenes living outside the main centre at Qumran were free to marry and to have children: 'And if they live in camps according to the rules of the land, marrying and begetting children, they shall act according to the Law and in accordance with the statute concerning binding vows, according to the rule of the Law which states [Numbers 30:17]: "Between a man and his wife, and between a father and his son".'

This statement of the Damascus Document must be seen

against the apparently contradictory observations by Pliny the Elder, who stated that the Essenes lived without women; by Philo of Alexandria, who claimed that the Essenes banned marriage because of a deep distrust of the female character; and by Josephus, who described mainline Essenism as decidedly celibate, but knew of one order of the Essenes who 'although in agreement with the others on their way of life, usages, and customs, are separated by them on the subject: for they believe that people who do not marry delete a very important part of life – the propagation of their species'.[31] What Josephus knew coincides with the passage from the Damascus Document above, but also with another statement from the same scroll which singles out an Essene Community in Jerusalem where celibate male priests were the only members:

'No man shall sleep with a woman in the City of the Sanctuary, for this would defile the City of the Sanctuary with their uncleanness' (CD 12:1).[32] If we try to reconcile these statements, rather than drive a wedge between them, we can see a kind of elitist and celibate group of priestly Essenes living in Jerusalem. But we can also see other groups elsewhere, including the centre at Qumran and its outskirts with the oasis at En Feshkha, where the prospect of starting a family was at least a possibility. The strictness of celibate elitism may have varied from time to time, but the text and – until recently (see pp. 209–10) – the archaeological discovery of a few women's and children's skeletal remains at a graveyard in the vicinity of Qumran suggested the conclusion that the Essene movement as such was not exclusively misogynous.

Is it possible to reconcile the different sources? To begin with, celibacy is a concept which has always been completely alien to Jewish men. In fact, it is a commandment going back to Genesis that men shall marry and have children. When the Damascus Document quotes Numbers 30:17, it does so because this *Torah* passage underlines the fulfilment of the original commandment or *mitzvah* that every man shall 'leave his father and his mother, and shall cleave unto his wife; and they shall be one flesh' – to quote the Authorized Version (Genesis 2:24). To this day, marriage is the first of the *mitzvoth*. A movement which saw itself as particularly pious and orthodox must have had very good reasons to abandon or modify it, and observers with a Jewish background and upbringing such as Philo and Josephus must have known there were such reasons – and they were comprehensible to *Torah*-reading Jews. Otherwise, it would be difficult to understand why they neither scrutinize nor criticize this quite unusual habit. The key to the solution may be found in the second book of the *Torah*, Exodus. At Mount Sinai, days before Moses received the ten commandments from God, he goes to the people of Israel and says, 'Be ready by the third day. Do not go near a woman' (Exodus 19:15). This could be interpreted as an order to be celibate at the holiest of places, closest to God. If the Essenes saw Jerusalem, the Holy City, with its Temple, as the embodiment of what Mount Sinai had been to Moses and Israel, celibacy could be argued a way of honouring God in the Mosaic tradition.

The Damascus Document does not refer to Qumran in this context. Only Jerusalem is singled out. But it is plausible enough that the inner priestly elite of perhaps around 100 men living at Qumran followed similar guidelines. If Qumran is Secacah, they could easily have regarded it as a holy place in its own right: God gave it to his people, as it is mentioned in the list of cities belonging to the tribe of Judah (Joshua 15:61). The Qumranites may have been more 'liberal' in allowing families to live nearby, but the fact remains all rules and regulations found among the Dead Sea Scrolls, those manuals of discipline meant to shape the core of the movement, do not refer to the behaviour, duties and obligations of women even once. It is as though women did not exist in the community framework of the scrolls. Celibacy under certain circumstances, demanded by priests, is further documented in 1 Samuel 21:4–5. It was, in other words, exceptional but not unknown. On the contrary, there were situations where it was demanded – or could be seen to be demanded – by holy scripture. There is one proviso, however: we do not have a biblical precedent where celibacy was lifelong. When the situation changed, marriage or the resumption of marriage seems to have been expected. Here, the Qumran texts could be interpreted in two directions: either the priestly elite stayed in Jerusalem or at Qumran all their lives. In that case, they continued to be close to God at a holy place and could justify their continuous celibacy by Mosaic law. Or they stayed at these places for a limited number of years (perhaps to be identified with the three-year probationary period) and later went to the so-called 'camps' or other Essene communities in the country, where they were free to marry – or to return to their wives left behind when they joined the 'training centres' at the Dead Sea and in Jerusalem.

A hitherto unknown fragment which will be published later in 2000, 4Q Serek ha-Edah (4Q 249e), may shed further light on the question. It confirms the principle of celibacy at Qumran, but seems to acknowledge that some married couples did live at, or near, Qumran. However, when they joined the movement at its educational centre, they had to promise celibacy in marriage. Thus, celibacy and marriage were not mutually exclusive. This appears to come close to what Paul writes to the Christians in Corinth (1 Corinthians 7:29): in eschatological times, 'those who have wives should live as if they did not'. The precise meaning of Paul's words remains controversial among New Testament scholars, and the forthcoming publication of the new Qumran fragment will probably provoke a lively debate about the practicalities involved in the eschatological teaching of the Essenes and the Christian Pharisee, Paul.

Philo and Pliny, who treated the Essenes as completely celibate, apparently wrote under an impression which was visually right, so to speak: looking at Jerusalem and Qumran, all one could see was celibate men. An observer or informer did not necessarily have to realize that these men changed places every three years or so, or that there were other forms of community life practised outside these two centres. As we saw above, Josephus, who was closest to them, knew at least that married Essenes may not have been the core elite, but that they were not a second-rate exception either. His description, quoted above, appears to assume a separate order of Essenes. And this may indeed have been his impression when he joined a training centre, at the age of sixteen, only to leave it some time later and decide on a career among the Pharisees. As a 'trainee' Essene at a celibate place, the celibate brotherhood must have been visible to him as the essence of the 'order' – not quite to his liking, as it turned out: Josephus married four times and had five sons.

Can we place Jesus and his disciples somewhere among these fellow Jews? Jesus was a lifelong celibate, but most certainly not a misogynist. Women were among his followers; he encouraged them, honoured them and was honoured by them. In John's Gospel, a woman, Mary of Magdala, was the first person to encounter the risen Christ. His decision against marriage was not a decision against the company of women. But since, in biblical terms, the purpose of marriage is the creation of a family, the Son of God was in a different category. From the point of view of sceptical onlookers, however – of people who may have accepted him as a rabbi, but not as the Son of God or the Messiah – his celibacy was unusual – still today, an unmarried rabbi would look like a walking contradiction in terms – but not impossible. The *Torah*, and Essene practice at his time, showed clearly it could be done. As for the disciples, they were married before they joined Jesus, left their families at his behest (Luke 18:28–29) and therefore became temporarily celibate, but returned to them in Galilee after the resurrection. As apostolic missionaries, they even took their wives with them on their journeys (1 Corinthians 9:5). Paul later developed a personal teaching which he carefully describes as his own, and not 'from the Lord' (1 Corinthians 7:25–40): unmarried men and women should ideally remain unmarried, following his own example. He does not condemn marriage – far from it. But he thinks, and here he is very close to the *Torah*'s case in Exodus 19:15 and its interpretation by the Essenes, that at a sanctified moment, at the end 'of the world as we know it' (1 Corinthians 7:29–31), marriage may be a distraction in one's devotion to the Lord (7:35). Not many Jewish Christians followed his advice, it seems, in spite of his model and the Essene teaching of which quite a few Jews would have been aware. But we can see and understand it was not plainly absurd and typical of the (alleged) misogynist Paul, as critics of Paul's attitude to women and marriage have often assumed. It had its place in contemporary Jewish thought and practice.

Encountering Essenes

Jesus, his disciples, and someone like Paul while still called Saul – or rather *Sha'oul*, the Pharisee – could have met Essenes anywhere, in Galilee, Samaria and Judea, in and around Jerusalem. There was certainly no need for them to go to Qumran if they wanted to find out who the Essenes were and what they taught. In Jerusalem, the 'City of the Sanctuary', Essenes were firmly established in New Testament times, so much so, that a small city gate on the south-west hill was called 'Gate of the Essenes' – a name duly recorded by Josephus.[33] The gate has been re-excavated,[34] and immediately behind it, on the hill which today is called Mount Zion, striking parallel purifying baths have been found, so-called *mikvaoth*, with further such *mikvaoth*, including the largest one ever found outside Qumran, in the vicinity. While purifying baths are not uncommon in Jewish towns, their number and architecture have been interpreted as typical of the Essenes who needed them for their frequent and daily self-purifications. What is more, Josephus links the Gate of the Essenes with a nearby *bethso*, which has been identified by historians as the latrines outside the city walls, again conforming to Essene rules.[35]

33

Josephus describes them in loving detail: he tells us the Essenes were not allowed to defecate on the seventh day and that they had to use mattocks to dig holes in the ground on the other days, at isolated sites (i.e. outside the confines of the settlement). 'They squat there and are covered by their cloaks so that they do not offend the rays of God. Afterwards, they push back the dug-up soil into the hole... Although the evacuation of the excrements is natural, they are used to washing themselves afterwards [in purifying baths] as though defiled.'[36]

Concerning the gate, the *mikvaoth* and the *bethso*, recent archaeology has shown Josephus to be well informed. At the time of writing, a team led by the archaeologists James Strange and Bargil Pixner is preparing further excavations near the abbey of Hagia Maria Sion (formerly Dormition Abbey) on Mount Zion, looking for houses, further *mikvaoth* and other traces such as mattocks for the excrements which would provide additional evidence for the existence of an Essene quarter virtually next door to the first Christian living quarters in Jerusalem. A very recent discovery of some tombs outside the walls of the ancient city of Jerusalem, as yet unpublished, may further corroborate this link of Essenes with the city of Jerusalem: a number of male skeletons have been found which show exactly the same positioning as those found at Qumran.

The archaeology of Qumran and Jerusalem will be portrayed in a later chapter. One recent discovery, however, has to be mentioned at this stage: we have tacitly assumed that Pliny, Philo, Josephus and others knew what they were doing when they described the people living at Secacah as 'Esseni' or 'Essaioi', etc. If this word can be explained etymologically, from Aramaic *hase*, 'pious', as 'the pious ones', as most scholars think, it may well describe a form of outstanding devotion, much like the modern terms 'Pietists' and 'Pietism' have been used to describe a particular type of Protestant devotional life in southern Germany and some other parts of Europe. But not a single example of the use of this description has been found among the Dead Sea Scrolls. Did the 'Essenes' themselves do without a proper name for themselves? Although they appear in the pages of the New Testament (see Chapter VII), we cannot identify them by name, because no name is given. In fact, those other messianic Jews, the Christians, had no group name of their own making, either. Strangers, observers in faraway Antioch, first had the idea to coin a phrase: they saw that those adherents of Jesus followed him as the Messiah, in Greek 'the Christ', and thus they were people 'belonging to Christ', *Christianoi*, Christians (Acts 11:26). The Essenes, too, were named first by distant observers: by Philo and Pliny.

However, recently published fragments from Qumran may indicate that the Hebrew word was used among the Essenes, after all. They belong to a Levitic text in Aramaic from Cave 4, 4Q Levi^{b}ar.[37] In line 6, we read, 'The name of the pious one(s) will for ever not be eradicated from their people.' One might object that 'pious ones' is a somewhat general description in Aramaic, as in any other language – whereas 'Essenes' was as unique a derivative as 'Pietists'. And indeed, in line 7, a different self-description of the movement occurs: they see themselves as the 'holy ones from among the people'. Much like the early Christians' self-description as followers of 'the way', these are communal labels, but they are not proper names. In 1996, a sensational discovery made not far from the steps to the plateau of Cave 7 presented a new possibility: a member of James Strange's team excavating at Qumran found two *ostraca* (inscribed potsherds). The larger one, broken in two parts, contained fifteen damaged and fragmentary lines in a Hebrew script which paralleled the handwriting on the scrolls from the early first century AD. It mentions several people, among them a certain Honi from Jericho and his servant Hisdai. And in line 8, it appears to say that this Honi had fulfilled his oath towards the *Yahad*, or, in English, 'Community' or 'Union'.[38] The document looks like a contract transferring some of Honi's possessions to the *Yahad* at Qumran. Since *Yahad* is a common term used in the Dead Sea Scrolls,[39] it may now be possible to identify it as the proper name of the movement. After all, there is an outsider who calls them by this name in an official document. The only remaining problem is the definitive identification of line 8. Some critics have doubted that the damaged word can be read as *Yahad*, and the present author witnessed a heated discussion between Norman Golb and Esther Eshel (one of the editors of the *ostraca*) during the International Dead Sea Scrolls Congress at Jerusalem in the summer of 1997, which divided the audience. It seems that most professional palaeographers agree with Eshel's reading – but more will be said (and published) in the foreseeable future.

Assuming that *Yahad* is indeed the solution to the quest for the Essene's own proper name, we can even find its traces in the pages of the New Testament: in the Acts of the Apostles, Luke describes the first Christian community as a *koinonia* (Acts 2:42–44). This Greek word comes as close as any translation can to *Yahad*, 'Community' or 'Union'. From other passages like Acts 5:1–11, which we will encounter later, it is obvious that the Christians in Jerusalem knew of Essene models of community discipline and were aware of a need to emulate those rigid standards if they wanted to convince their neighbours the Christian *Yahad* was the true one. Luke's idiom, so early in this sequel to his gospel, may well contain an implicit claim: the *Yahad/Koinonia* must be understood as messianic. We, the Christians – still Jews – proclaim the one and only Messiah, Jesus. Therefore, our *Yahad/Koinonia* is the one to belong to, particularly for pious Jews. Not much later, in Acts 6:7, we may have a reference to the remarkable success of this strategy.[40]

If a close relationship between the Essenes and Jerusalem can be shown, both from archaeology and literature, what finally, and without going into details left to later chapters, can be said about the relationship between the Essene *settlement* at Qumran and the Qumran *caves*? Assuming the case for the identification of Qumran/Secacah with the settlement of the Essenes referred to by ancient authors is overwhelmingly strong, how strong is the case for their use of the caves? What may look like an absurd question to most visitors who have seen the area of Qumran, is a far-from-settled one. Some obscure theories, for which there is no shred of archaeological evidence, have turned Qumran into a fortress or into a winter villa, with inhabitants blissfully unaware of the library caves and their scrolls. Other scholars have assumed that the caves contained the library of the Temple, taken to the caves near the Dead Sea for safe keeping just before the Roman onslaught on Jerusalem, and while Qumran was still active – that is, before AD 68. But the Temple library must have contained at least some representative writings of the Sadducees, the priestly movement in charge of Temple worship. So far, however, not a single Qumran scroll could be identified as undoubtedly Sadducean. Still others have denied any link between the Essenes and the caves and have treated the scrolls as a collection of different libraries, a kind of representative cross-section of Jewish theology. But it would be practically impossible to ignore a relationship between the inhabitants of Qumran and the caves: Caves 4, 5 and 6 were within a few hundred yards of the settlement, and their entrances were visible. No one could have approached them without being noticed by the inhabitants. Cave 7, the only cave with nothing but Greek texts exclusively on papyrus, was situated underneath the northern end of the plateau of Qumran. No one could reach it without going through the inhabited area. Remnants of the ancient steps to the cave can still be seen. Caves 8, 9 and 10 are also within walking distance of Qumran. That leaves only Caves 1, 2, 3 and 11 which could conceivably have been used unnoticed by the Qumran inhabitants. And since Cave 4 is the major library cave, with two-thirds of all scrolls, the very fact of its immediate vicinity to the settlement of Qumran is in itself a decisive argument against a separation of caves and Qumran Essenes.

Needless to say, this does not mean that the Essenes wrote all the texts found in these caves, or that they are a monolithic entity. We shall see later that some texts were certainly imported for study purposes.[41] Others may represent a theological development among the Essene movement from its beginnings in the mid-second century BC to the mid-first century AD, when the last Hebrew and Aramaic scrolls were written. But as a rule, we should apply what the Qumran scholar and theologian, Frank M. Cross, put in a nutshell many years ago: 'If the people of the scrolls were not the Essenes, they were a similar sect, living in the same centre, in the same area'.[42] In other words, the logical working hypothesis is still to call them Essenes and treat them as directly involved with the caves and their scrolls. Alternative theories remind one of the old joke about the works of Shakespeare written by a different person of the same name. Or, to quote Cross again, any scholars who hesitate to identify the inhabitants of Qumran with the Essenes (and the use of the caves) place themselves in an astonishing position. For, as Cross states, with the acerbic pen of a long-suffering observer, such scholars

> must suggest seriously that two major parties each formed communistic religious communities in the same district of the Dead Sea and lived together in effect for two centuries, holding similar bizarre views, performing similar or rather identical lustrations, ritual meals, and ceremonies. Further, the scholar[s] must suppose that one community, carefully described by classical authors, disappeared without leaving building remains or even potsherds behind; while the other community, systematically ignored by the classical sources, left extensive ruins and even a great library![43]

Recent excavations by Yizhak Hirschfeld at En Gedi, not yet published,[44] have led some observers to the risky hypothesis that the true Essene settlement was discovered, and that therefore Pliny the Elder's account should be reinterpreted. His Essenes, Hirschfeld suggested, did not live north of En Gedi (i.e. at Qumran/Secacah), but above it.[45] Hirschfeld discovered some twenty-five houses of approximately two by three metres, the type of building one might associate with resident fieldworkers at the border of the oasis. There are not enough of them to house a community like the Essenes. And, so far, no traces of the typical *mikvaoth*, the numerous purifying baths demanded by the Essene Community Rule (and evident in abundance at Qumran and near the Gate of the Essenes on Jerusalem's south-west hill) have been found at the En Gedi site. Irrespective of the lack of any evidence to prove that these archaeological traces can be identified with the period of Essene activities – they are probably early second century, some forty to fifty years after the destruction of the Essene sites by the Romans and the end of the Essene movement – there is an historical argument which should be taken into consideration. During the Jewish uprising against the Romans, which began in AD 66 and ended with the destruction of Jerusalem and the Temple in AD 70, followed by Roman mopping-up operations including the conquest of the fortress of Masada in AD 73/74, some Essenes took refuge on that southern fortress. Their literature was known among the zealots; fragments of their texts, including the popular Songs of the Sabbath Sacrifice,[46] were discovered among the scant remains of the Masada library. Josephus, however, tells us that the Masada defenders raided the settlement at En Gedi and killed the fellow Jewish inhabitants.[47] It is inconceivable that they would have done so if the En Gedi area had been the Dead Sea headquarters of the Essenes.

Our sources, fragmentary as they are, may not tell us exactly what happened at Qumran and in Jerusalem, but they have already given us a multifaceted picture of a community which evolved and spread widely, around two centres: Qumran and, in New Testament times, the south-west hill of Jerusalem, and which seems to have allowed for a certain variety of lifestyles within the law. This last

II

Scrolls and Caves
Near Jericho

THE CASE OF A MAN CALLED ORIGEN

None of the ancient authors tells us anything about Essene libraries. To many people, therefore, the discovery of the caves with their scrolls in 1946 or 1947 (accounts vary!) came as a complete surprise. But everyone could have guessed at their existence. In the early third century AD, a famous Christian philosopher and librarian called Origen commented on his own edition of the Hebrew and Greek Old Testament and said that he used a scroll for the Hebrew text which had come from a jar in a cave near Jericho. Even in the ninth century AD, Timothy I, a Nestorian bishop, referred to such scrolls as a matter of course.

This chapter tells the story of 'knowledge gained and lost', and develops the general scenario of the archaeology of Qumran and the sites where scrolls were found near the Dead Sea – at places like Masada, the Nahal Hever, the Wadi Murabba'at and others.

Origen's origins

In the summer of 1997, scholars from all over the world assembled in Jerusalem to celebrate the fiftieth anniversary of the discovery of the Qumran caves. It was a somewhat artificial, and some would say even fictitious, year, as 1946 or even a considerably earlier date have been suggested. Nowadays, most would agree that Cave 1 was discovered in November or December 1946, by one or up to three Bedouins from the Ta'amireh tribe – Muhammad ed-Dibh ('the wolf'), Juma

Muhammad and Khalik Musa. They took a few manuscripts and jars. The news spread, though not publicly at first. On 25 November 1947, the Jewish scholar Eleazar Sukenik, professor of archaeology at the Hebrew University, Jerusalem, and father of the famous soldier and archaeologist Yigael Yadin, heard about these first finds and began his own inquest. It was, in a manner of speaking, the 'year zero' of Dead Sea Scroll studies. But without the Bedouins, and in an attempt to overtake them, it took soldiers of the Arab legion under Captain Akkash el-Zebn more than two years to find the same cave again on 28 January 1949.

This rediscovery of a rediscovery heralded the beginning of serious archaeological work, although the Bedouins continued to outwit the professional archaeologists more than once. It was the rediscovery of a rediscovery indeed, for caves with jars and scrolls in the northern Dead Sea region have been known of since the early third century AD. It is one of the enigmas of archaeology that no one took the earliest sources seriously enough. In fact, the accidental discovery by some Bedouins remains a stigma on the face of classical archaeology. Everyone knows many sensational discoveries have come about by pure chance, and most of us have read about farmers or building workers who happened upon priceless treasures or ancient walls. But in the case of the Dead Sea caves, the literary evidence for their existence has been so blatantly obvious that it is difficult to find an apology for the lack of archaeological enterprise. Ancient sources refer to Hebrew scrolls in caves near Jericho. Could it be that neither the Muslim powers ruling over this area since the early Middle Ages, nor the pro-Arab Christian scholars resident in Jerusalem and Amman were particularly motivated to look for such documents? It would at least give them a political and pseudo-religious reason (even though a decidedly flawed one). Otherwise, we would feel tempted to accuse them of ignorance and incompetence.

The 'political' aspect remained in force even after the first discoveries; only the handful of scrolls eventually obtained by the Israelis could be studied by Jewish experts and were eventually publicly displayed at the Israel Museum. The vast majority, including those thousands of fragments from Cave 4, went to East Jerusalem, which at that time was occupied by Jordan, and some, like the Copper Scroll from Cave 3, went straight to Amman, with the explicit strategy of excluding all Jewish scholars from access to their heritage. Only after the reunification of Jerusalem in 1967 was it possible to give Jewish and non-Jewish experts alike open access to the scrolls and fragments. And from then on, the only yardstick was a proven track record in linguistic and papyrological competence, and a willingness to accept academic 'copyright'. All those so-called scandals about 'hidden scrolls' were artificially created by outsiders like Robert Eisenman and their journalistic followers, such as Michael Baigent and Richard Leigh. There never was a Vatican conspiracy – or any other attempt at hiding sensitive material. But it was obvious to any open-minded observer that the editorial process was slow and cumbersome; only a handful of scholars were qualified to cope with the sheer amount of unknown, fragmented material; they had to train a new generation of students (now fully at work), and the real experts, the Jewish scholars, who had published their scrolls within a few years, were barred from access by the Jordanians and their committee until 1967. When the Israelis finally overcame their policy of observing the pre-1967 'status quo' and changed the whole structure of the editorial committee in the early 1990s, gratefully yielding to international pressure, it was like changing from first to fourth gear. Meanwhile, the 'copyright' problem remains unsolved. Pirated editions of scroll fragments entrusted to qualified scholars have led to legal actions, the most famous case involving Professor Elisha Quimron of the Ben-Gurion University of the Negev, Beer-Sheva, who was granted compensation for an unauthorized pre-emptive edition of a Qumran scroll on which he had spent years of painstaking work.

Back to the early centuries: a man called Origen appeared on the international scene, teaching in Alexandria, Caesarea, Athens, Rome and Jerusalem. He lived from c. AD 185 to c. 253 and was one of the most fascinating characters of the early church – and 'early church' means Christendom before the reign of Constantine the Great (AD 312–37) who ended almost three centuries of empire-wide, but precarious, development, which had been marked by intermittent persecutions, and gave Christianity the status of a legitimate, even preferred religion. Before Constantine, public Christian activities were always risky, and Origen had himself paid the price. During the persecution under Emperor Decius in AD 250–51, he was tortured so brutally that he died from the after-effects. He was a famous man by then, director of the library at Caesarea Maritima and founder of an academy which was so prestigious that even non-Christians came to study at his feet. Origen was anything but orthodox, and the Roman Catholic Church later refused to accord him the status of a teacher, let alone sainthood, but the Bishop of Caesarea ordained him presbyter and invited him to preach on all the books of the Bible. Origen travelled widely to meet important men such as Hippolytus in Rome, and to obtain scrolls for his library. In Athens, for example, he acquired a Greek translation of the Old Testament. And he did not treat his sources as secrets. Let us assume he was proud of his successes, or he simply wanted to help others. In any case, he informed his readers about a find which could have opened up a whole new market – if only it had been taken seriously.

Compiling his greatest philological work, the *Hexapla* – a six-column edition of the Old Testament – he collected the available and reliable manuscripts. Apart from the Hebrew text, he needed those of the Septuagint, which was the standard Greek text used by all Greek-speaking Jews (including the New Testament authors) since the third century BC. But there were rival editions of the Greek text, and they had begun to replace the Septuagint in some Jewish circles; the very fact that the Septuagint – which Philo of Alexandria had called

Antoninus, the son of Severus'.³ In other words, Eusebius knew Origen's own account. There appear to be two differences between the two: Origen refers to Hebrew and Greek scrolls in that cave, whereas Eusebius, talking about translations, only mentions the Greek text. And, perhaps more significantly, the location varies slightly: was that cave *in* or *near* Jericho?

Scholars such as the papyrologist Josef Milik and the first director of Qumran excavations, the Dominican Roland de Vaux (1904–71), who for a long time acted as director of the École Biblique et Archéologique Française de Jérusalem, were ready to identify Origen's cave with the first cave discovered at Qumran. This was a convenient solution. After all, Eusebius with his '*in* Jericho' did not make much sense, since there are no caves *in* Jericho. But from the perspective of Caesarea in the north, where Origen wrote (and Eusebius after him, for that matter), Qumran/Secacah was certainly *near* Jericho. Be this as it may, Jericho was the nearest town anyone would choose to describe the position of caves at Qumran, which in the days of Origen was a derelict former Roman garrison unworthy of any topographical reference. However, this does not amount to evidence that 'near Jericho' means 'at Qumran'. There are in fact caves near Jericho proper, and the caves south of Qumran, in the Nahal Hever or the Wadi Murabba'at – where Greek Old Testament scrolls were indeed discovered! – do also measure up to the geographical yardstick of Origen. To put it bluntly, the whole stretch between Jericho and the Wadi Murabba'at, and indeed further south towards Masada, was full of caves with jars and scrolls, not necessarily preceding the fall of Jerusalem in AD 70, but certainly older than the period of Antoninus, the son of Severus. And what is more, the way Origen and Eusebius refer to one of these caves is sober, matter-of-fact, without the slightest hint of sensationalism. They do not seem to be surprised. A scroll or two with an old Hebrew and Greek biblical text – so what? We get the impression that everyone knew about these things – in those days, at least. Could it be that this is one of the reasons why only such a small amount has been rediscovered since 1946/47? Most of the sites mentioned in the Copper Scroll from Cave 3 have been identified, but so far, none of the treasures mentioned in that scroll has been found. Small wonder, if people knew about hiding places and cave libraries and (as some scholars think) had access to many more copies – including copies of the Copper Scroll – than have survived today.

After all, we are talking about a period of almost 200 years between the end of the Qumran settlement and the time of Origen – a period when even the Romans, who had occupied the area between AD 68 and the early second century, and all those who came after them, could easily have found the caves, if only by accident.[4] And as though it was all about adding insult to injury, modern archaeologists were confronted by another source of embarrassment: not only Origen and Eusebius, but, some 500 years later, another eminent witness corroborated the story about scrolls in caves near Jericho. In c. AD 800, when Charlemagne was crowned emperor by Pope Leo III in Rome, when the legendary Harun al-Rashid (763–809), the hero of the *Arabian Nights*, was an Abbassid Caliph and made Charlemagne protector of the Christian sites in Jerusalem, a Christian bishop mentioned 'pious Jews' who had told him about such a cave.

That bishop was Timothy I, Patriarch of the Nestorians at Seleukeia-Ktesiphon, some 60 km north-east of ancient Babylon on both sides of the River Tigris. Timothy was a highly respected, learned theologian and diplomat. His correspondence with Caliph al-Mahdi remains an outstanding document of Christian–Muslim dialogue. He encouraged missionary activities in countries such as China and India, and taught mainly by way of letters (of which some 200 have survived) on questions of biblical studies, philosophy and the Nestorian theology. The one letter which concerns us most was addressed to Sergius/Mar Sargis, the metropolitan bishop of Elam.

Writing in Chaldean, a form of Aramaic which has survived until today, Timothy informs his correspondent about the complicated process of copying different editions of the *Hexapla*. He complains about the incompetence of quarrelsome scribes, and describes his own role as corrector. So difficult was this work, he says, he nearly lost his sight. And then, all of a sudden, he tells a fascinating story:

> We learned from trustworthy Jews who have just been taught the
> Christian faith, as catechumens, that books were found in a cave
> near Jericho ten years ago. It is said that the dog of a hunting Arab
> went into a cave, chasing an animal, and did not return. Its master
> followed the dog and found a cave among the rocks, and in it
> many books. The hunter went to Jerusalem and told other Jews
> about his discovery. Many of them came to the place and found
> the books of the Old Testament and other writings, in the Hebrew
> language.[5]

Timothy emphasizes the role of the Jews – no Bedouins here! And although the story of the discovery has one parallel in the Bedouin legend of 1946/47 – an animal lost in the hills – it is remarkably down to earth and ecumenical. A Christian bishop, living under a Caliphate, looks after Jewish converts who apparently remain in contact with orthodox Jews in Jerusalem. The hunter who made the discovery was an Arab, but he went to Jerusalem to inform the Jews whose language, it seems, he had recognized on the scrolls. What a story, and what a lesson! But where are those scrolls?

In his letter, Timothy tells Sergius/Mar Sargis what he did next: full of hope that these scrolls would help him to identify the sources of some New Testament quotations which he could not find in his Hebrew Old Testament, he asked his Jewish informants, and they told him such quotations could indeed be found in those texts.[6] In fact, one of the Jews told Timothy there were 'more than two hundred Psalms of David' among the finds. So the bishop wrote to trusted Christian colleagues, among them a royal adviser and the metropolitan bishop of Damascus; apparently, he assumed them to have access to the scrolls.[7] However, as Timothy complains in his letter, 'I never received a reply, and I do not have a suitable man whom I could send. It moves my heart like a fire which burns and glows in my bones.' No trace of these scrolls has remained. If they were taken to Jewish libraries, or to any other archive for that matter, they would have been destroyed by strife, wars and conquests, or they may simply have fallen apart like most manuscripts from antiquity which were not protected by jars in caves, arid heaps of refuse and earth (as at Nag Hammadi, Oxyrhynchus and other Egyptian sites) or volcanic lava (as in Herculaneum). Origen's Hebrew scroll has not survived either, nor has any of the more than 30,000 scrolls he had assembled in his academic library at Caesarea Maritima. The one detail to which Timothy refers does take us back to Qumran, however.

One of the peculiarities of the biblical scrolls at Qumran is several collections of additional psalms. The Thanksgiving Hymns (1QH and 4Q 427–33) are twenty-five psalms, and eight scrolls of them were found at Qumran. A collection called the Psalms of Joshua (4Q 378–79) was found twice. Further psalm-like poems and prayers were found in Cave 4 (4Q 286–93; 4Q 392–93; 4Q 434–56). In some cases, the authors are anonymous; in others, David or Manasseh are mentioned. The most spectacular discoveries were the scroll fragments with 'apocryphal psalms' (4Q 88; 4Q 380–81; 4Q 448; 11Q 5, 22; 11Q 11): not only do they indicate that the Jews of the late Second Temple period creatively extended the classical collection of the 150 psalms included in the *Tanakh*;[8] three of the psalms discovered in the caves are the Hebrew versions of texts previously only known as part of the Syriac (!) psalter which has the five additional psalms, 151–55. They are 4Q 88, 4Q 448 and 11Q 5, with Psalm 151 (identified in the text as a psalm 'of David'), Psalm 154 and Psalm 155. In each case, the scrolls contained other texts as well – 4Q 448, for example, also has the famous Prayer for King Jonathan. But the most striking observation concerns the potential context: these new Hebrew psalms were known from the Syriac Christian Bible, and it was a 'Syriac' bishop, Timothy I, who told the story of scroll discoveries near Jericho, including numerous psalms. Could it be that the Syriac Church owed their additional psalms to the same source which was behind the collection in that cave 'near Jericho'? If so, the link between Qumran and a strand of the Christian tradition could be very close indeed. Once again, we do not know if 'near Jericho' should be interpreted as 'at Qumran' in modern topography. But it is a distinct possibility.

Here are two examples from these new, additional psalms, first the beginning of Psalm 151, in which David, the shepherd, joins in with trees and herds to praise the Lord who had chosen him, followed by the end of Psalm 155, a psalm of trust in the Lord, the just judge and Saviour:

> *Hallelujah. By David, the Son of Jesse.*
> *I was smaller than my brothers*
>> *and I was the youngest of my father's sons.*
> *And he made me the shepherd of his flock,*
>> *and the ruler over his children.*
> *My hands made an instrument, my fingers built a lyre,*
>> *and I glorified God.*
> *Thus I said to myself:*
> *The mountains do not testify to him,*
>> *and the hills do not tell of him.*
> *[But] the trees agree to my words,*
>> *and the herds to my deeds.*
> *For who tells and who names and who describes the works of God?*
>> *God sees everything, he hears everything, he notices everything.*

I trust you, Lord.

I called, 'Lord', and he answered me,
and he healed my broken heart.

I slept, and I slumbered, I dreamt, but I woke up.

Lord, you helped my stricken heart,
and I called upon you, Lord, my Saviour.

I relied on you, and I was not disappointed.

Redeem Israel, your pious ones, Lord,
and the House of Jacob, your elect.

Karaites, cavemen and the Jews of Cairo

A few decades before Timothy I, in c. AD 767, a Persian Jew called Anan Ben David established a Jewish movement, the Ananites. Others soon called them *Quara'im*, or 'Karaites', and *Bene miqrah*, the 'Sons of scripture'. Confronted by the political and religious unrest of the Muslim conquest of Persia, and an all-too-flexible rabbinical Judaism, these Karaites, as they came to be known, attempted to consolidate orthodox faith. It was a return to strictest rules, and it was built upon the sole authority of the Old Testament. Talmud and Mishnah or, in other words, the traditions of rabbinical teaching, were excluded. The regulations for the sabbath, for circumcision, cultic purity and marriage were tightened, and there were variations in several observances of *kashrut* regulations and the festal calendar.

After the death of their founder, the Karaites split into various groups, but continued to spread to the Holy Land, to Egypt and into the Byzantine empire. About AD 850, Daniel al-Qumiqi led the Karaites to Jerusalem where they soon established a missionary presence, reaching even Muslim Spain, via northern Africa. There was a messianic strategy behind this: all Jews were invited to return to the promised Holy Land, so as to hasten the coming of the Messiah. We owe to the Karaites of this period one of the most important surviving codices of the Hebrew Old Testament: the so-called Codex Cairensis

(Cairo Codex), which comprises the books of the Prophets and was written in Tiberias, in AD 895, by a certain Moses Ben Asher. The date and the name are mentioned in editorial endnotes (colophons) by the writer himself; this makes the Cairo Codex the oldest dated manuscript of the Hebrew Bible. Moses was one of the members of the Ben Asher 'clan' who also engendered the even more famous tenth-century Bible edition called the Aleppo Codex and established the Hebrew text of the *Masorah*.[9] Moses Ben Asher's codex was given to the Karaite community of Jerusalem and requisitioned by the Crusaders in 1099. Through unknown channels, it was eventually released and handed over to the Karaites of Cairo who still own it.[10]

It has been supposed – but is far from certain – that the Ben Asher family were themselves Karaites. Eventually, in the seventeenth and eighteenth centuries, many Karaites settled in Lithuania and the Crimean peninsula. Since 1948, thousands have emigrated to Israel, mainly from Islamic countries and, more recently, from the former Soviet Union. And what appears to be a minor facet of Jewish religious history turns out to offer yet another surprising glimpse into the history of the Dead Sea Scrolls, from the centuries prior to their rediscovery. For the Karaites themselves are convinced that Anan Ben David may have established their movement, but its groundwork was laid during the late Second Temple period; the Judaism of the diaspora in Egypt (of which Philo of Alexandria was the most famous exponent), and particularly the thought of what we call the Essene movement, are claimed as spiritual cornerstones.

In or about AD 937, the Karaite historian Qirqisani said that Zadok, the progenitor of the Sadducees, had written a book which prohibits (among other things) the marriage of a man with his niece, and Anan Ben David had quoted it in his 'Book of Rules'. It is a rule which appears literally in the Damascus Document (5:8–11). Thus, it may be supposed that the Karaites knew the Damascus Document or other texts of the same persuasion which could be linked to Zadok.

And the so-called 'Sons of Zadok', descendants of the Zadokite priesthood, were indeed the rulers of the Essene movement – at least for a certain period of time, and at Qumran, if not everywhere else.[11] And Qirqisani provides us with further evidence: he names a source of his information, a certain David Ibn Merwan, who had written about the sect of the 'cavemen', so-called because their writings were found in caves. It is difficult to escape the conclusion that he meant the caves of the Dead Sea, 'near Jericho', at Qumran.[12] Qirqisani's hints include certain Essene aspects – for example, his reference to their different calendar, and the place he gives them in his own chronological history. The 'cavemen' and their texts are mentioned after the Sadducees and before Jesus and his followers – that new Jewish movement of the first century. In other words, he places them precisely at the time when they had their main 'headquarters' at Qumran, near the caves.

More than any other writing, the Damascus Document (CD) and the Community Rule (1QS) underline the importance of the Sons of Zadok for the Essenes. To most Christians, however, Zadok is a mere name from the lineage of Jesus (Matthew 1:14), and a musical experience thanks to Handel's coronation anthem *Zadok the Priest*. But it is no accident that Matthew inserts Zadok, the great high priest at the time of David and Solomon, into his selective genealogy of Jesus Christ. He heavily and consciously relies on his 'priestly source', the priestly genealogy of 1 Chronicles, to establish the pedigree of the Messiah.[13] Jesus himself shared certain attitudes towards the written law of the *Torah* with the Zadokite priesthood, and indeed with the later Karaites. The most remarkable point is perhaps the refusal to accept 'the traditions of men' if they do not coincide with the explicit 'commands of God' (Mark 7:8). The scribes and Pharisees are seen as propagators of a false piety which puts human authority – oral law – over God's word. The Essene Teacher of Righteousness, a man with Zadokite links, introduced and developed such precepts: in the only letter which has been found at Qumran, and which has been attributed to this Teacher, we read about the final authority of the law given to Moses and preserved in writing, and about the 'doing of the *Torah*'.

Scholars have named this letter 'Miqsat Ma'ase ha-Torah' (4Q MMT), 'something about the doing of the *Torah*'. When Jesus says, 'My mothers and brothers are those who hear God's Word and put it into practice' (Luke 8:21), he echoes this thinking of the Zadokites. The Apostle Paul uses the Greek equivalent to the Aramaic 'works/doings of the Law' in the Qumran text no less than seven times in two of his letters (Romans 2:15; 3:20; 3:28; Galatians 2:16; 3:2; 3:5; 3:10), albeit with his distinctive personal emphasis. The decisive link between Jesus, the Zadokite Essenes and Paul – which also protects us from misunderstanding Paul as an outright opponent of 'works' – is Galatians 3:10–12: 'Cursed is everyone who does not continue to do everything written in the Book of the Law.' Clearly no one is justified before God by the Law, because the 'righteous will live by faith'. The law is not based on faith; on the contrary, 'The man who does these things will live by them.' The first quote used by Paul is from Deuteronomy 27:26. The second comes from Habakkuk 2:11, and the third from Leviticus 18:5. In other words, *doing it* is the teaching of the *Torah*, of the five Mosaic books, and this remains so even if we, unlike Jesus, never achieve a status of complete obedience and fulfilment.[14] Nothing could be closer to the letter of James, a brother of Jesus (e.g. James 1:22: 'Do not merely listen to the word and so deceive yourselves. Do what it says.')

No one claims – indeed, no Qumran writing does – that works are on their own a road towards justification. But the written law of God remains the unshakeable basis, as Jesus himself had taught:

> *Do not think that I have come to abolish the law or the prophets:*
> *I have not come to abolish them, but to fulfil them. I tell you the*

truth, until heaven and earth disappear, not the smallest letter, not the least stroke of a pen will by any means disappear from the law until everything is accomplished. Anyone who breaks one of the least of these commandments and teaches others to do the same will be called least in the kingdom of heaven, but whoever practises and teaches these commands will be called great in the kingdom of heaven.

(Matthew 5:17–19 – and see the application in Luke 10:25–28, where Leviticus 18:5 is referred to by Jesus, much as Paul quotes it in Galatians 3:12!)

Paul may have had to differentiate carefully between faith and works, and the way to salvation, treading on difficult ground among the recipients of his letters in Galatia and Rome, but the teaching of Jesus is clear enough, and the apostle does not deny it. Further Qumran writings, such as the Damascus Document (CD) itself, the Community Rule (1QS), the Habakkuk Pesher (1Q pHab) and the eschatological Florilegium (4Q flor) confirm an action-orientated attitude towards the law. But it should be obvious by now: the similarity between the Teacher of Righteousness and his Essene Zadokites on the one hand, and Jesus and the apostles on the other, is anything but the relationship between an original thinker and his epigones. They all drew upon the same source: the *Torah* itself. And they emphasized it, against a 'spirit of the times' which appeared to deflect from it.[15]

Should we assume, tentatively at least, that the Karaites were the only Jewish movement of Judaism after the destruction of the Second Temple which could make sense of Essene literature, and therefore cherished and preserved it? But if this were the case, these Jews must have had a continuous history until they suddenly blossomed into a proper movement from the eighth century onwards. And this is indeed how the Karaites see it themselves. However – if they were not recognizable as Karaites before they were given a structure by Anan Ben David, who were they? We do not know, and this is not the place (nor the book) for the detective work needed to disentangle such a question. It could well be that the eighth-century discovery of caves with scrolls near Jericho – the very discovery mentioned by Timothy I, and with or without dogs chasing animals – revealed texts which triggered off the consolidation of this new orthodoxy. Jewish contacts between Jerusalem (where the scrolls were first studied by Jews, as Timothy tells us) and the Persian diaspora were uncomplicated at that time. If the Damascus Document was among the scrolls, it would soon have been obvious that it offered alternatives to rabbinic Judaism. And these 'alternatives' seem to have been irresistibly attractive, not only to the Karaites. Fifty years before the Qumran caves were rediscovered, a scholar from Cambridge University, Solomon Schechter, found a copy of the Damascus Document in the forgotten *genizah* of the Ben-Ezra Synagogue in Fostat, Old Cairo.

A *genizah* is a storage room in synagogues, where worn-out scrolls and books, and other objects of worship and ritual, are kept for a solemn burial at a later time. Some archaeologists think the room behind the *Torah* niche in the first-century BC/AD synagogue on the fortress of Masada, where scrolls of the prophet Ezekiel and Essene writings were discovered, could have been such a *genizah*. But the one which has become proverbially famous was discovered by accident, in 1896, when two women from Scotland bought some Hebrew manuscripts in Cairo and showed them to Solomon Schechter, who identified one of them as the lost Hebrew original of Ecclesiasticus (Ben Sira) and in 1887 went to Cairo himself to investigate. The *genizah* of that synagogue, which until the ninth century had been the Christian church of St Michael's, had simply been forgotten, walled up and accidentally found during some restoration work. Scrolls were sold, to Scottish women and many other collectors, and when Schechter arrived, he managed to buy more than 140,000 fragments for Cambridge University. Other books and fragments, an estimated 60,000, had gone to archives and museums all over the world before Schechter reached Cairo. Most of them could later be traced at the library of St Petersburg (intermittently called Leningrad). There and at the Taylor-Schechter Genizah Research Unit, Cambridge University Library, scholars are still working on these fragments, although most of the major works have long been edited and published.

The priceless treasures in Cambridge include personal manuscripts of Maimonides, one of the great Jewish teachers of the late Middle Ages (1135–1204), who lived in Fostat/Old Cairo as head of the Jewish community from 1177 until his death. Countless texts, many of them previously unknown, were identified, ranging from the Bible to rabbinical exegesis (*midrashim*), the Talmud (particularly the Jerusalem Talmud or *Talmud Yerushalmi*), Karaite writings and, strikingly, documents which could be connected with the scrolls mentioned by the Nestorian bishop Timothy I and the Jewish Karaite historian Qirqisani. The oldest manuscripts could be dated to the fifth century AD, but most of them were copies of much older documents. It took Schechter years to decipher and publish the first of his finds – and the editorial problems were not caused by texts which were already known (if only, as for Ben Sira/Ecclesiasticus, in translations), but by completely unknown new discoveries. This, in fact, has remained a problem for other editors, notably those of the Oxyrhynchus discoveries (which began in the same year), and of the Dead Sea Scrolls: fragments of which there are no complete copies or originals elsewhere cannot be compared to such published 'models'. Every attempt at reconstruction must be tentative. And if there are gaps, missing words and lines, lost beginnings or ends, how is one to know what to insert? Intuition, a vast knowledge of the relevant literature, and years of combining bits and pieces of circumstantial evidence must come together. Even then, there will be many hypothetical approaches and suggestions.

Schechter edited the surviving fragments of the 'Zadokite Work', originally two separate and complete copies, in 1910.[16] From its text, he identified it as a writing in the tradition of the Zadokite priesthood – hence the name he gave it. And we can understand how tempting it must have been to see the links between this find and Qirqisani's comments. But how did two copies of what came to be known as the Damascus Document (CD) reach the Ben-Ezra synagogue in Cairo? Remember that the building, previously the church of St Michael's, only became a synagogue in the ninth century – in 882, to be precise. This roughly coincides with the initial heyday of the Karaite movement in Egypt and the Levant, preceded by the rediscovery of those caves near Jericho mentioned by Timothy I. For the tentative dates given to the actual Cairo fragments, which are of course copies of copies of copies, are ninth to tenth century (the time of Timothy I) for the first, and eleventh to twelfth century (the time of Qirqisani) for the second; in both cases, the earlier dates are more likely. It could be argued, of course, that a single Essene text, the Damascus Document, outstandingly important as it is, does not suffice as proof of a link between the caves and the *genizah*. After all, good old biblical precedent demands 'two or three witnesses'. And indeed, there is at least one other text which was discovered both in the *genizah* and in the Qumran caves: the so-called Testament of Levi.

Most scholars assume there once was a work called the Testaments of the Twelve Patriarchs. Its Greek version was completed towards the end of the first century AD, with one Testament for each of the twelve sons of Jacob. But while the completed work did not exist during the lifetime of the Qumran community, this composition had Hebrew and Aramaic precursors, of which a few have been found at Qumran: a Testament of Naphtali (4Q 215), a Testament of Judah (minute fragments tentatively identified from 3Q 7; 4Q 484; 4Q 538), a Testament of Joseph (4Q 538–39?), and a Testament of Levi which existed in at least three separate Aramaic copies (1Q 21; 4Q 213;

4Q 214), related perhaps to a third and fourth fragment (4Q 537; 4Q 541). The Levi manuscripts have been dated to the third century BC – which makes them one of the oldest, if not the oldest, non-biblical texts found at Qumran. This further highlights their outstanding importance. What is more, the Testament of Levi is explicitly quoted in the Damascus Document (4:15). Small wonder, perhaps. After all, it is about Levi and the institution of the Levite priesthood, the very origins of a tradition which was the yardstick for the Zadokite priests behind (and in) the Damascus Document. Like all the other testaments, it is a valedictory speech, but Levi gives it nineteen years before his death. Decisively, the text also deals with his investiture as priest. Levi is singled out among his brothers: his descendants will form the priestly family. The Qumran fragments of the Testament of Levi are very close indeed to the lengthy fragmentary manuscripts found half a century earlier in Cairo (and now housed in Cambridge and Oxford).[17] It seems there was a continuous, reliable awareness of this work among Jews interested in priestly origins and traditions.

The sheer wealth of manuscripts discovered in the Cairo *genizah* has been overshadowed by the discovery of the Qumran caves. This is unfortunate, and it is unjustified. But for our present purposes, suffice it to say the story of the caves near Jericho and the treasure of the Ben-Ezra synagogue seem to prove that the knowledge of the 'Qumran' or 'Dead Sea' literature was never completely lost. Archaeologists may have been incredibly slow to understand and to grasp their opportunities – it is difficult to believe, for example, that even after the discovery of Cave 1 in 1946/47, most scholars thought it was a 'one off' and did not initiate any further search until the Bedouins – again! – discovered caves in the Wadi Murabba'at some 18 km south of Qumran in 1951 and a further cave at Qumran itself in 1952 (2Q). In March 1952, serious archaeological work finally began, and Cave 3 was discovered. But Cave 4, the enormous library cave just opposite the settlement of Qumran, was once more found by

III

Goats, Arms and Revolutionaries

THE CASE OF THE MODERN DISCOVERIES

The rediscovery of the first Qumran caves by Bedouins has been surrounded by popular legends about shepherd boys and their goats. The historical reality is much more intriguing and takes us back into a world of arms trading, caches and gun-running in the final years of the British Mandate.

This chapter briefly describes the struggle for the scrolls, between the Bedouins, the Israelis, the Jordanians and some Christians, in the years from 1947 to 1956, when the last fragments were found. What happened when the settlement or *Khirbet* of Qumran with its mysterious structure was discovered and further caves were found in the south? There is more behind the Dead Sea Scrolls than Qumran and its caves.

For a gun and a wife

The discovery of the caves at Qumran has been hailed as the greatest archaeological success story of the twentieth century. Books about Qumran, the Essenes, Jesus and early Christianity have become instant bestsellers. And there certainly is no other discovery which has produced so many different journals, articles, TV programmes and conferences, still going strong after more than fifty years. And yet, as we have seen, the discovery itself was not only unspectacular, it was a complete embarrassment. The three Ta'amireh Bedouins, Muhammad ed-Dibh, Juma Muhammad and Khalik Musa, turned out to be far-from-harmless shepherds who innocently stumbled upon a cave, and equally innocently upon further caves almost at leisure, outwitting professional archaeologists as they went along. Their tribe had been in the smuggling business for generations. And the rugged cliffs along the Dead Sea, with their deep wadis and seemingly inaccessible caves, were ideal depots for contraband – much as they had been hiding places for the revolutionaries under Bar Kokhba in the second century. The Bedouins had sheep and goat herds with them, near their home region around Bethlehem in the summer, and at the Dead Sea during the winter months. Such herds were their regular livelihood. They could sell the milk, the wool and the meat in Bethlehem, Jericho and the villages. And at the same time, these herds provided perfect cover for their more clandestine activities. Looking for caves was a regular activity. They could serve as storage places, or they could already contain treasures left by others before them. It is no secret that Ta'amireh Bedouins had been selling ancient coins and other artefacts to workers at the budding Dead Sea industrial plants since the 1930s. It is equally well known that the French excavator of Wadi Churetun – also called Wadi Chareitun and, in Hebrew, Nahal Tekoa[1] – 1 km south of the Herodeion, Consul René Neuville, employed Ta'amireh Bedouins who sold him the ancient objects they had found in other wadis. And thanks to Neuville, the Ta'amireh acquired archaeological techniques. In brief, when they found a cave which turned out to contain jars with scrolls, later labelled Qumran Cave 1, they knew exactly what they were going to do. Scrolls in a – to them – more or less indecipherable writing may not have been as appealing as coins, but it was obvious enough that they were very old and therefore intrinsically valuable.

Whether it took them a few days or a couple of weeks (their recollections differ on points of detail), they eventually did approach a dealer in Bethlehem, one Ibrahim Ijha who in turn went to a professional salesman, Feidi al-Alami, who had a name as an antiquities expert. Both were sceptical, and al-Alami regarded the manuscripts he was shown as stolen Jewish property, refusing point blank to deal with them. In other words, the Bedouins and the Arabs in Bethlehem emerge from the initial stages of the story with some credit. Should we really expect them to have approached the Jews, or one of the western parties – the French or British – diplomatically and militarily ill at ease at a time of internecine strife, Arab-Jewish unrest and a looming world crisis over plans to establish a state of Israel? In fact, going to one of these players was the last idea that would have crossed a Ta'amireh Bedouin's mind. After all, they played a highly dangerous game behind and between the lines themselves, smuggling arms and ammunition. The intricacies of the plot only developed when the first Christians became involved: two Syrian-Orthodox Arabs from Jerusalem and Bethlehem, George Shaya and Khalil Iskander Shahin. The first, also known as George Isaiah ('Shaya' is Arabic for Isaiah), had helped the Ta'amireh sell their merchandise in Jerusalem. When Juma Muhammad told George about those conspicuous scrolls, the Christian immediately thought of another Syrian-Orthodox man with friends in high places: Khalil, better known as Kando, a shoemaker in Bethlehem. And Kando knew the right person: the young Syrian-Orthodox bishop at St Mark's Monastery in Jerusalem, between the Armenian and Jewish quarters of the city, Mar Athanasius Yeshue Samuel, a keen collector of old manuscripts for the monastery's famous library.

The rest, as they say, is history. Well, not quite – the bishop was no expert in ancient Hebrew. He consulted scholars at the Hebrew University of Jerusalem. They identified the longest of the scrolls as Isaiah – it was in fact the great Isaiah scroll of the second century BC, 7.43 m long – but rejected any thoughts that it might be older than medieval. The bishop, however, persisted, and his efforts to get the scrolls properly validated were fed back to Kando who realized his

Ta'amireh friends had discovered a potential treasure trove. Two of the Bedouins and the Syrian-Orthodox Christian George Shaya returned to Cave 1 and found further scrolls, with some jars. Suddenly, there was a market for these things. Shaya sold his share, and the scrolls of the first find, to Bishop Samuel. And the Bedouins returned to Feidi al-Alami, who bought three scrolls for seven pounds sterling. Not much later, the Bedouins would demand – and get! – twenty pounds for a single square centimetre. With Feidi al-Alami, the decisive turning point in the archaeological drama was reached – for he had an associate in Jerusalem who happened to know Eleazar Sukenik, another professor at the Hebrew University of Jerusalem. This associate, Nasri Ohan, was neither Jew nor Arab, but another Christian, though an Armenian one, for a change. Sukenik was shown the scrolls on 25 November 1947. And he, an outstanding expert in ancient Hebrew epigraphy – inscriptions on stones, ossuaries, etc. – realized immediately that these scrolls were genuine and very old indeed. The Christian merchant Nasri Ohan and the Jewish epigrapher Sukenik went to Bethlehem on the day when the United Nations voted on the establishment of the State of Israel, 29 November 1947, and they came back with two further scrolls. Later, still restricted by modest funds but blessed with tactical patience, Sukenik managed to acquire even more scrolls.

Meanwhile, the Syrian-Orthodox bishop had not managed to find anyone who was prepared to believe in the authenticity of his scrolls. In January 1948, he contacted Sukenik, who analysed them and declared them the most valuable ones so far discovered. But he could not raise the money to buy them, and the bishop was 'advised' to cease negotiations with Jews in such uncertain times and to turn to the Americans who ran the American School of Oriental Research (ASOR) in Jerusalem. With scholars such as John Trever and William Brownlee, who knew next to nothing about ancient Hebrew script, but took excellent photographs of the scrolls Bishop Samuel showed them (the long Isaiah scroll, the Community Rule and the Habakkuk Pesher), but were later joined by Millar Burrows, who was a qualified Hebrew scholar, another major player had entered the scene – the Americans. And soon, after Israel and Jordan were established as new states, the Jordanians, who occupied the Dead Sea area, became a further power to be reckoned with. But outside intrigue and politics, the decisive date was 11 April 1948: on that day, the US headquarters of the American Schools of Oriental Research in New Haven released a press report about Bishop Samuel's scrolls, highlighting the oldest surviving Isaiah scroll. The following day, it was in all major American and European newspapers. Suddenly, the Dead Sea Scrolls were a media sensation. Whatever happened next – and whole libraries have been written about it – this event helped to seal the incessant, bitter rivalry between the parties. From then on, it was a scholarly fight about access to the scrolls and first publications; it was a struggle between archaeologists and Bedouins, between Israel and Jordan, and, unfortunately, also between Jewish and Christian experts, a conflict which simmered under the surface of public attention until the director of the editorial team in East Jerusalem, John Strugnell, was sacked in 1990, after blatantly anti-Semitic remarks in an interview published by the Israeli daily Ha'Aretz, and was replaced by a team under Jewish-Israeli leadership. (The new top man, Emanuel Tov, is an excellent scholar and administrator.) What could have been an ecumenical story, reminiscent of Timothy I and his Arab and Jewish sources, had already turned sour when the American Christian scholars outwitted both Eleazar Sukenik and, in a way, Bishop Samuel, and published three scrolls on the basis of Trever's photographs,[2] and when Kando and his Bedouins began to play them all off against each other, for even more pounds and dollars. Gone were the days when Muhammad ed-Dibh, 'the wolf', was satisfied with enough money to buy a gun – and a wife.

Desert hideouts for lawyers and revolutionaries

In the autumn of 1951, while the quest for more caves and scrolls was in full flow – among the Bedouins, at least – sudden light was shed on the area south of Qumran, when Ta'amireh Bedouins found manuscripts in the Nahal Darga. This cleft, with its more common Arabic name Wadi Murabba'at was, in a way, natural Bedouin hunting ground – it stretched from the desert of Bethlehem down to the Dead Sea.[3] The Ta'amireh sold their first finds, and when the archaeologists arrived on the scene – no Jews among them[4] – a total of four caves was searched (two of which are accessible to intrepid climbers, from the path south of Kibbutz Mitzpe Shalom). It soon became obvious they had been used by refugees, revolutionaries and smugglers since the Chalcolithic Age (c. 4000 BC and later). Artefacts such as ceramic and scarabs belonged to the Middle Bronze Age, c. 2000 BC. The oldest manuscript, an administrative papyrus (P. Murabba'at 17), could be dated to the Late Iron Age, c. 650 BC, the period of the last kings of Judah. It was written in palaeo-Hebrew – the ancient Hebrew script which remained in use much later, in some of the Qumran scrolls of the second and first century BC, for the holy and unspeakable name of God, the tetragram YHWH. The latest finds in those caves included Arabic texts and other Arab objects from the seventh to the fourteenth century AD. It seems Arab tribes found and used the caves several centuries after the last Jews and Romans had left them. For the decisive periods of use were neither the Iron Age nor the Muslim–Arab occupation, but the time of the first and the second Jewish revolts against the Romans.

Some of those who had fled from Qumran, or from the Bethlehem area north-west of the wadi during the first revolt between AD 66 and AD 73, and who had not made it to Masada, found refuge in the caves. But in the later stages of that revolt, when the Romans had occupied Jerusalem and were approaching Masada, some of the Jews up there left the fortress and took shelter in the caves. It is quite possible that those who left were ordinary inhabitants who did not want to join the zealots in their both desperate and ruthless actions in the final stage of the revolt, when Jerusalem had fallen to the Romans. A promissory note, a marriage contract and a divorce certificate were discovered (Murabba'at 18, 19 and 20), all three in Aramaic, and since one of these, the divorce certificate, describes the couple as resident on Masada, while the other two documents are in a near-identical, moderately older script, it has rightly been assumed that they all came from the fortress, perhaps as a once-complete legal archive – of which only these three pieces have survived.

The divorce certificate can be dated to the month of October (Heshvan) in the sixth year of Masada – 71 AD.[5] It is signed by the husband, Joseph, son of Naqsan, who dismisses and expels his wife, Mariam, daughter of Jonathan, according to Jewish law, and it is signed by three witnesses, Eliezer, son of Malka, Joseph, son of Malka, and Eleazar, son of Hanana. The former husband declares he does it of his own free will and pays his ex-wife in coins for all loss of her own property. As from now on, Joseph declares, Mariam is free to marry any Jewish man she likes. The lawyer who kept what would have been his filing-cabinet copy of the original given to Mariam (with a further copy for Joseph) evidently came to Masada from a place where he had been used to dating his documents in Roman terms. Both the promissory note and the marriage contract are dated to the relevant years of Emperor Nero's reign: the note is dated to the second year of Nero (13 October 55–12 October 56; day and month were also mentioned, but are lost on the fragment). And the contract is dated 'Seventh Adar in the eleventh year...' This cannot be the eleventh year of Masada, since the fortress only lasted eight years under zealot rule until the Romans took it, and it has therefore been assumed that the damaged part of the manuscript mentioned Nero. Hence, the date would be February/March AD 64. All three documents seem to be valuable evidence for a continuation of Jewish civil and religious law under the Roman occupation of Palestine. The marriage contract explicitly refers to a wedding 'according to the law of Moses'. And it had taken place in Haradona, the home town of the husband, 'Judah, son of Jo[...], son of Manasseh the Eliashibite' (cf. 1 Chronicles 24:12 for the oldest reference to this priestly family), some 5 km south-east of Jerusalem.[6]

These three texts coincide with the New Testament period, and they help us to understand passages in the gospels. In Luke 16:1–7, we encounter a promissory note. It is the parable of the rich man and his dishonest manager who summons his master's debtors. 'How much do you owe my master?' the manager asks the first debtor. 'A hundred jars of olive oil.' He said to him, 'Take your promissory note [in Greek, ta grammata][7], sit down quickly, and make it fifty.' Then he asked another, 'And how much do you owe?' He replied, 'A hundred containers of wheat.' He said to him, 'Take your promissory note and make it eighty.' In the note from the Nahal Darga, we read that Absalom from Kfar Sagana (in southern Galilee) had lent twenty Sus (sixty-eight grams) of silver to Zechariah from Kasalon (17 km west of Jerusalem). Zechariah promises to pay his debts by a certain date; otherwise he will pay a surcharge of one-fifth. He puts in pawn the equivalent value of his property and his future earnings. The promissory note is signed by the scribe (Zechariah cannot write) and three male witnesses. As in the divorce certificate mentioned above, a certain number of witnesses was such a common ingredient of legal procedures that we meet it on several occasions in the Bible: in the almost proverbial 'two or three' witnesses of Deuteronomy 17:6 and 19:15; Matthew 18:16; 2 Corinthians 13:1; 1 Timothy 5:19; and Hebrews 10:28 (only John 8:17 and Revelation 11:3 are satisfied with the minimum of two witnesses, whereas another Johannine writing, 1 John 5:7, retains the trio). It is this awareness of legal precedents and expectations which convinced the early church that all three synoptic gospels of Matthew, Mark and Luke should be kept in the canon of the New Testament, in spite of their overwhelming doublets and similarities. Well, not in spite, but because of them. These similarities, with the added authenticity of unharmonized, quite normal differences and nuances, fulfilled the requirements of the law. For the words and deeds of Jesus, for his death on the cross, and most importantly for his resurrection, the one gospel of Jesus Christ had to be protocolled and signed by 'two or three' closely corroborative witnesses.[8] And the two documents from the caves which have preserved their endnotes with the signatures, and which are dated to the later gospel period, emphasize the contemporary practice: if possible, get three rather than merely two witnesses.

The divorce certificate, too, illuminates a gospel text. Some Pharisees came to test Jesus, and they asked, 'Is it lawful for a man to divorce his wife?' He answered them, 'What did Moses command you?' They said, 'Moses allowed a man to write a certificate of dismissal and to divorce her.' But Jesus said to them, 'Because of your hardness of heart he wrote this commandment for you. But from the beginning of creation, God made them male and female. For this reason a man shall leave his father and mother and be joined to his wife, and the two shall become one flesh. So they are no longer two, but one flesh. Therefore what God has joined together, let no one separate' (Mark 10:2–9; cf. Matthew 5:31; 19:3–9). The reference to the law of Moses is based on Deuteronomy 24:1–4, and the divorce certificate from the Nahal Darga/Wadi Murabba'at, with its dismissal of the wife, is therefore quite unobjectionable in historical Jewish terms. Remarkably, Jesus tries to explain why this was so, but he also explains to his opponents that God's will for mankind moves in a completely different direction.

On a more positive note, the marriage contract is a surprisingly modern and caring document, for the benefit of the wife, their children, and for the time of a possible widowhood. Thus Judah, the husband, declares that his wife (her name is not extant on the fragment), should she survive him, will be entitled to live in his house, and be fed and clothed from his estate, in perpetuity. Twice the husband appeals to 'the law of Moses of the Jews'. And twice the formula 'for ever/in perpetuity' is used. This husband does not even consider the eventuality of a divorce, as partners in a late-twentieth-century marriage contract are encouraged to do by efficient lawyers. He would have understood and appreciated the punchline of Jesus' reply to the Pharisees in Mark 10:2–9.

More famous by far, at least in the eyes of the public, are the Nahal Darga discoveries from the second Jewish revolt, under Bar Kokhba, AD 132–35. It was the time of Emperor Hadrian (117–138), whom many classical scholars appreciate as an enlightened, poetically gifted administrator and builder. In and near Rome alone, four of the most impressive buildings which have survived from antiquity are his: the villa at Tivoli, the Pantheon, his mausoleum (the Castel S. Angelo) and the Aelian Bridge (Ponte S. Angelo) opposite the mausoleum. A certain Simon Bar Kosiba assembled a group of resistance fighters against the Romans who had continuously suppressed Jewish freedom after the first revolt and the destruction of Jerusalem, which Hadrian was about to turn into a Roman city called Aelia Capitolina. Soon he was hailed as the Messiah by important Jewish teachers such as Rabbi Aquiba. Aquiba taught that Simon was the fulfilment of Balaam's prophecy in Numbers 24:15–19: 'A star shall come out of Jacob, and a sceptre shall rise out of Israel' to destroy the enemies of the people. Thus Simon's family name 'son of Kosiba' was soon turned into the Aramaic byname 'Bar Kokhba', the Son of the Star. But obviously, Jewish Christians were among the Jews who did not follow this false Messiah; they called him 'Bar Koziba', the Son of the Lie. It took the Romans almost four years to suppress the revolt, and there appears to be some evidence for Roman losses and exhaustion behind Hadrian's decision to drop the standard formula, 'I and my legions are well' (*mihi et legionibus bene*) in his report to the senate in Rome.[9] And Hadrian's revenge was ruthless: no Jew was allowed to settle in Jerusalem; the city was rebuilt as a garrison town with temples to Roman godheads covering the site of the Temple, of Golgotha and the empty tomb; and a giant statue of Hadrian in the centre of town. Circumcision was forbidden, and some later rabbinical sources mention the prohibition of sabbath observance and the reading of the *Torah*.[10] During the final, desperate period of the revolt, Bar Kokhba and his people regrouped in the Judean desert. In the Nahal Darga, they lived in the caves and left wax tablets, everyday tools and cooking implements; a *tefilin* box (for a biblical verse to be worn on the left arm or on the forehead) and coins minted by the Bar Kokhba adherents, with a palaeo-Hebrew inscription calling him 'Shimon Nasi Yisrael', 'Simon the Prince of Israel' – plainly a messianic title. But most importantly, there was a host of Hebrew, Aramaic, Greek and Latin manuscripts in those caves, among them a marriage contract of AD 135 (Muraba'at 21), leases, sales contracts and promissory notes of AD 131 to 135 (Murabba'at 25–26, 27–28, 31–33, 38).

The leases are dated to the equivalent year 'of the liberation of Jerusalem under Shimon Ben (!) Kosiba, Prince of Israel', and they name the 'Nasi' as the legal owner. The most fascinating documents from those caves, however, are two letters (Murabba'at 43 and 44), written by Bar Kokhba in his own hand, as he states himself at the end (cf. Paul's usage in 1 Corinthians 16:21; Galatians 6:11; Colossians 4:18; 2 Thessalonians 3:17). They are addressed to one of his commanders, Yeshua Ben Galgula, who apparently took them with him when he pitched camp in the Nahal. Even with the pretty hopeless situation of his troops at this stage, Bar Kokhba insists on the holiness of the sabbath; in the second letter, he tells Yeshua to welcome members of his family for the sabbath and to expect a delivery of wheat once the sabbath is over.

The Romans soon found the caves, starved out the defenders, took them prisoner or killed them on the spot. One cohort under the centurion Annaeus stayed in the caves: a Roman lance, some fragments of Latin documents and a wooden seal of 'Gargilius from the cohort of Annaeus' were found by archaeologists. It seems the Romans kept a sentry in this area until the reign of Emperor Commodus (AD 180–193 – this follows from a military papyrus in Greek, P. Murabba'at 117). During their presence, they found manuscripts left behind by the revolutionaries and wilfully tore them up, notably biblical texts copied in the early second century (Murabba'at 1–3), from the *Torah* (Genesis, Exodus, Leviticus) and Isaiah, of which a few fragments were found. But the Nahal Darga/Wadi Murabba'at offered three finds which have remained among the most important and most puzzling Dead Sea manuscripts: a Hebrew scroll of the twelve minor prophets, a papyrus fragment of an unknown Greek comedy, and a leather document in Greek shorthand.

The Hebrew scroll was discovered by the Bedouins in 1955, in a fifth Murabba'at cave which had been used as a tomb. Dated to the early second century, the Hebrew text is astonishingly close to the edited Hebrew Bible of the eighth-century Masoretes. And since this closeness is much more consistent than in the Qumran scrolls, a far-reaching conclusion has been drawn: the biblical scrolls at Qumran, which precede the year AD 68, belonged to a period of flexibility in style, vocabulary and syntax. But after AD 70, when Jewish religious leaders and scribes reorganized themselves, one of their most urgent tasks was the codification of the Hebrew Bible, establishing a unified – and unifying – literary form and structure. The scroll of the minor prophets from Cave 5 in the Wadi Murabba'at could be the earliest surviving piece of evidence for this authoritative standard text.

A different literary surprise was the discovery of a Greek papyrus fragment in the typical metre of Greek dramatic dialogue, iambic trimeters. The papyrologists dated it to the middle or second half of the first century AD, give or take a few years. When papyrus P. Mur. 108 was published by the Wadi Murabba'at editors, they thought it was a philosophical text.[11] But because of its metre, and although no line is complete enough to make an exact analysis possible, the British classical scholar and papyrologist Colin Austin identified it as a fragment of a lost Greek comedy.[12] Both suggestions point in a similar direction, however: someone must have taken Greek literature of a certain cultural standard (be it philosophy or comedy) to the rocks and caves of the Dead Sea. It was no accident, since three further unidentified Greek literary papyrus fragments of the same date were found nearby (P. Mur. 109–111), and in all likelihood – given the date of the papyri – they were deposited during or soon after the first Jewish revolt, rather than at the time of Bar Kokhba or later. Should we assume that the revolutionaries browsed through comedies and neo-Platonic treatises while the Roman legions were surrounding their hideouts? It sounds somewhat unlikely. But there may be a solution, not too far away, if we look at these finds in the Wadi Murabba'at and compare them to similar fragments at another Dead Sea site, the fortress of Masada, some 27 km to the south.

A Roman officer and a Jewish playwright

Masada, like the Nahal Darga/Wadi Murabba'at, has a long history of habitation. First fortified in the second century BC, it was enlarged and beautified by Herod the Great, who built a terraced, three-storey palace, the remains of which can still be visited. The Romans took it over in AD 6, but since AD 66, it had been in the hands of Jewish rebels. Masada is in everyone's imagination, of course, thanks to the almost mythical story of a mass suicide of more than 900 Jewish defenders, men, women and children, in the winter of AD 73/74, when the Romans were about to conquer the fortress. Not so many years ago, recruits of the Israeli Defence Force, the IDF, took their vows on Masada, and visitors could buy caps with the evocative inscription, 'Masada Shan't Fall Again'. The heroic account of Josephus, complete with famous last words, has very recently been questioned by Israeli archaeologists and historians. But whatever the scholarly debate may yield one day, the fact remains that there was a battle between zealot defenders and Roman attackers, and that several caches and deposits with manuscripts were found when Yigael Yadin, the son of Eleazar Sukenik, undertook his archaeological campaign between 1963 and 1965. Two sites aroused enthusiastic interest: first, the place where the first Jewish manuscripts were discovered, and second, not far away, another *locus* with Latin papyri.

Those Jewish manuscripts were found in the synagogue of Masada, in a room behind the 'Aaron ha-Kodesh', the niche for the *Torah* scroll. Some scholars think it was a kind of *genizah*, like the one at the Ben-Ezra Synagogue in Old Cairo. But it is much more likely that it was the study library of the synagogue.[13] In any case, one of the fragments rescued by the archaeologists contained Ezekiel 37:1–14, the prophecy of the dry bones, and a fragment from Deuteronomy 33–34, with the final blessing of Moses. When the Romans approached, the scrolls were hastily buried under the floor, and when the Romans arrived and found the synagogue, they burnt furniture and other objects and threw them into that room. The scrolls survived underneath the rubble.

Other Jewish fragments found on Masada include the Angelic Liturgy, later called the Songs of the Sabbath Sacrifice,[14] which were also found in Qumran and have been used by scholars to argue that Qumran Essenes escaped to Masada with some of their texts – or, at least as likely, Masada was one of the places which received copies of Qumran writings as a matter of course. Numerous Greek and Aramaic papyri and *ostraca* (potsherds) were found, with letters, names and instructions about the distribution of food and drink. All of these texts could safely be dated to the period before the Roman occupation. The ramparts? One thing is certain: for every text that can be assigned to the Jews on Masada, the latest possible date is AD 73/74, when the Romans took over. And Virgil? It might just about be possible to suggest a certain knowledge of Greek literature among highly educated Jews at this time and in this part of the world – witness Paul who knew at least some lines from Menander, Aratus and Aeschylus, perhaps also from Euripides, Callimachus and (Pseudo-)Epimenides.[17] We may even assume some working knowledge of Latin for everyday purposes – after all, the administrative language of the Romans was Latin, not Greek. But for Palestine, there is no trace of literary Latin in Jewish hands. Not even the theatre, a welcome form of entertainment in Caesarea, Sepphoris, Jerusalem and elsewhere, could have introduced the Jewish population to this cultural language; all performances were in Greek.[18] Thus Hannah Cotton and Joseph Geiger, the editors of the Masada Virgil, are right: this line from the *Aeneid* was written by a Roman officer, probably just after the conquest. It is a conclusion with a clue in the text itself, for the fragment could be reconstructed as *Aeneid* 4:9, a line from Dido's first speech: *Anna, soror, quae me suspensam insomnia terrent* – 'Anna, sister, why are these nightmares frightening me?' A Roman officer, faced by hundreds of dead bodies among the debris of Masada, could well have had a sleepless night or two. And a famous line of an educated Roman's staple diet, Virgil's *Aeneid*, could easily have come to mind. It seems he wrote down a similar line on the other side of the papyrus, but although enough letters have survived, it cannot be identified; the Roman poem to which it belongs is no longer extant. However, the central word is *titubantia* which means 'swaying/stammering', and thus suggests a comparable context. The man who quoted these lines was a perturbed Roman seeking solace in poetry. And, as it happens, there is similar evidence for the role of Virgil among battle-worn Romans: at Vindolanda, the Roman garrison town near Hadrian's wall, thousands of slivers of wood with writings from the end of the first century were discovered, and among the private and military texts, there was one piece of literature: Virgil. Yet again, it was from his *Aeneid*, a later passage, 9:473. Heads dripping with blood, and the news of the killings spreading to the camp. Gory stuff, sublimated in poetry.[19] Virgil on Masada, the oldest surviving papyrus of the *Aeneid* on a Jewish fortress – riddles with a plausible solution. And thus, the Greek comedy fragment found in the Nahal Dagar/Wadi Murabba'at, datable to more or the less the same period as the Masada Virgil, could be explained on the same grounds: here was an educated Roman officer, who read his Greek authors in his spare time, and who needed some light, but poetically refined (iambic trimeter!) mental refreshment after a hard day's work.

It is a solution which fits our knowledge of the wide-ranging education of the Roman officer class. But it is almost too tempting to be satisfied with it. Let us pause for a moment and look at the Greek fragment from the Murabba'at caves again, attempting some detective work. Not much has survived, no complete lines, few complete words. The fragments consist of six scraps. Fragment A has, among other legible and distinctive words, 'God' in line 6 (θεος). In line 8 we have δεσμε, which belongs to a verb, 'to bind together', 'to put in chains'. In line 9, there is φευγ from 'taking flight', 'fleeing from something'. Line 10 has a form of ελεεω, 'to have/show/obtain pity/mercy'. In line 11, we read γυναικα, 'woman' (accusative). Line 16 identifies a speaker who talks about himself: εγω, 'I'. In line 20, we read αναφ, which could come from the verb for 'to offer (occasionally, 'at the altar'), or 'to bear/sustain', αναφερω. In line 22, something happens about marriage (γαμουμεναις). Fragment B has, among others, νεκρ in line 2, derived from νεκρος, 'dead', or some other Greek word connected with death. In line 4, we can read clearly η φυσις, παλει, καλει, 'nature', followed by forms of 'to be disabled' (or, if -ει is a misspelling for -αι, 'long ago/in times past'), and 'to summon/ invite/call by name'. Something is turned round or changed in line 5 (ετρεψεν), and taken into the arms (ηναγκα). In line 6, νομω refers to law, a fragmentary word preceded by εχειν – someone out there is having a law. Fragments C to F are single letters, with the exception of a word on fragment C, φερουσι, connected with 'carrying/ bringing/bearing/enduring'. This, without going into grammatical details, is the substance of what there is. But what is it?

One's first impression is not particularly comical, in spite of Colin Austin's metric suggestion. It rather looks like a theological or philosophical text, albeit in poetic form. In fact, all these words occur in the Greek Bible (Septuagint/New Testament). Just to provide an example: in the story of Jesus and the healing of the Gerasene demoniac (Luke 8:26–39), and the ensuing story of the woman with haemorrhages (Luke 8:43–48), we encounter God, someone in chains, demons 'summoning/beseeching' (παρα–καλεω), swineherds taking flight, a woman, Jesus saying εγω, 'I', about himself – and so forth. Needless to say, this is not to suggest that our Greek text from the desert caves is a kind of philosophical paraphrase of Luke 8:26–48. But even if we add the words missing in this Lukan story, chosen at random – there are other New Testament passages with a similar score, and words about marriage and the law are archetypal biblical terminology – it should be obvious that there is nothing in these papyrus fragments which could not have occurred to a Greek-speaking Jew immersed in biblical language. Poetic forms are common throughout the Old Testament – in the Psalms, in Job, in Ecclesiastes and the Song of Songs, to name but a few. So-called lyric metres occur in the New Testament – in the gospels and in Paul's letters. And thus our virtual Roman officer evaporates in the desert air of the Nahal Dagar. He may have been at work in Latin, up there on Masada, but we do not need him behind this Greek papyrus.

Let us go one step further. The evidence on Masada told us Greek was a natural second language to Jews at this time and not least in this area. Greek literary learning was available, and the examples given above, from Paul and Luke, speak for themselves.[20] Here is a proposition: the metric fragments P. Mur. 108 could belong to a lost play of the only known Jewish dramatist, Ezekiel the Tragedian. Some 269 lines of one of his plays have survived, quoted by Alexander Polyhistor and the Christian authors Clement of Alexandria, Pseudo-Eustathius of Antiochia and Eusebius of Caesarea.[21] The *Exagôgê* or *The Leading Out*, a drama about Moses and the Exodus, was written in iambic trimeters – the metre of the Murabba'at fragments – competently and with a gift for faithfulness to the biblical account (in the Greek Septuagint version) combined with dramatic effects. It is a play about Moses and his encounter with God (who has an off-stage speech), and it includes effective summaries of past events, notably Jacob's and Joseph's adventures in Egypt, then goes on to dwell on the marital bliss of Zipporah and Moses, before Moses dreams about his journey to Mount Sinai and finally meets God at the burning bush. This dramatic encounter, needless to say, would have been the third act. Act 4 dramatizes the flight from Egypt. An Egyptian survivor returns and tells the story – a brilliant piece of playwriting, modelled on Aeschylus' *Persians*, 353–514. Finally, the last act is placed at the palms of Elim. The oasis and the beauty of a phoenix are described in glowing terms by a fascinated visitor; it is paradise for Moses who will not see the end of the 'leading out' into the Promised Land. There must have been much more, but this is all we can still glean from the fragments which have survived in the quotes of others. We do not even know when Ezekiel lived, nor where. Most scholars assume he lived in or near Alexandria, and he must have written before the mid-first century BC, for that is when Alexander Polyhistor wrote, the first author to quote him by name. But his continuous literary presence, at least among the *cognoscenti*, is documented by Clement and Eusebius, who still knew both Alexander and Eusebius in the late second and early fourth centuries AD.[22] All Greek words or related word-forms on the Murabba'at fragments occur in the book of Genesis.[23] And they otherwise unknown and probably individual shorthand system.[25] In fact, not much is known about ancient shorthand.[26] Scholars agree it was introduced on a systematic basis in Rome, by Cicero's secretary Tiro – hence the name for the most popular system, which was later developed into Carolingian shorthand, the 'Tironian notes'. That was in the 60s of the first century BC. But even the surviving Latin shorthand manuscripts remain so difficult to decipher that the editors of five shorthand texts on slivers of wood which were discovered at Vindolanda near Hadrian's Wall, and belong to the late first century AD, admitted defeat with a self-deprecating sense of humour: 'We should warn the reader that in some cases the "writing" is so enigmatic that we cannot be sure that the plates present the tablet the right way up.'[27] Shorthand did not begin with Tiro, however. It can be traced back to the Greek-speaking Jewry of the third century BC at least, for there is an indirect but conclusive reference in the Septuagint version of a psalm.

In Psalm 45:1, we read, 'My tongue runs swiftly like the pen of an expert scribe' (Revised English Bible). In the Greek Bible, the word used for the swift expert scribe is *oxygraphos*, a shorthand writer. The person who translated that psalm from Hebrew into Greek apparently knew what he was doing, for he used this Greek word for the Hebrew *sofer macher*, but preferred a different Greek expression, *grammateus tachis* for the same Hebrew words in Ezra 7:6 – a passage about Ezra, the skilful scribe of the law of Moses, the *Torah*. In other words, he clearly distinguishes between a skilled writer and a shorthand writer. And since he does this with different translations of the same Hebrew word, we may draw a tentative conclusion: a certain kind of shorthand writing was so well known among Jewish Bible readers in the diaspora that a technical term for it could be used in a translation. And, as we all know, translations serve the purpose of rendering a text understandable in another idiom. The word would not have been employed if the target group, ordinary Jewish readers, could not have known what it meant.

The most surprising – and recognizable – symbol on this tachygraphic leather fragment occurs in line 11. It is a clear and unmistakable *chi-rho*, known to Christians as the Christ monogram, with the two initial letters of 'Christ' in Greek, XPICTOC, pronounced 'chi' and 'rho', intertwined to look like a P crossed by an X. As a Christian symbol, it is definitely documented since the mid-second century, although its meteoric rise to empire-wide popularity followed Constantine's vision of a 'chi-rho' before his victorious battle against Maxentius at Milvian Bridge in AD 312.[28] But the 'chi-rho' could also be used as a non-Christian scribal sign, a so-called *Chrêsis*, *Chrêston* or *Chrêsimon*, written in the margins of manuscripts to alert readers to an important, even memorable and quotable passage in that line or paragraph. However, in the case of our leather text from the Wadi Murabba'at, the *chi-rho* occurs nowhere near a margin, but in the very centre. Could it be a Jewish-Christian shorthand text?

There are, it seems, other pieces of circumstantial evidence which might point in this direction.[29] Provocative as it may sound, this is perfectly reconcilable with our knowledge of the early development of Christian signs and symbols in the papyri, and above all with the active knowledge of shorthand among Jews – and Jewish Christians. It has been emphasized more than once, for example, that Matthew-Levi, the tax and customs official, belonged to a professional sphere where shorthand knowledge was essential.[30] Another obvious candidate for shorthand knowledge in the earliest Christian circles is Tertius, the man who wrote Paul's letter to the Romans (Romans 16:22).[31] And there even is a 'scenario' which would explain the existence of a (Jewish-)Christian shorthand manuscript among those finds which belong to the period of Bar Kokhba at the latest. Disappointed by the Jewish Christians' refusal to participate in the armed revolt against the Christians, the revolutionaries persecuted Jewish followers of Jesus and probably also raided their communities, confiscating their literature.[32] A Jewish-Christian manuscript torn and turned into a leather pouch by Bar Kokhba revolutionaries – it would fit the circumstances.

But again, this may remain an unanswerable question for some time to come. Suffice it for now to remember the fundamental basis: there is a Greek shorthand leather fragment, written sometime between the mid-first and early second century AD, with a 'chi-rho', discovered among the finds of the Nahal Dagar/Wadi Murabba'at caves. Together with the other manuscript discoveries, it underlines the amazing variety of literature and literary culture present among the Dead Sea Scrolls.

Skeletons, bones of contention, and a woman called Babata

And there is more to come: Qumran apart, Masada and the Nahal Dagar/Wadi Murabba'at are only two of many camps and hiding places in the hills of the Judean desert near the Dead Sea. The Nahals Arugot, Asael, David, Hardof, Hever, Holed, Mishmar and Zeelim between En Gedi and Masada were explored, and traces of habitation as ancient as the Chalcolithic period were found. Skulls, whole skeletons, arrows, Israelite and Roman forts, coins, phylacteries with Exodus 12:2–10 and 12:11–16 (from God's institution of the Passover), even a few damaged leather and papyrus fragments were duly catalogued in the Nahal Hardof/Nahal Zeelim region, and the archaeologists felt inspired enough to give the caves names such as 'Cave of Arrows', 'Cave of Skulls and 'Cave of Scrolls'. But by far the most important discoveries were made in the Nahal Mishmar ('Cave of the Treasure') and in the Nahal Hever ('Cave of Horrors', 'Cave of Letters'). Israeli soldiers with minesweepers helped to locate these objects under the soil of the cave. The magnificent hoard of 416 stone, metal and ivory objects from the fourth millennium BC which were found in the Cave of the Treasure are on display at the Israel Museum, Jerusalem, as are Roman items from the Cave of Letters – bronze pans, bowls and jugs, apparently taken by revolutionaries in more successful days.

A riveting little detail became visible on a Roman libation bowl: it had been decorated with Thetis, the mother of the Greek hero Achilles, shown riding Triton, a kind of mer*man* (rather than mermaid). Greek myth, unpalatable to pious Jews who knew of a teaching later passed on in the mishnaic collection of the Talmud: 'How do you profane an idol?' 'It is profaned when you cut off a piece of an earlobe, or the tip of the nose, or of a fingertip, or when it is dented, even if nothing is broken off.'[33] And this is exactly what they did with the faces of the figures on the medallions of the bowl. They did not dent it though – after all, it was a useful kitchen implement. Most cultic utensils belong to the period before the Israelite conquest, and the reason why they were hidden, let alone their everyday or cultic purposes, remains unclear. Some scholars assume they belonged to a Chalcolithic sanctuary at En Gedi and were hidden during a war. In the context of the Dead Sea Scrolls, however, the Cave of Horrors and the Cave of Letters are particularly interesting. Both contained numerous manuscripts, and although not all of them contribute to a deeper understanding of the period of early Christianity, some have proved to be of enormous value.

In the Cave of Horrors, the bones of some forty men, women and children were found in 1961, starved to death by the Romans. During the last days of their lives, these Bar Kokhba people had burnt everything, with one exception – their scrolls of holy scripture. And the surprise was complete: here were nine fragments of a Greek leather scroll of the twelve minor prophets, damaged, but legible. They clearly belonged to fragments which the Bedouins had found before and which had been provisionally edited in 1953. It was a pleasing discovery, but also a politically sensitive one, for the Bedouins who had been raiding these caves since the early 1950s had crossed the border (technically the armistice line) from Jordanian territory. The Israeli archaeologists worked with the logistic help and military protection of the army, and this kept the Bedouins at bay until all caves in the Nahal Hever were searched so thoroughly that nothing of substance was ever found after this archaeological campaign.[34] Enough of six prophets (Jonah, Micah, Nahum, Habakkuk, Zephaniah and Zechariah) remained, and the scholarly editions started an unending debate.[35] The writing was dated to the period between 50 BC and AD 50, with a definite tendency towards the later end of this spectrum. In other words, they coincide with the dates of the Greek papyri from Qumran Caves 4 and 7 and therefore help us to see that the Greek papyri and leather scrolls kept in the libraries of Qumran were no exception. Even the Bible in Greek, the Septuagint, belonged to the supply of scripture used by orthodox Jews in the Holy Land. The Bar Kokhba revolutionaries had brought the Twelve Prophets' Scroll with them to the cave in the Nahal Hever; it was much used when they brought it, but still good enough to be kept for spiritual nourishment at a time of impending death.

The Greek text of the scroll is the result of thoughtful editorial work, based on the Septuagint, but here and there it is trying to get closer to the Hebrew original. It was a pious translation: the holy tetragram of God's unspeakable name, YHWH, is inserted in ancient Hebrew script, the palaeo-Hebrew of the time before the Babylonian exile.[36] Whoever it was who stood behind that scroll of the twelve prophets, a community, a rabbi, a sanhedrin, he or they invested careful philological energy in the comparative study of both languages. Astounding as it may sound, the first half or middle of the first century – the probable date of this scroll – was already a time of active Greek scholarship in the Jewish homeland. And even if we assume that this scroll was imported, from Egypt for example, we would still have to accept that orthodox Jews in Judea consciously opted for this 'revised' version of the Greek text and remained satisfied users for some eighty years, until their cruel death in AD 135.

Almost disappointingly, there is only a sober, unromantic name for that other exciting cave in the Nahal Hever, the 'Cave of Letters'. It could have been called the 'Cave of Bats', because of the thick layers of foul-smelling bat dung which covered the floor of the cave, or the 'Cave of the Psalms' because of a Hebrew leather fragment with verses from Psalm 14 and the beginning of Psalm 15, in meticulous square Hebrew letters and with an interesting variant in the text.[37] Or it could have been called the 'Cave of Bar Kokhba', because fifteen of his letters were found here in an ancient waterskin, carefully tied together, four of them on slivers of wood, in Hebrew and Aramaic, rallying the few remaining zealots and ordering them to get the fruit for Sukkoth, the Feast of Tabernacles, in AD 134. Two of the letters are in Greek. 'We have no one here who understands Hebrew,' it says in one of them.[38] Ardent orthodox Jews and freedom fighters with not even enough Hebrew or Aramaic to understand and write letters in these languages – obviously the 'ideal' users of the Greek Twelve Prophets' Scroll and other Greek Bible scrolls, as they were found along the Dead Sea. Then again, this cave could have been called the 'Cave of Babata', because of a unique manuscript discovery – an archive of thirty-seven Aramaic, Nabatean and Greek documents named after Babata, a woman from Makhoza/Maoza in the region of Zo(o)ra/Zoar, also called Egaltein, just south of the southern tip of the Dead Sea, who was a wealthy supporter of the revolutionaries and had brought jewellery, a beautiful mirror and her legal correspondence to this hiding place.

At first glance, such an archive does not sound all that mouth-watering. Babata survived two husbands – the first was called 'Jesus, son of Jesus' – and spent a lot of time in legal battles, some of them in more than one language, and she did so from c. AD 94 to c. AD 132, decades after the gospels and apostolic letters. But one of these documents has influenced the course of historical Jesus research. Every enlightened student of the gospels knows that the story of Jesus' birth is a late legend, invented by second- or third-generation community committees called 'Matthew' and 'Luke', etc. This, at any rate, is the impression an innocent observer gets when he or she opens a mainstream gospel commentary. One of the suspicious elements is the census organized by Quirinius, the very reason why Mary and Joseph left Nazareth and went to Bethlehem (Luke 2:1–5). It has been observed that Luke's account does not tally with any outside information about Quirinius and his activities. Or so it seemed. Historians have patiently explained how a Roman census worked, and there is no insurmountable problem in synchronizing the known information about year-long censuses under Augustus, and their chronology, particularly in this part of the Roman empire, with the sparse, abbreviated account in Luke. But the real breakthrough came when the Greek documents of the Babata archive were published in 1989. It turned out that Babata's tax declaration confirms the way in which Luke followed a precise Roman formula for an official census registration.

The document, Papyrus Yadin 16, is an attested copy of her statement of property and tax declaration of 2 December AD 127. It begins with the full titular address of the emperor and the consuls, followed by the area of the province of Arabia and the names of the imperial legates in charge. After that, we have the name of a local Roman commander, skipped by Luke, but nonetheless documented elsewhere, not least for the Syrian provincial part of the census under Quirinius some 134 years earlier.[39] The text from Babata's archive documents that she and her husband had to leave their town of residence, Makhoza/Maoza, to go to Rabbath – probably Rabbat-Moab to the north-east, or perhaps even Rabbat-Ammon, modern Amman, where she had her original landed property, now shared by her second husband. He, Judah Ben Eleazar, owned further estates and plantations at En Gedi, his own home town. The Babata form uses the same Greek word as Luke in his gospel, *apografestai*, to (be) register(ed) (Luke 2:3, 5). And interestingly, Babata and her husband travelled in December, the same season traditionally assumed for Mary and Joseph. The punchline is obvious: every reader of Luke's

Gospel knew such forms; they had been an element of continuous Roman administrative practice since the first century BC, not least in this part of the empire. Our problems with the requirements of the Quirinius census are artificial and unrelated to what Luke, what his sources – including, needless to say, relatives of Jesus who were members of the first Jewish-Christian community in Jerusalem – and what his readers knew from their own experience.[40] Even journeys of more than one day had to be undertaken if a census was organized to establish (among other things) the liability for taxation. If Joseph and Mary had come from Bethlehem, we may ask what had made them move to relatively faraway Nazareth, or what made Babata and her husband move from Rabbat(h) to Maoza. We do not know, as the sources do not tell us.[41] But mobility and flexibility are certainly an underestimated aspect of life among the entrepreneurial and working classes in Roman Palestine.

IV

Order, Order

THE CASE OF THE BOOKS AND THE LIBRARIES

The manuscripts from the caves of the Wadi Murabba'at, of Masada and of the Nahals look like accidental collections, or to put it differently, we cannot detect librarians and a system of cataloguing at work. This may be an erroneous impression – on Masada in particular, the synagogue appears to have possessed its own library. Qumran, however, was different. The community who lived near the caves was well-organized, and its discipline seems to have extended to the structure of the manuscript collections. What exactly was the literature collected in these caves? Was it 'sectarian', or does it represent a broader spectrum of literature read by Jews (including future Christians) at this period?

But where are the houses? And who made the jars?

Even before re-examining the time-honoured questions, 'Who wrote the texts,' and, 'Where did they come from?' observers of the literature can detect a kind of Qumran Cave filing system consisting of three different main categories: the writings collected at Qumran were biblical, exegetical, pastoral. Or, if this sounds too much like a Christian theological seminar library, there were first of all copies of the Hebrew Bible, and of its Greek translation, the so-called Septuagint, and the Aramaic translations of original Hebrew texts, the *Targums*. A second category comprised texts ascribed to authors such as Enoch and Baruch which were not part of the Hebrew canon, but were considered by many Jews to be inspired – let us call them, in plain English, pseudepigraphal writings. A subcategory is the apocryphal or deuterocanonical writings. It is a subcategory, for there may have been a consensus about the nucleus of the Bible at that time, but there was no authoritatively fixed Hebrew canon. And we should not force later yardsticks on the Qumran collections. In a third category, there were commentaries on these writings. For these, there are two Jewish terms, *midrashim* and *pesharim*, and we shall see what this meant in practice. Within this category of new, previously unknown texts, we have what are for many readers the most important of all Qumran finds: the complex rules and regulations of community life, organizational structures and the manifold definitions of hopes and goals. There will be more about these categories shortly.

Not so very long ago, most scholars thought the scrolls in all three of them were 'home-made' Essene manuscripts. Others later suggested none of them was actually written at Qumran, but that they formed the library of the Temple, taken to the caves before the Roman onslaught during the first Jewish revolt. Today, it seems the community at Qumran did write some, if not most of the texts, but collected others, in order to study the thought of different Jewish movements. In any case, it seems as though even caves with texts which are plainly non-Essene, such as the exclusively Greek papyrus collection from Cave 7, presented the same 'three-tiered' system. And we could add one further observation at this stage: the closer a cave was to the settlement, the more it conformed to the structure of a systematic library; the further away it was, the more idiosyncratic the texts found in it appeared to be.

But even if we take this as a mere starting point, it all depends on the identification of the people who lived at the settlement with those who filled the caves with jars and scrolls. Some basic historical and literary points were made in Chapter I. Here are a few considerations which give us the 'hands-on' perspective. How, after all, could one prove such a link in archaeological terms? And if not prove it, then at least make it look more plausible than any conceivable alternatives? Two types of tangible artefacts come to mind: first, the inkpots; and second, the jars. The inkpots were found at the settlement, or *Khirbet* (which is Arabic for 'ruin'), of Qumran/Secacah; the jars were found in the caves. Remarkably, no fewer than six inkpots have been found to date, some of them with dried ink still inside.[1] The ink in the pots is identical to the ink on some of the scrolls. In other words, a minimal result, merely on the basis of what has survived, implies that at least some of the scrolls were written at Qumran. The precise provenance of two of the inkpots is unknown – they were bought from Kando, the ubiquitous Bethlehem shoemaker. But the others were found at a place now commonly called the *scriptorium*, a room in the centre of the settlement. In actual fact, the writing room was on the first floor of a two-storey building, but since this has collapsed, the ground floor is shown to visitors as 'the' *scriptorium*. Apart from inkpots, the archaeologists discovered a number of low benches and higher tables which they explained as stools and writing tables for the scribes. This explanation has been disputed by other scholars who proffered a novel theory: Qumran was either a kind of military establishment or, alternatively, a winter villa.[2]

Needless to say, archaeological objections were raised immediately. One of them pointed at the insufficient width of the walls for defensive military purposes. And these objections have been supplemented by important evidence against all military fortress or winter villa theories, thanks to recent discoveries by Esther Eshel and Magen Broshi. In 1996, they found nine new caves near the settlement which were not part of the actual habitat or study centre, but served as living quarters for members of the community. The newly discovered Cave 'C' contained pots, pans and jugs – the typical traces of daily life. Coins were also found, and the latest was struck in

AD 67. None of the typical Bar Kokhba coins, which were discovered at the settlement itself, could be traced. It seems these live-in caves were only used until the occupation of the area by the Romans in AD 68. Shoe nails along the paths linking these caves with the settlement suggest regular 'commuting' from one place to the other. Nearby, stone circles were found which had served as base borders for tents.[3] Not for the Essenes the luxury of houses or Roman-style *insulae* – they made do with caves and tents. However – and this is an important caveat – the comparative examples of residential caves all over ancient Israel (there are impressive remnants from first-century Nazareth, for example) down to late twentieth-century Bedouin tents show to the open-minded visitor that such living conditions should not be taken for signs of poverty. Voluntary simplicity – that goes without saying – but enforced impoverishment must be ruled out. And yet, on the basis of the 'winter villa' theory, we are supposed to believe that the objects found in the *scriptorium* were part of the furniture in a dining room or banqueting hall, a so-called *triclinium*, and that the 'writing tables' were in reality the reclining seats or couches, according to Roman dining habits. But with a maximum width of 50 cm, with a base of just 18 cm, and made of a kind of mortar mudbrick, they would have collapsed under the weight of an average adult, unless of course that person would have rolled or slid down first. As Alexander Schick, Otto Betz and Frank M. Cross joked in a recent book, if that room was a banqueting hall, the inkpots found nearby must have been those of the waiters, busily writing bills.[4] In a more serious vein though, it seems to be certain enough that the immediate vicinity of numerous inkpots and tables, which do make sense as writing surfaces for scrolls with a width of up to 30 cm, justifies the description of these rooms as a *scriptorium*.[5] There is a direct link with scrolls in the caves – although we cannot tell, on this basis alone, how many of the scrolls and fragments found in the caves were written *in situ*.

The second direct link between caves, scrolls and settlement was established by a technique which smacks of twenty-first-century science fiction: Neutron Activation Analysis (NAA). And yet, even this technique is a servant, not a master. All science, after all, and all methods of application, serve the purpose of answering questions, and not, as has been thought from time to time in some circles, of determining the answers before the questions have been asked. Far from being the proverbial sorcerer's apprentices, the scholars who operate the Neutron Activation Analysis do not approach their subjects with ready-made theories. And as far as Qumran is concerned, the stage is set by a passage in the book of Jeremiah, 32:14. 'Take these deeds, both this sealed deed of purchase and this open deed, and put them in an earthenware jar, in order that they may last for a long time.' The Lord speaks to Jeremiah, and the prophet passes the message on to Baruch, son of Neriah. Scrolls in jars – not a funny idea of some desert 'monks', but a command of the Lord. Pious as they were, the librarians of the Qumran caves knew and obeyed it. Not for all scrolls, it must be said, but for those which possessed an outstanding value to the collectors at Qumran.

This fact alone, the fact that scrolls were found in jars, rules out the 'panic theory', according to which the Qumran scrolls were hastily hidden in the caves when the Roman tenth legion Fretensis approached from Jericho. There would not have been time to find or make suitable jars in a hurry, to select the appropriate scrolls and to organize an orderly storage process. On the contrary, it seems that valuable 'master copies' of biblical books and internal documents were always kept in jars – carrying out God's command to the letter – whereas everyday reading material was kept in niches and on shelves.[6] But who made the jars, and where? Who placed the scrolls in these jars, and where? Essenes at Qumran? Priests in Jerusalem, at the Temple library, just before the Roman siege began, when Qumran looked safe? Diaspora Jews in Rome, supplying their poorer brethren back home with well-made scrolls, particularly those in Greek? This is where Neutron Activation Analysis has provided the conclusive answer, and the results were first made public by a scholar from the Hebrew University, Jerusalem, Jan Gunneweg, at a Dead Sea Scrolls congress in Prague, in April 1999.

As Gunneweg explained in his as yet unpublished paper,[7] pottery can be traced, through its chemical composition, to the pottery manufacturing centre where it was made. To the technically minded, the procedure sounds straightforward enough: a pottery sample is taken by grinding off 100 mg of ceramic. The powder is then mixed with pure cellulose (50 mg) as a binder and is pressed into a pellet of uniform size and thickness. The pellets (which represent potsherds or complete vessels) are wrapped in pure aluminium and placed into an aluminium capsule which is submitted to a neutron flux in a nuclear reactor. The capsule undergoes a predetermined period of irradiation, which depends on the length of the half-life of the elements to be detected. Every single pellet is measured for its gamma rays by using a pure germanium detector, and the spectrum is then stored in an analyser. The gamma rays are converted to electric pulses which are strictly proportional to the energy of the gamma rays. The pulses are amplified and go into an 'Analogue-to-Digital Converter' (ADC) which sorts out the pulses from each gamma ray – according to their energy – and stores them in the memory of a 'Pulse-Height-Analyser' which is set to accumulate data for a predetermined interval of time. A computer program converts the quantities of each chemical element which is present in the fabric of the vessel into measurable data. Gunneweg explains that the technique is based on the presumption that every clay source on earth has its own chemical composition – and therefore pottery which was made from any given clay source can be recognized accordingly. Once the chemical quantities are known, one can compare them with analyses of fired clay and waste from kilns which are 'site specific'. A match means one has found the place where the pottery was made. In other words, it is a kind of 'chemical fingerprint'.

Jan Gunneweg and his colleague Marta Balla of the Technical University, Budapest, are hoping for answers to five questions: is there a difference between the pottery found in the settlement complex of Qumran and in the caves? Was all or part of the sampled pottery made locally at Qumran? And, related to the first two, if the jars were brought in from places such as Jerusalem, Bethlehem, Jericho, Masada or from any other site for which NAA data are available, are there matches to link them to a specific place of origin? Will it be possible to trace and geographically locate the interrelations which certainly did take place (pottery or no pottery) between the people at Qumran and other populations, so that Qumran would get an archaeological link with other sites in the region? Finally, what can we learn about different techniques of pottery manufacture? The NAA results must be compared stylistically to check whether the differences in chemistry correspond to those in the stylistic appearance of the jars – or, to put it the other way round, if vessels from the same kilns show similar or identical stylistic features. This has always been an important part of pottery studies in archaeology, and archaeologists have known for a long time that the pottery found at Qumran and in the caves has a specific, identical form.[8]

While the details of Jan Gunneweg's pioneering work will be set out in his own forthcoming publication at the Orion Institute, the gist, as presented at the Prague Congress,[9] is straightforward and conclusive. None of the jars samples so far from the Qumran finds was made anywhere else but at Qumran itself, with the remnants of the kiln still there to show where it was done. Gunneweg's single most important example is the famous jar found in Cave 7. With a height of 40 cm, it weighs 10 kg.[10] On its neck, it twice has the Hebrew inscription *RWM'* (in letters: *resh, wahw, mem, aleph*).[11] Ever since one of the pioneers of modern Aramaic and Hebrew studies, John

Fitzmyer, suggested the word is the Hebrew transliteration of Latin ROMA or Greek POMH, both meaning Rome, scholars have been intrigued by a tempting possibility: this jar was imported from the capital of the Roman empire, with scrolls inside.[12] Admittedly, its shape varies slightly from other Qumran jars – it is slightly more bulbous – but it has the usual opening which is big and practical enough for scrolls. Thus, why not assume different origins? It would fit in nicely with the identification of two of the Greek papyrus fragments found in Cave 7 as verses from Mark's Gospel and the first epistle to Timothy (see Chapter VII). Mark has always been associated with Rome, at least according to the majority opinion of conservative and less conservative scholars, and for 1 Timothy, a Roman origin is at least a possibility. Gunneweg, however, managed to prove that the jar from Cave 7, like all the other Qumran jars, was local produce.

It is a result which helps us to focus on two different aspects of Dead Sea Scrolls research. To begin with, even a jar from a cave which contained imported scrolls – all papyri, all in Greek – was made at the site. This means that there remains no reasonable doubt about one conclusion: it was the conscious decision of the Qumranites to place (some of the) scrolls in jars, in accordance with Jeremiah 32:14. They did it themselves, and they did it with their own jars. But second, why did they mark this particular jar with a Hebrew inscription? At a place like Qumran, a theory of some scholars who have doubted an association of the Cave 7 scrolls with Rome must be ruled out: the inscription cannot refer to a Nabatean individual called 'Ruma' or something similar, as the first editors of the Cave 7 finds had assumed in 1962. The scrolls at Qumran were not owned by individuals; they belonged to the community. In fact, jars with inscriptions have been found elsewhere, from Roman and pre-Roman Palestine, and there are at least four known examples where it is obvious that not a person, but a place is named: jars from Gibeon, Jerusalem, Socoh and Ziph.[13] As a contemporary place name, 'Ruma' occurs once in the

caves at Qumran, the question, 'But where was the library?' would be tinged with the same bemused blankness. But there are scholars who think there was an actual separate library building at the settlement itself – not a bad idea if one assumes that the members of the Essene elite would have wanted at least some of the scrolls next to their central assembly room. An open-shelf reference library on the plateau of the *Khirbet* sounds intriguing. Where was it and what did it look like?

One theory points to the room underneath the so-called *scriptorium*, but although this room was found in relatively good condition, there were no traces of stands for books, wooden racks, or even holes in the walls for a shelving system (as were found in Cave 4). Hypothetically, the scrolls could have been kept in two niches in the southern wall. But they are too small for more than a very few scrolls. The Qumran library, after all, was not conceived like the new British Library at St Pancras where hundreds of square metres are luxuriously bookless walking space, with most of the books completely invisible. If, however, a scholar like Hartmut Stegemann is right, the three adjacent rooms next to the *scriptorium* should be interpreted as a proper library, consisting of a storage room for about 1,000(!) scrolls which were later hidden in the caves, a reading room, and an issue/return room. The storage room included a smaller chamber for disused scrolls, archive material and similar objects.[15] However, the problem with this attractive theory is obvious: not a single implement (let alone a scrap of leather or papyrus) was found in any part of this supposedly so elaborate, three-room library complex, not even a metre under the present surface (where scrolls were found in Cave 5, for example). And although the absence of evidence should never be taken for the evidence of absence, it is too much to accept that some 1,000 scrolls with their shelving and storage systems, their adjacent archive and so forth, did not leave even the tiniest scrap of circumstantial evidence, whereas the caves nearby, some of them within easy walking distance, provide all that evidence.

To salvage his idea, Stegemann suggested that a mousehole-sized opening in one of the walls was used by petitioners asking for permission to enter the library, throwing a stone with their name on it through the hole into a kind of hollow inside. One such pebble, with the name 'Joseph' on it, was indeed found. Fortunately though, Stegemann himself at least mentions the much more plausible explanation first given by the excavator, Roland de Vaux (without giving him credit for it, however): this small hollow basin carved into the wall, which could be filled from outside, should be understood as a feature designed for closed sessions in which those taking part did not wish to be disturbed. Since the room has a low bench installed round its walls, it looks like a typical assembly room.[16] Members of the community who had temporarily been excluded from assemblies, because of some misdemeanour or other – there are detailed regulations in the scrolls[17] – could not just walk in. It almost sounds like a face check at a modern club or disco; but it seems this room had no windows – those who met in here did not want to be seen or overheard during their meetings. However, what about a bench in the 'reading room'? Stegemann assumes this was used by the librarians to unroll a scroll for users next door, find the required place, pass it through a 'hatch' and then re-roll the scroll when it was returned. To handle those scrolls, some of which were seven or more metres long (e.g. 7.43 m for the Isaiah scroll found in Cave 1), the expert knowledge of a librarian was needed. And an opening in the wall, 1.60 m above ground and 80 cm high, is interpreted as a kind of serving hatch.

This, at any rate, is the theory. And it is of course plausible enough, even almost mandatory, that an inner circle of assembled Qumranites needed quick access to a reference library during their deliberations – and why not have a librarian at hand who would quickly and knowingly find the required passage? But all this is far removed from any trace of a main library. The space was much too small for the number of scrolls discovered in the caves, and the 'reading room' was too small for any sizeable number of studying Essenes. It makes much more sense to see the caves themselves, with their separate collections, as storage rooms-cum-reading rooms. And the caves had a decisive advantage over the supposed 'library' next door to the *scriptorium*: with their wide openings, they provided sufficient light – and it was indirect light, ideal for readers, never falling directly on the leather or papyrus. The rooms next to the *scriptorium*, on the other hand, possessed no outside windows. Even during the day, nothing could be seen, let alone read, without oil lamps. If the Qumranites read at night, which they obviously did from time to time,[18] they had to use lamps wherever they went. But to do so during the day, with all those alternatives flooded by wonderful natural light, smacks of architectural and administrative incompetence. And this would be somewhat untypical of the Essenes, to put it mildly.

A key to the caves

The eleven caves where scrolls and scroll fragments were found have been numbered 1Q to 11Q; the individual texts or particles carry numbers allocated to them, or, in the case of the very first discoveries from Cave 1, abbreviated names only (1Q Isa[a] for the complete Isaiah scroll for example, 1Q Isa[b] for the fragmentary Isaiah scroll, 1QS for the Community Rule, which, to make it more complicated, was previously called the Manual of Discipline, and so forth). Such names were originally given to most fragments from all eleven caves, but with the exception of the great scrolls from Cave 1, the numbering system has replaced the old procedure. Occasionally, this causes problems. For example, when the famous Aramaic 'Son of God' fragment, 4Q 246, made the headlines in 1992, purportedly proving that Luke's claim of originality in calling Jesus the 'Son of God' (Luke 1:32–35) was plagiarism of Essene thought, bringing down one of the pillars of the Christian faith in the process of its discovery,[19] many people overlooked the fact that most of it had already been known for some thirty years as Pseudo-Dan^d, finally seen in context with the fragments Pseudo-Dan$^{a–c}$ or 4Q 243–45. The first of these fragments, under the slightly different name of 4Q ps DanA^a, had already been noted as completely unsurprising in a commentary on Luke's Gospel as early as 1978.[20]

It is impossible to give a complete and annotated overview in this book.[21] But there is a recognizable framework, even if we accept, as we must, that only a small percentage of all scrolls originally deposited in the caves have been discovered. Let us take Cave 1 as a typical example. It contained scrolls with biblical texts (Isaiah, twice), a Genesis Apocryphon (a writing 'appended' or added to the biblical text, and therefore presupposing the existence of a Genesis scroll), a commentary on Habakkuk, Thanksgiving Hymns, the Community Rule and the War Scroll. It further contained fragments of several biblical books – Genesis, Exodus, Leviticus, Deuteronomy (the absence of Numbers from these *Torah* fragments must be an archaeological 'accident'), Judges, 1 and 2 Samuel, Isaiah, Ezekiel, the Psalms and Daniel. There are commentaries on Micah, Zephaniah, the Psalms and books which do not belong to the Hebrew Canon: the Book of Jubilees, a Book of Noah, the Testament of Levi, Sayings of Moses, the Book of Giants (based on the Book of Enoch, chapter 6).[22] And there are writings not known from anywhere else: an apocryphal prophecy, a wisdom text, a book of mysteries and benedictions (both annexes to the Community Rule), several liturgical texts, hymns and prayers, a text on the New Jerusalem, and several unidentifiable Hebrew fragments.

If we group these scrolls and fragments, we have:

1. Biblical texts Books of what was to become the definitive Hebrew canon of the Masoretes. This category includes *Targums* (Aramaic translations of Hebrew books; at Qumran the most important one is the almost complete *Targum* of Job), and occasional *tefilin* (also called phylacteries – one was found in Cave 1, twenty-one in Cave 4, etc.) – with small boxes in which passages from Exodus and Deuteronomy are placed and then tied to the forehead or the left arm – a practice still observed by orthodox Jews. *Mezuzoth* were also found: with passages from the same *Torah* books, they were (and are) attached to the doorposts of houses, apartments or offices. Seven were found in Cave 4, one in Cave 8. Both *tefilin* and *mezuzoth* are applied in accordance with Deuteronomy 6:8–9, and they are important witnesses to the textual tradition of the Hebrew text.

2. Pseudepigraphical books So-called because most of them are ascribed to a person or group who certainly did not write them themselves. They are writings which were theologically instructive and popular, often with important theological messages and teachings (see, from Cave 1, particularly 'Enoch' which was very popular at Qumran), which also existed outside Essene circles and were occasionally quoted by Jewish writers such as the authors of the New Testament texts, but did not belong to the core collection of the Hebrew Bible, the later 'canon'. In Cave 1, we have the Book of Jubilees, Book of Noah, the Genesis Apocryphon, the Testament of Levi, Sayings of Moses and the Book of Giants/Enoch. More of the same, and further writings of this sub-group were found in other caves.

2a. Apocrypha Known from the wider tradition of the Greek, pre-Christian Septuagint, they were not found in Cave 1 but in other caves: Ecclesiasticus (Ben Sira) in Cave 2, Tobit, Susannah (4Q 551, identification not quite certain) in Cave 4, and the Letter of Jeremiah (Baruch 6) in Cave 7. It is, however, fair to say that these writings did not play any sizeable role at Qumran. With the exception of Tobit (one Hebrew, four Aramaic fragments), only one fragment each of the aforementioned texts was found, the one of the Letter of Jeremiah only in a Greek translation, but Esdras, Judith, the Additions to Esther, Wisdom, Baruch, The Song of the Three Children, Bel and the Dragon, the two books of Maccabees and the Prayer of Manasseh[23] were not found at all. Since we do not know for certain whether there was a fixed 'canon' of the Hebrew Bible at the time of the Qumran collections, we cannot treat these books as we would treat the Apocrypha in Protestant Bibles – more or less surplus to requirements, but harmless enough to be included in some editions styled 'with Apocrypha'. The only collection of books that was absolutely binding and compulsive reading were the five books of Moses, the *Torah*, also called (from the Greek) the Pentateuch.

3. Unknown new writings The individual, 'group-specific' texts of the Essenes (or, which is still under debate, of course, of other Jewish groups as well), previously unknown and often called the 'sectarian writings'. Many more than those in Cave 1 have been found. The Community Rule from Cave 1, the Copper Scroll from Cave 3, the Damascus Document and the Letter of the Teacher of Righteousness ('Miqsat Ma'ase ha-Torah') from Cave 4, and the Temple Scroll from Cave 11 are probably the most famous and most controversial. Psalms and hymns like the Thanksgiving Hymns from Cave 1 are the most moving and beautiful of these writings.

3a. The commentaries Commonly called *pesharim* (plural of *pesher*, commentary), like the Habakkuk Pesher from Cave 1. They have not been found for all biblical books (judging by what has survived), and not in all caves – in Caves 2, 5, 6 and 11 no *pesharim* are extant (unless the unidentified small fragments 2Q 27–33, 5Q 16–25, 6Q 21–31 and 11Q 21–23 belonged to such commentaries). But they belong to Category 3 since they interpret the biblical books from the perspective of the Essenes, often defending the Teacher of Righteousness on the basis of an authoritative passage, and so forth.

These three main categories will be recognized in all other major caves.[24] Cave 4, of course, the great library cave with 575 numbered scrolls and fragments, has it all in abundance. But even the microcosm of caves such as 1, 2, 3, 5, 6 and 11 reflects the system. And we shall see in Chapter VI whether this is also true of the odd one out among the caves of Qumran, Cave 7, with its unique collection of eighteen Greek papyrus fragments and one inverse image imprint of papyrus on hardened soil. But even at this stage, it should be obvious that the Qumran librarians operated with a recognizable system. Any user of any of the caves could work with texts from these three categories. For the Qumranites, they were interrelated. This may not be news to modern, regular Bible readers who read the biblical books next to a collection of, say, C.S. Lewis stories and essays (which to us today are roughly at the same chronological distance as the Pseudepigrapha and Apocrypha were to the Essenes of the first centuries BC and AD), consult commentaries from Bultmann to Bruce and then go on to read the latest *Alpha* manual. But in all seriousness, the study system which we can detect in the Qumran library was demanding and wide-ranging. Admittedly, the guiding tenets of the community were at the centre, coming a close second to the *Torah*, but it must be said that these collections were inclusive, not exclusive. Cave 7, but not only this special cave alone, may well provide an answer to the quest for the nature of this inclusiveness.

But before we reach this stage, we have to tackle one question which, among other things, also concerns the background to early Christian attitudes towards the 'Old' Testament: what about the one biblical book which, as everyone agrees, has not been found at Qumran? Is there a hidden message behind the absence of Esther?

Come Esther, Come Nehemiah

THE CASE OF THE MISSING SCROLLS

If the Qumran caves were the library of an orthodox group, or a study centre for contemporary Jewish thought, how come the book of Esther was not found among the scrolls? This is one of the few facts almost everyone knows about Qumran, and it has provoked much speculation. Did the Essenes dislike the feast of Purim, based on Esther? Did they object to the apparent fact that God is not mentioned in this book by name? But then again, is this not the one book which Maimonides taught would be the only one to survive – together with the *Torah* – when the Messiah comes? The absence of Esther is as puzzling as it is helpful for our understanding of the Dead Sea Scrolls, a case study which tells us much about Jewish thought, and about our own presuppositions. The 'missing links' have their own story to tell about God's presence in a book of the Tanakh from which he appears to be absent.

Desperately seeking Esther

The caves at Secacah/Qumran were a library of Jewish thought. At its core, there was the basic, inalienable collection of writings: holy scripture, the *Tanakh*. But what was holy scripture at the time of the Essene movement? If we look at a Hebrew Old Testament today, or at the pre-Christian Greek translation – the so-called Septuagint – or at Roman Catholic and Protestant versions, the answer is different each time. The number of writings included, and their order, and sometimes their names, differ considerably. This is not the place to write a book within a book to do justice to the intricate question of the 'canon' of the Old Testament and its development. All we can safely say is this: the five books of Moses, also called the *Torah*, or in Greek, the Pentateuch, have always been the pièce de résistance. They are the holiest of the holy, and the textual history of these five books, including the evidence of the Qumran scrolls, tells us that their contents, the style, the exact vocabulary and syntax, were fixed long before that of any other biblical writing. After the *Torah*, the next section in the Hebrew Bible contains the Prophets, the *Nevi'im*, in three subsections: Joshua, Judges, 1 and 2 Samuel and 1 and 2 Kings (that is, the so-called Former Prophets or *Nevi'im Rishonim*), followed by Isaiah, Jeremiah and Ezekiel – the Latter Prophets or *Nevi'im Acharonim*, and finally the twelve Minor Prophets or *Tree Asar*: Hosea, Joel, Amos, Obadiah, Jonah, Micah, Nahum, Habakkuk, Zephaniah, Haggai, Zechariah and Malachi. The twelve minor prophets were usually collected in one scroll, and one of these scrolls, dated to the first century AD, was found near Qumran, in the Nahal Hever. The third group of writings is called *Ketuvim* and includes the Psalms, Lamentations, Song of Songs, Proverbs, Job, Ecclesiastes, Ruth, 1 and 2 Chronicles, Esther, Ezra, Nehemiah and Daniel. These thirteen books were not immediately arranged in a fixed order, but one group among them soon acquired a name and role of its own: the so-called *Megilloth* or Five Scrolls. They are:

❑ Song of Songs, read in the synagogues at Passover;

❑ Ruth, read at Shavuot (Pentecost);

❑ Lamentations, read at Tisha be'Av, the ninth day of the fifth month, July/August, which originally commemorated the destruction of Solomon's Temple by the Babylonians under

106

Nebuchadnezzar in 586 BC, but later also the destruction of the Second Temple by the Romans under Titus in AD 70, and – because it became associated with the same day in the Jewish calendar – the end of Bar Kokhba's revolt against the Romans in AD 135 and King Edward I's edict expelling all Jews from his realm on 18 July 1290, the first such measure in European history;

❑ Ecclesiastes, read at Sukkoth (Tabernacles, celebrated at full moon in the month of Tishri, September/October);

❑ Esther, read at Purim, the most popular Jewish festival, which is celebrated on the 14th/15th Adar (February/March). Of these five books, only one is still read from a scroll: Esther.

And yet Esther, given this special status among the *Megilloth* in synagogues everywhere in the world, was not found among the Dead Sea Scrolls. This undeniable fact has led to numerous speculations. Why was it not found, if whole scrolls or at least some fragments of all other biblical (Old Testament) books were discovered between 1947 and 1956? The *absence* of this book has raised almost more questions than the *presence* of all the others. Could the inhabitants of Qumran, and those Jews who collected and hid the books in the caves, have had theological objections to it? Was Esther perhaps too joyful – not in the bulk of the book, where we encounter stiff court rituals and occasionally quite extravagant cruelties, but at the end, which gave rise to the institution of the exuberant Purim festivities (Esther 9:19; 10:28)? A tractate of the Talmud, *Megillah* 7b, stipulates that a man should get drunk at Purim until he can no longer distinguish between *Arur Haman* ('Cursed be Haman') and *Barukh Mordekhai* ('Blessed be Mordecai'). Although this is a later rabbinical teaching, Purim appears to have been a boisterous affair at least from the time of the Maccabees. In other words, it was well established by the time the Essenes settled at Qumran, and it would not really have been the right stuff for this ultra-orthodox, sober and celibate movement. This, in any case, is what many commentators still think. Another explanation could be seen in the 'foreignness' of Esther. It is a book of the distant diaspora, set in Persia, with no hint at attempts to make *alya*, to come home to the land of the Temple.

Yet another reason has been found in a further peculiarity of Esther: it is a book which does not mention God. Or so it seems. And a pious community would refuse to acknowledge a writing which is, as it were, God-less. Much like the first two theories, this is guesswork based on preconceived assumptions. Scholars who think the Essene community, guardians of the scrolls, lived and behaved like a monastic order will find it difficult to envisage a day or two of dancing, noise-making and boundless drinking at Qumran or on Jerusalem's south-west hill, with no reference to God whatsoever. In fact, all Jewish festivals are mentioned in the scrolls, with one exception: Purim. But even if we let this pass, how does it follow that such people did not study and store a book which (without even describing them) initiates such festivities? In fact, the celebration of a Jewish victory in Persia, far from Jerusalem and the Temple, could rather be seen as a good reason to cherish Esther – after all, the Essenes themselves had left the Temple, to find God's presence outside its precincts, in the diaspora of the 'land of Damascus', before they returned to Judea. And, as we shall see, God is not even truly absent from the book of Esther. But let us first go to the Qumran caves, for here we realize that some of the basic assumptions about the absence of Esther and the presence of the others are wrong to begin with.

The users of the Qumran caves favoured the *Torah* and the Psalms. At the last count, and without speculating about the number of lost scrolls, there were thirty-six scrolls of the Psalms, and eighty-two of the *Torah*: twenty-nine scrolls of Deuteronomy, seventeen of Exodus, fifteen of Genesis, thirteen of Leviticus and eight of Numbers.

The only other book of the Hebrew canon that reaches a two-digit number is Isaiah with 21 scrolls. At the other extreme, there is only one scroll (a fragment) of 1 and 2 Chronicles, and only one fragment of Ezra. It does not take much imagination to see how easy it would have been for each of these single fragments to disappear without trace before Bedouins and archaeologists reached the caves. Conversely, there is no fragment at all of Esther – nor of Nehemiah. For the absence of Nehemiah, most scholars have agreed to offer an elegant but suspicious way out: the Hebrew Bible of the Masoretes, which was developed in the eighth century AD – or, in other words, some 800 to 900 years after the Dead Sea Scrolls – treats Ezra and Nehemiah as one book. Therefore, it is assumed that the practice of the Masoretes, which has since become normative, was already in existence at Qumran. If that was the case, the one solitary Ezra fragment could be adduced as evidence for the presence of both Ezra and Nehemiah at Qumran. It is a generally accepted theory. But if we take this one step further, would it not imply that the discovery of four of the *Megilloth*, the collection of the Five Scrolls (Song of Songs: four Qumran fragments; Ruth: four fragments; Lamentations: four fragments; Ecclesiastes: three fragments) suggests the presence of the fifth *Megilloth* text, Esther, as well?

But we should not operate like this. The fact remains that there is no evidence whatsoever of a single scroll of Ezra-cum-Nehemiah prior to the editorial decision of the Masoretes to turn them into one. On the contrary, as late as the early third century AD, the Christian theologian and textual critic Origen, director of the library at Caesarea Maritima, kept to the separation of Ezra and Nehemiah when he edited his *Hexapla*, the six-column Bible with the Hebrew text and its Greek versions. In the Hebrew text of the Bible as we have it today, Nehemiah begins with its own title. Origen himself worked with an accepted Hebrew text of the Bible; he knew what he was doing. In fact, as we saw in Chapter II, he claimed he had obtained a Hebrew scroll from a jar found in a cave near Jericho. It is a moot point why the Masoretes of the Ben Asher family decided to 'roll' Ezra and Nehemiah into one six centuries later. The tradition of the Greek Septuagint could have influenced them, or a number of other considerations. But whatever the reasons may have been, we must not jump to conclusions. We have to acknowledge that Nehemiah, like Esther, was not found at Qumran.

This is an archaeological fact, but it should not be overinterpreted theologically. To put it differently, Esther (and Nehemiah) were not found simply because they were not found. Or, to quote James Charlesworth of Princeton, one of the acknowledged experts in Dead Sea Scrolls studies:

> It is preposterous to build upon the claim that Esther was not found among the fragments of Cave IV and the other Qumran caves. We need to consider how little we have from what was hidden in the Caves about or before 68 BCE. I have asked many scholars this question: 'What percentage of what was hidden is now in our hands?' The answer is usually 60 or 70%. This is incorrect. We have less than 6% of what was hidden in the Caves. Moreover, some biblical books are preserved only by minuscule fragments that easily turn to dust if pushed or moved too abruptly.[1]

Help from another place

To find out more, we have to look at the question of God's presence in the other scrolls. It is far from certain that Esther is the only book of the biblical canon which does not mention God by name. Most Jewish scholars and the vast majority of Christian Old Testament theologians assume he is not mentioned in another of the *Megilloth*, the *Shir ha-Shirim* or Song of Songs, either. The question centres on chapter 8, verse 6. The New English Bible and the New Revised Standard Version, for example, show no trace of God in their translations, whereas the New Jerusalem Bible, for example, has 'Yahweh'. Choose between 'It [love] blazes up like blazing fire, fiercer than any flame' (NEB) and, 'The flash of it [love] is a flash of fire, a flame of Yahweh himself' (NJB). Those who think God is mentioned have to see him in the Hebrew *shalhebeth-yah*. At first sight, this is rather unlikely. The syllable *yah* does not look like an abbreviation of God's name, but rather like a superlative, the 'most vehement flame' (RSV). And yet, could it be that the writer of the Songs of Songs consciously 'played' with the double meaning, intending his readers to see God in this love? If so, it would be a double entendre of some importance for the acceptance of this book at Qumran, and indirectly, as we shall see in a moment, for Esther as well. Interestingly, the Song of Songs was read intensively by the compilers of the Qumran library; four scroll fragments have survived. Risky as it may be to argue with statistics, this means there are two more surviving scrolls of the Song of Songs than of Joshua and Proverbs, and one more than of Judges and Ecclesiastes. And the Song of Songs was never above suspicion: in some circles, it was marginalized or even rejected because of its explicit sexuality and its delight in visual eroticism. During the rabbinical period at the latest, this unease had reached such an extent that allegorical interpretations became the fashion, and the loving couple was seen as an image of God and Israel. Christian interpreters later understood it as an allegory of Christ and the church. However, there is no trace anywhere in the Dead Sea Scrolls which might indicate that the Essenes or any other group behind the biblical scrolls ever read the Song of Songs other than literally.

Rabbi Akiva Ben Joseph (Rabbi Aquiba), one of the earliest sources quoted in the Talmud (he lived from c. AD 45 to 135), praised the *Shir ha-Shirim* beyond all measure. It is 'the holy of holies', he taught, and he added, 'the whole world attained its supreme value only on the day when the Song of Songs was given to Israel'.[2] Similar praise was heaped upon the 'God-less' book of Esther, by the most influential Jewish thinker of the high Middle Ages, the revered Rambam, also called Maimonides.³ He taught that only six books would remain after the coming of the Messiah: the five books of the *Torah* – and Esther.⁴ Maimonides does not go into detail, but one of the reasons could well be its liturgical format: only the *Torah* and Esther were (and are) still read from scrolls in the synagogues, whereas the early Middle Ages, particularly after the introduction of the Masoretic text of the Hebrew Bible from the eighth century onwards, saw a change from scroll to codex for all other biblical books. There was, however, also a good dose of theological reasoning in favour of Esther: a whole tractate of the Talmud, *Megillah*, is dedicated to Esther and its use. Admittedly, a few voices were indeed raised against this book. At one stage, Rav Judah, speaking in the name of Shmu'el, intended to declare the scroll of Esther uninspired. But the others, referring to Rabbi Shmu'el Ben Judah himself, replied that Esther was written under the inspiration of the *Ruach ha-Kodesh*, the Holy Spirit.⁵ Against this rabbinical vote, modern scholars have followed Rav Judah, and continue to miss God, the laws of the *Torah*, other subjects like prayer, grace and forgiveness, the regulations of *Kashrut* (*kosher* eating and drinking), and so forth. But obviously, not all of these are mentioned in the other biblical books all the time. And even when and where they are mentioned, they often appear indirectly, in allusions which a contemporary reader would have understood without difficulty.⁶ It is evident from the Talmud that orthodox Jews did not miss them at all in Esther. The very presence of God among his people is made abundantly clear in the *Megillah*, the Talmud tractate dedicated to Esther:

'*I do not reject them* – in the days of the Chaldeans, when I made Daniel, Hananya, Misael and Asarya rise for them; *I do not despise them* – in the days of the Greek, when I made Shimon the Reliable and the Hasmonean and his sons and Mattathias, the high priest, rise for them; *as to destroy them utterly* – in the days of Haman, when I made Mordecai and Esther rise for them... for *I am the Lord, their God*'

(*Megillah* 11a). Each statement is introduced by a quotation from the *Torah*, Leviticus 26: 44–45 – printed here in italics. The combination of the *Torah* and its application to the history of the Jews clearly implies that Mordecai and Esther, the chief protagonists in the Esther scroll who are mentioned as the culmination of this list, are seen as God's agents, and that God himself is there with them.

Can we say even more? Is there a starting point somewhere in the text where we can discover the hidden God, perhaps even by name, after all? Let us remember how the story unfolds, how it presupposes Persian history as we know it from classical sources (mainly Herodotus) and shapes it with the narrative art of the author. The Persian king Ahasuerus (Xerxes) celebrates a feast, but his queen, Vashti, refuses to take part. No reasons are given for her refusal. Xerxes/Ahasuerus follows the advice of his astrologers and deposes her. Years of warfare with Greek armies follow – they include the famous battles of Thermopylae and Salamis. Only later, probably in 479 BC, Ahasuerus finds time to look for a new queen. Many young women go to the capital, but in the end, the king chooses Esther, who happens to be Jewish, although her name is Persian (it means 'Star'; her Hebrew name is Hadassah, 'Myrtle': see 2:7). She is an orphan, and a cousin of the courtier Mordecai, who acts as her foster parent. Mordecai hears of an assassination plot against the king. He informs Esther who tells Ahasuerus; thus, they both save the king. In a separate development, the king makes another courtier, Haman, his grand vizier. Haman demands the oriental-style veneration: everyone is supposed to bow down and prostrate themselves. Mordecai refuses. Again, no reasons are given. 3:5–6 seems to imply that the Jew Mordecai refused to honour any man with the exception of the king himself. Haman decides to punish all people of Mordecai's race in the Persian empire. He attempts the first recorded genocide of the Jews. Mordecai hears of his plans and implores Esther to enlighten the king. She hesitates at first, since on pain of death she can only go to

Ahasuerus when he asks her to come, but Mordecai's insistence persuades her to risk her life for their people. Ahasuerus grants her every wish she may have, even half of his kingdom. She asks him to attend a dinner which she is going to prepare for him and his grand vizier. In the meantime, Haman has a gallows erected for Mordecai. During a sleepless night, the king reads the imperial records and finds a reference to Mordecai's action which had saved his life. He sends for Haman and asks him how a man should be treated whom the king wants to honour. Haman, who thinks the king intends to distinguish his grand vizier – Haman himself – suggests the most extravagant procedures and is told he should bestow them upon Mordecai. He obeys and realizes this is the beginning of his end. At the dinner, Esther unmasks him, and Haman is hanged on the gallows he had prepared for Mordecai. The edicts against the Jews are revoked, and a new edict, drafted by Mordecai, the newly appointed grand vizier, grants them the right to armed self-defence against any enemies and attackers. With the full assent of the king, 75,800 people are killed throughout Persia (15,800 according to the Greek text of Esther), among them Haman's ten sons. To commemorate this chain of events, it is determined that the 14th and 15th Adar (February/March) each year will be celebrated as the feast of 'Purim' ('lots', after the casting of lots which had determined the day of Haman's thwarted decree against the Jews).[7] And, poignantly, Purim is preceded by *Ta'anit Esther*, a day of fasting, just as Esther had fasted before she went to the king.

It is a story of suspense, intrigue, sex and crime (at one stage, Ahasuerus/Xerxes even thinks that Haman was going to rape Esther), of justice, revenge, cruelty and feasting. Where indeed is there a place for God? Where did and do orthodox Jews, from the Essenes at Qumran via the compilers of the Talmud and Maimonides, to the rabbis and worshippers of today, see him in this story? We find the clue in a Hebrew word which could turn out to be the very key to the presence of the 'hidden' God in times of adversity – a subject of some importance to the Essenes and to all Jews throughout the ages. The decisive passage is 4:12–14. Mordecai had just informed Esther about Haman's plans and his edict against the Jews and had implored her 'to go into the king's presence to beg for mercy and plead with him for his people'. Esther had refused because she knew she 'would be put to death', according to the law, if she went to the king without being summoned. In this tense and dangerous situation, Mordecai sent the king's eunuch Hathach to her with a second message:

> When Esther's words were reported to Mordecai, he sent back his
> answer: 'Do not think that because you are in the king's house you
> alone of all Jews will escape. For if you remain silent at this time,
> relief and deliverance for the Jews will arise from another place,
> but you and your father's family will perish. And who knows but
> that you have come to the royal position for such a time as this?'
> (NIV).

In other words, if you do not act, you will have forfeited your privileged role, given to you by none other than God himself at this hour of need, and you and your family will be punished for it – by the One who acts from his place, and who will help his people. Help will come from another *place*. The Hebrew word is *maqom*, and while this could simply mean 'place' in normal, everyday contexts, in the highly charged atmosphere of this dialogue, it reverberates with the message of the *Torah*: the *maqom* is God's place, as he revealed it in Genesis 28:16–17; Exodus 3:5; 20:24; Deuteronomy 12:21; 14:24, and other passages of the Hebrew Bible. Read, for example, the following:

> In every place [maqom] where I cause my name to be
> remembered, I will come to you and bless you (Exodus 20:24).

*Then God said [to Moses]: 'Come no closer! Remove the sandals
from your feet, for the place [maqom] on which you are standing
is holy ground' (Exodus 3:5).*

*Then Jacob woke from his sleep and said, 'Surely the Lord is in
this place [maqom] – and I did not know it!' (Genesis 28:16,
NRSV).*

These, and the other instances of *maqom* indicate that it is not
one single, determined place. God is not where believers may have
fixed his abode; wherever God himself decides to reveal himself, there
we can see his place. Consequently, the Hebrew word *maqom* became
one of the names of God. He is where his place is; his place and his
presence become synonymous, and it is God who decides. In the
Talmud, the popular and much-quoted *Pirqe Avot* ('Sayings of the
Fathers') call God *maqom* almost to the exclusion of any other name.[8]
And we can follow this thread from Esther and the Talmud to the
present day. At funerals, the mourners greet the relatives of the
deceased with the Hebrew sentence, 'Ha Maqom y'nachem etchem
betoch shar aveley zion v' yerushalayim': 'May the Omnipresent One
[He who is everywhere at His place] comfort you among the mourners
of Zion and Jerusalem.'[9] And when Josephus, the Pharisee-turned-
Roman historian who had spent some time among the Essenes as a
young man, told the story of Esther in his *Jewish Antiquities* soon after
AD 70, he was so certain of the identity of *maqom* and God that he did
not even comment on it: 'Mordecai ordered the eunuch who had
brought this message to him from Esther to tell her not to look out for
her own safety so much as the common safety of their nation; for if
she now neglected them, they would surely receive help from God...'[10]

Why, if Esther 4:14 can be seen to refer to God almost self-
evidently, and even by name, did the author of the book prefer such a
detour? Could it be that Mordecai did not trust the eunuch Hathach,

and therefore gave him a coded message which only the Jewess Esther/Hadassah would be able to decode? Could it be that the exiled Jews in the Persian diaspora avoided the more obvious names of God in public or in the presence of non-Jews – and that our passage would be an historically accurate depiction of this situation? Two other explanations were offered in a Jewish commentary on the *Megilloth*:

> *Perhaps, since the* Megillah *[the Esther Scroll] was to be read
> at the annual merry-making of Purim, when considerable licence
> was permitted, the author feared that the Divine Name might
> be profaned, if it occurred in the reading. Perhaps he feared that
> the Book might be profanely treated by Gentiles, because of its
> story of triumph of the Jews over their enemies. But whatever the
> reason for the omission of the Name of God, the sense of Divine
> Providence pervades the Book. The statement of Mordecai in iv.14
> shows unfailing trust in God's providential care for His people.*[11]

Do call upon the Lord!

A further clue, which takes us back to text of the Bible at Qumran and other Dead Sea caves, and to Josephus, the Jewish-Roman historian, can be detected in the Septuagint, the Jewish translation of the Hebrew Bible into Greek. This version came into being in northern Egypt in the third and second centuries BC and had reached the status of the widely accepted New International Version of the Bible before the turn of the century. Although only a few Greek scrolls – or rather fragments of scrolls – were found at Qumran, six in Cave 4 and nineteen in Cave 7, the Wadi Murabba'at with its magnificent Greek Twelve Prophets' Scroll of the mid-first century AD and other, smaller finds confirm that the Greek Bible was known even at the Dead Sea. As for the rest of the Jewish world, the Greek version soon became increasingly popular and important. During the first decades of early Christianity, the Jews who decided to follow Jesus, and wrote what was to become the New Testament, quoted almost exclusively from this Septuagint in Greek. The book of Esther has a fascinating Greek track record. Again and again, the text was 'improved' by extensive additions, some of which are produced in modern translations of the Bible 'with Apocrypha', where they are called 'The Rest of the Chapters of the Book of Esther' or 'Additions to the Book of Esther'. But the oldest Greek version, belonging to the original Septuagint, was written only a few decades or so after the Hebrew original. And in this Greek version, God is not 'hidden' behind a name like *maqom*.[12] He makes his entrance as *kyrios*, the Lord. This is Esther 4:8, in the Greek version of the early second century BC:

> And he [Mordecai, in Greek, Mardochaeus] gave him [the servant
> Hathach, in Greek, Achrathaeus] the copy [of Haman's, in
> Greek, Aman's, edict], which was published in Susa concerning
> their [the Jews'] annihilation, to show it to Esther. And he told him
> to charge her to go and implore the king, and to beg him for the
> people. 'Remember the days of your low estate,' [he told Esther],
> 'how you were nursed by me, for Aman, who is the king's closest
> adviser, has spoken against us, demanding our death. Do call upon
> the Lord, and speak to the king, concerning us, to deliver us from
> death.'

The decisive variant, apart from a couple of minor additions, occurs at the end. 'Do call upon the Lord, and speak to the king.' Who is the Lord? Greek usage is quite unequivocal: 'calling upon', *epikaleô*, is used in literary, philosophical and theological texts for calling upon the Godhead.[13] Exceptionally, it can be used for the invocation of a ruler, but this must be ruled out in Esther 4:8 – the king, or in Greek, *basileus*, is mentioned in the second part of two consecutive actions. And Greek grammar demands that the active voice would have to be employed, instead of the medium or middle voice which we have in this verse, if, in spite of the sentence structure, 'lord' and 'king' were supposed to be identical. Does this sound too technical, too complicated? Only if we forget that the Greek and the Hebrew texts of the Old Testament were written by people who knew what they were doing. The vagaries of the textual tradition may have obscured some of the nuances, but more often than not, we can rescue them. Readers of the Bible have learnt to see the text in its context. 'To call upon' (*epikaleô*), combined with 'God' (*theos*) is standard language in the Septuagint, the Greek Bible of pre-Christian and Christian times.[14] What is more, *kyrios*, Lord, was the most common way of rendering the holy, unspeakable tetragram YHWH. Greek Esther 4:8, with *kyrios* = the Lord = God, an integral part of the canonical Greek version, prepares the way for later additions. Long prayers of Mordecai and Esther, referring to God, and other bits and pieces were added.[15] But if we leave these later additions aside, the earliest Greek text on its own is persuasive enough. Are we allowed to observe that the most striking difference between Greek Esther and Hebrew Esther is the 'fragmentariness' of Hebrew Esther? There is an abundance of 'Lord' and 'God' in the former, and only the one 'name', *maqom*, in the latter.

And, at this stage, we have to admit we just do not know what we do not know. Could it be that the Greek text of the third/second century BC Septuagint was based on a Hebrew text which was older than the standard version of the eighth-century-AD Masoretes? The Qumran discoveries seem to indicate this possibility.[16] If so, God the *kyrios* and God the *theos* were not added to the Greek text, but deleted from the (later) Hebrew editions. Since there is not a single Hebrew fragment of Esther which precedes the eighth-century-AD Masoretic edition of the Hebrew Bible, the question may be asked, even though it cannot be answered conclusively. Remember Professor Goldman's explanation: in the Hebrew text of Esther, the direct naming of God was avoided (shall we say, deleted) because of a fear of profanation by the Purim extravaganzas, and by pagan readers averse to the violent Jewish triumph in the diaspora. The latter reason would make sense at the time of the Masoretes. After all, the Hebrew edition of the Masoretes was put together precisely so as to give minority Jews in the diaspora a unifying bond. Revelling in an armed slaughter of opponents in this very diaspora, as a kind of response to prayers to the God of the Jews, would have been somewhat counterproductive. But the definitive answer eludes us. All we do know for certain is this: in the Hebrew text, *maqom* could be understood as a name of God. A man who had studied with Essenes, Sadducees and Pharisees – Josephus – knew *maqom* meant God. And the Greek version of Esther, which existed before the Essenes assembled at Qumran, refers to God as Lord (*kyrios*) and directly as God (*theos*). To put it differently, God is in Esther, by inference, by name and by action. He is the God of the diaspora, helping his people when everything else seems to fail.

Back at Qumran, we notice that the missing Esther scroll is only half the story. It may be one of those sobering facts of archaeology that Esther was not found in any of the caves, but the story of Esther was known, and studied. Several Aramaic fragments discovered in Cave 4 belong to what one scholar, Josef Milik, called 'Proto-Esther', and another, James Charlesworth, a 'Commentary on Esther'.[17] Those fragments are known as 4Q prEst ar ('ar' stands for Aramaic), or Proto-Esther 4Q 550, and they have been dated to the second half of the first century BC. The complete text once contained more than an account of the Esther story: as the fragments tell us, it comprised references to the time of Darius I, the father and predecessor of Ahasuerus/Xerxes, who lived from 521 to 486 BC. In other words, it placed Esther even more firmly in the history of the ancient near east. All of this belongs to the realm where ancient history, the Bible and the Dead Sea Scrolls come together. For Darius was the true successor of Cyrus, and Cyrus was the first of the Persians to appear in the pages of the Old Testament. As Dorothy L. Sayers put in her timeless essay,

'A Vote of Thanks to Cyrus', recalling her first encounter, as a young girl, with this peculiar form of ancient cross-fertilization:

> *Cyrus was pigeon-holed in my mind with the Greeks and Romans.*
> *So for a long time he remained. And then, one day, I realized*
> *with a shock as of sacrilege, that... he had marched clean out*
> *of Herodotus and slap into the Bible. Mene, mene, tekel*
> *upharsin – the palace wall had blazed with the exploits of Cyrus,*
> *and Belshazzar's feast had broken up in disorder under the stern*
> *and warning eye of the prophet Daniel. But Daniel and Belshazzar*
> *did not live in 'the classics' at all. They lived in the Church, with*
> *Adam and Abraham and Elijah, and were dressed like Bible*
> *characters, especially Daniel. And here was God – not Zeus*
> *or Apollo or any of the Olympian crowd, but the fierce and*
> *dishevelled old gentleman from Mount Sinai – bursting into Greek*
> *history in a most uncharacteristic way, and taking an interest in*
> *events and people that seemed altogether outside His province.*
> *It was disconcerting. And there was Esther. She lived in a book*
> *called* Stories from the Old Testament, *and had done very*
> *well for God's Chosen People by her diplomatic approach to*
> *King Ahasuerus. A good Old-Testament-sounding name,*
> *Ahasuerus, reminding one of Ahab and Ahaz and Ahaziah.*
> *I cannot remember in what out-of-the-way primer of general*
> *knowledge I came across the astonishing equation, thrown out*
> *casually in a passing phrase, 'Ahasuerus (or Xerxes)'. Xerxes! –*
> *but one knew all about Xerxes. He was not just 'classics', but*
> *real history; it was against Xerxes that the Greeks had made their*
> *desperate and heroic stand at Thermopylae. There was none of the*
> *fairy-tale atmosphere of Cyrus about him – no dreams, no oracles,*
> *no faithful herdsmen – only the noise and dust of armies trampling*
> *through the hard outlines and clear colours of a Grecian land-*
> *scape, where the sun always shone so much more vividly than it*

*did in the Bible. I think it was chiefly Cyrus and Ahasuerus who
prodded me into the belated conviction that history was all of a
piece, and that the Bible was part of it.*[18]

Darius, and Xerxes after him, set the scene for a pro-Jewish attitude at the Persian court. And even if people not known from any of the other scrolls appear on the scene, men like Bagasro, Patireza and Bagoshi, Dorothy L. Sayer's insight is borne out: the odd one out, that 'missing' scroll of Esther, is very present and very real indeed, in Jewish history, textual tradition and among the Dead Sea Scrolls. Josef Milik reconstructed the name of Esther in one of the fragments from Cave 4. And perhaps, according to another scholar, Klaus Beyer, the text even claims Xerxes/Ahasuerus (eventually) worshipped the God of the Jews.[19] From a Persian perspective, God is described as 'the Most High' (Fragment *d*):

*The Most High whom you [the Jews] fear and worship rules o[ver
the whole e]arth. Everyone whom he wishes [comes] near.*

These 'Proto-Esther' fragments are not, and never were, original components of the biblical book, whatever else they may have been. But they help us to understand that the literary and religious 'intake' of the Qumran librarians was far from narrow-minded. By the early first century, while Jesus was a young man growing up in Nazareth, the library caves had accumulated a wealth of texts in Hebrew and Aramaic. There is no reason whatsoever to suppose that Esther, of all texts, was excluded. Once again, we appreciate the truth of that old adage: the absence of evidence must not be mistaken for the evidence of absence. From time to time, circumstantial evidence is all we have, and we must take it seriously. If, for example, someone were to ask if the book of Esther was accepted and appreciated by the Jewish authors of the New Testament and its first Jewish readers, our initial reply might be: no, probably not. But Mark's Gospel tells a different story. When Herod implores his step-daughter (the one called Salome in later tradition) to dance for him, he promises her everything she might demand, even half of his kingdom (Mark 6:23–24). The girl consults her mother and demands the head of John the Baptist. Herod's promise is practically word-identical with Ahasuerus'/Xerxes' promise to Esther, repeated no less than three times (Esther 5:3, 6; 7:2). Queen Esther uses the first two opportunities to unmask Haman. On the third occasion, she asks the king for her life and for that of her people. As in Mark's Gospel, the consequence is death: the death of Haman, the grand vizier who had plotted the genocide of the Persian Jews. But every reader of Mark's Gospel was – and is – invited to understand the difference: the step-daughter of Herod acted out of spite, goaded by her mother, and against the king's intentions. Esther, however, a God-fearing Jewess, acted because she wanted to save lives, in the interest of the king and in obedience to God. Esther and 'Salome', Ahasuerus/Xerxes and Herod are models of contrast. Any reader of Mark's Gospel who knew the Hebrew Tanakh, or the Greek Septuagint – and this was the vast majority of the first generation of gospel readers – had the means to understand the punchline.

'We Ourselves Are Jews by Birth'

THE CASE OF CAVE 7

The writings of the New Testament belong to the Jewish Library of the late Second Temple period. Identifying fragments from Qumran Cave 7 as passages from Jewish-Christian writings (Mark, 1 Timothy) means that this library has grown. Mark, 1 Timothy and other writings of what later became known as the New Testament are no less Jewish in origin than the writings of the Essenes and other groups whose texts may be among the scroll fragments at Qumran. The later development of a Christian church, and of a Christian 'world mission' which was to target people from non-Jewish cultures, should not deflect our attention from the fact the Christian documents of the first generation were written by Jews, about another Jew, Jesus of Nazareth, as the incarnation of two Jewish concepts: Son of God and Messiah. Today, there are Jewish scholars who say we should assume the presence of the first Christian texts at Qumran even if not a single fragment had been found: it was a natural place for them to be studied.

This chapter gives an up-to-date presentation of the case for and against the identification of fragments in Cave 7 and the consequences of such identifications for our understanding of that period and the origins of the New Testament.

A Greek surprise

By 1955, the first wave of Qumran enthusiasm was over. When Cave 7 was discovered on 5 February of that year, the archaeologists did not bat an eyelid. No journalist was alerted, no press conference was given. Eighteen tiny fragments, one piece of seemingly illegible writing on clay, a few pieces of pottery: how could this possibly change the course of studies on the great Caves 1, 3 and 4? But in terms of Qumran research, and remembering the flowery language which had been employed to describe previous finds, Cave 7 was truly sensational. Together with Caves 8 and 9, it was the cave closest to the settlement, it had a jar with a legible Hebrew name, its manuscripts were exclusively Greek, and all of them were papyri.[1] At that stage of Qumran archaeology, only one other cave with an inscription on a jar had been opened, and it was illegible. Only in Cave 4 had a few other Greek scroll fragments been found – unedited until 1992 – hardly noticeable, it seemed, among thousands of scraps from some 570 scrolls. In the edition of the Greek texts from Cave 4, just two of these six manuscripts are papyri.[2] And papyrus as a writing material plays a minor role in just one further cave, Cave 6, where five papyri were found, none of them in Greek.[3] As for the Greek texts in Cave 4, they are fragments of:

❑ Leviticus, 4Q 119/4Q LXXLev^a (leather); and 4Q 120/pap4Q LXXLev^b (papyrus);

❑ Numbers, 4Q 121/4Q LXXNum (leather);

❑ Deuteronomy, 4Q 122/4Q LXXDeut (leather);

❑ Exegetical paraphrase on Exodus, 4Q 127/4Q papPara Ex gr (papyrus).

Exodus proper and Genesis were not found – but there is a Greek Exodus fragment in Cave 7, so one might say that at Qumran, all books of the *Torah* with the exception of Genesis were found in Greek.

❑ Unidentified Greek leather fragments in Cave 4, published under one number, 4Q 126/4Q Unid gr.

Given the sporadic appearance of Greek *and* papyrus, let alone Greek *on* papyrus, in Cave 4, a certain lack of perspicacity on the part of the first editors should be admitted. Whatever the precise nature of the texts in Cave 7 may be, and even before the full extent of Greek texts and papyrus fragments in Cave 4 became known, it should have been obvious from the beginning that Cave 7 was a special collection, a library within the library system of Qumran – and in this sense, the second most important cave after the great Cave 4. What is more, the curiosity of scholars should have been aroused by yet another aspect: since the papyri were undoubtedly written in Greek, they could have contained – and, as it turned out, they did contain – texts from the Greek Bible, the Septuagint. This version, as we have seen repeatedly in previous chapters, was immensely popular at the time, particularly in the diaspora, and had become an accepted part of worship and teaching, even if orthodox Jews in Roman Palestine would have insisted on the liturgical use of the Hebrew text. The discovery of the Greek Bible at the piously orthodox study and community centre of Qumran was a breakthrough – or would have been, if it had been recognized for its true importance. Other manuscripts of the Septuagint, known before the Qumran discoveries, or found more or less simultaneously, were rare exceptions (see the Nahal Hever and Nahal Dagar/Wadi Murabba'at discoveries described in Chapter III); and the vast majority of the other surviving papyri belonged to the later Christian tradition of the Greek Bible.[4] But the chance was missed.[5] In fact, although the mere existence of Greek fragments in Cave 4 had been known of since the first survey after the discovery of the cave in 1952, they were, as we just saw, not properly edited until 1992, and when the Cave 7 papyri were edited in 1962, the two fragments which were identified as scraps from the Septuagint, 7Q 1 (Exodus 28:4–7) and 7Q 2 (Letter of Jeremiah/Baruch 6:43–44), were drowned under the mass of material published in that volume; no effort was made to 'rescue' them.[6]

In Cave 4, the Greek scroll fragments show us almost the whole variety of Hebrew and Aramaic Qumran categories. There is the Bible, and it is the *Torah* minus Genesis (i.e. Exodus, Leviticus, Numbers, and Deuteronomy); there is a commentary, 4Q 127; and there are unidentified texts, which are legible enough to betray traces of 'group-specific' literature: whatever they once were, they dealt with theological and pastoral questions, within a Jewish context. Thus, though they are Greek, they are not alien to the nature of the Qumran system. What makes them different is the language – but then again, it was the common language of Jews all over the Roman empire and beyond, at least since the first century BC. And it is certainly noteworthy that the Greek finds from Cave 4 have been dated precisely to the period from the first century BC to the early first century AD. Even an orthodox library, proud of its Hebrew and Aramaic stock, had to get at least a few Greek scrolls. For one thing, there was a growing number of Jews who became interested in the Essene movement, but did not have fluent Hebrew any more; and for another, the Essenes simply had to know what the 'rest' of their fellow Jews out there were doing, reading and studying. They had to know – either so as to find out how to attract them, or, conversely, to find out to refute them. And they may have been relieved to find that orthodoxy was preserved in the Greek *Torah* versions: the holy and unspeakable name of God, YHWH, if it was not translated into Greek as *kyrios*, 'Lord' – which was the most common rendering in the Greek Bible – was 'protected' by a vocalized abbreviation, i – a – o.[7]

A much more important and momentous consequence of the Greek discoveries in Cave 4 concerned the text itself. In the above chapter on Esther, we noted in passing that there is a tendency, at least among some scholars, to assume there was an original Hebrew text which was considerably older than the eighth-century text of the Masoretes – the text which became the modern standard. And we noted that this older Hebrew text was – in parts, at least – quite different from the medieval and modern standard editions. The Qumran discoveries provided the proof. They showed that the Greek translations of the Septuagint and its followers used different Hebrew models. In the case of the two Isaiah scrolls from Cave 1, it was evident enough how divergent the style, syntax and vocabulary of one and the same Hebrew book found in one and the same place could be, without interfering with the content. The scrolls of the *Torah* were much less affected by these variations, but even here, a certain flexibility was evident. What the Greek fragments from Cave 4 also showed was a surprising variety of readings among the extant Greek manuscripts themselves.

The pre-Christian Septuagint was a kind of work in progress, with constant revisions. Eugene Ulrich counted no fewer than fifteen variants (excluding orthographic changes) in the Leviticus fragment 4Q LXXLev^a, over against the edited text of the Septuagint, and one more in comparison with the Hebrew text of the Masoretes. In 4Q LXXNum, he counted seventeen variants.[8] Ulrich himself was amazed to the extent of using an exclamation mark in his comment on the Leviticus manuscript: 'Fifteen variants in twenty-eight less-than-half-extant lines of manuscript! But none of these variants is an error. All are sensible readings, constituting an alternate text or translation.'[9] He goes on to show that seven of these fifteen variants are unique, and three others are attested by only one or two manuscripts. These are observations which have not been popular among those who prefer cut-and-dry scenarios, but such idylls never were the real world of textual history and criticism. Ulrich's conclusions will be useful when we turn to Cave 7. For, in the debate about the contents of this cave, they have been conveniently forgotten by most critics of the proposed Christian identification of at least two of its papyri.

Before we move to Cave 7 with its entertaining examples of multiple variants in the two Septuagint papyri, 7Q 1 and 7Q 2, just two examples for the insights gained by comparing the Hebrew texts

The settlement (*Khirbet*) of Qumran,
with the Dead Sea and the
mountains of Moab in the east

Picture: Carsten Peter Thiede

Two Qumran caves: Cave 4 in the centre,
and, bottom left, the remnants of Cave 7.
To the left, the Wadi Qumran (Nahal Secacah)

Picture: Carsten Peter Thiede

The synagogue on Masada, where Dead Sea Scrolls were found. The architecture explains the seating order presupposed by the epistle of James 2:2–4

Picture: Carsten Peter Thiede

**Example of a Reconstruction:
7Q5, the Fifth Fragment from
Qumran Cave 7**

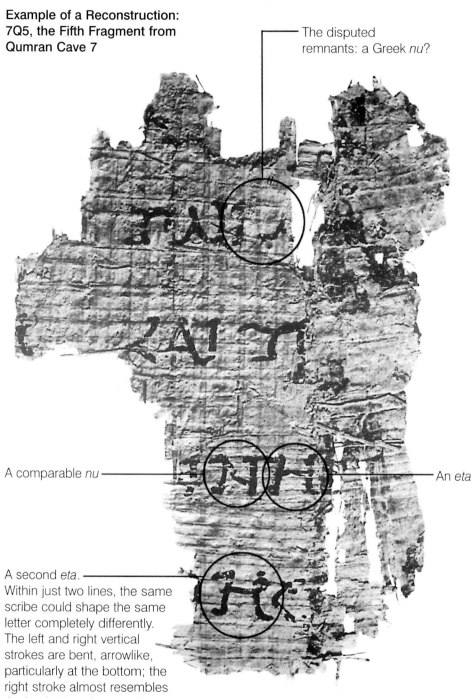

The disputed remnants: a Greek *nu*?

A comparable *nu*

An *eta*

A second *eta*.
Within just two lines, the same scribe could shape the same letter completely differently. The left and right vertical strokes are bent, arrowlike, particularly at the bottom; the right stroke almost resembles the beginning of an *epsilon*

The reconstructed *nu*

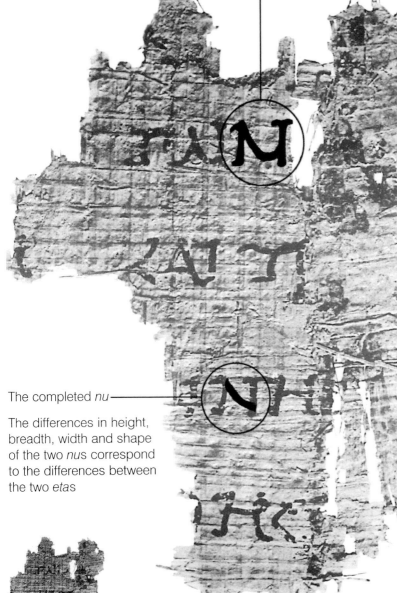

The completed *nu*

The differences in height, breadth, width and shape of the two *nus* correspond to the differences between the two *etas*

7Q5 in its original size

Picture: David Rubinger, Jerusalem

The most controversial fragment of the 'War Scroll':
4Q 285 – a slain or slaying Messiah?

Picture: Israel Antiquities Authority, Jerusalem

Confocal Laser Scanning Microscopy: Pnina Shor of
the Israel Antiquities Authority and Carsten Peter Thiede,
analysing Plate 789 with the fragments from Cave 7

Picture: Carsten Peter Thiede

Qumran fragment 7Q4:
1 Timothy 3:16 – 4:3
or 1 Enoch 103:3–4?

Picture: David Rubinger, Jerusalem

found at Qumran to the Greek text of the Septuagint. The first example takes us into the New Testament. In Acts 7:14, Stephen delivers his great valedictory address. He mentions seventy-five family members and relatives invited by Joseph to visit him in Egypt. It is the text of the Greek Bible which Stephen, the Greek-speaking Jew or 'Hellenist', must have used. But the Hebrew text of the Masoretes mentions only seventy people in Genesis 46:27, Exodus 1:5 and Deuteronomy 10:22. The fragmentary first leather scroll from the Cave 4 finds, 4Q 1/4Q Ex^a, however, also has seventy-five relatives. In other words, Luke in Acts and the Greek Septuagint are not in error. They used an older Hebrew text of Exodus than the one which is represented in the edition of the Masoretes. The Qumran discovery shows the textual accuracy in Stephen's speech and in the pre-Christian Greek translation of the Hebrew original.[10]

The second example is even more famous. In 1952, a Hebrew fragment of the books of Samuel was found in a deep cavity of Cave 4: 4Q 51/4Q Sam^a. Damaged and badly soiled by animal urine, it had to be cleansed in a very slow and careful process. And to the surprise of the scholars, the legible text turned out to be extremely close to the Greek Bible. Why was this such a sensational discovery? Until then, the Masoretic text – and hence the printed Hebrew editions used by Jewish and Christian Bible scholars – was the only available version of the Samuel books. And it varied from the Septuagint (LXX) to such an extent that most scholars thought the Septuagint was a somewhat sloppy translation, a paraphrase rather than a proper rendering. But now it could be shown that the Greek translators had been admirably accurate. They had simply used a different Hebrew text – the text rediscovered in Cave 4. There are many similar cases at Qumran, and it is one of the regrets of scholars and translators that there are no complete copies of all biblical books. As Emanuel Tov, one of the pioneers of the comparison between the Greek and Hebrew Bible texts at Qumran, and currently head of the Dead Sea Scrolls editorial team in Jerusalem, put it: 'Unique agreements between the Septuagint and the Qumran scrolls... abound in all books of the Bible. The reason that only a relatively small amount of such evidence is known is that only a limited number of texts have been preserved in the Judean Desert.'[11] Generalizations are therefore impossible. The Septuagint does include additions and translations which verge on paraphrase and comment. But it is no longer possible to claim that the Greek Bible, which was the one almost exclusively used by Jews outside the Holy Land in New Testament times – and by the authors of the New Testament themselves – is almost automatically less authentic, less reliable when it differs from the standard Hebrew text and its modern translations.

Your brother Aaron

Exodus and the Letter of Jeremiah: an incongruous combination – and that is exactly where the first editors of the texts found in Cave 7 left it in 1962. The other seventeen fragments were treated as unidentifiable – certainly as unidentifiable with any text of the Greek Old Testament. Even so, this meagre result was surprising enough. No other Greek fragment of Exodus was found anywhere else at Qumran, and of the apocryphal Letter of Jeremiah, neither Hebrew nor Aramaic nor Greek fragments were found in any other cave. Obviously, the book of Exodus was a natural part of the Qumran library, and its discovery should not surprise us. When the archaeologists found the cave on 5 February 1955, its roof had already collapsed, and most of the cave had disappeared into the wadi underneath. Some of the fragments, such as 7Q 5, had been wilfully damaged in antiquity (it was old, not recent damage), as though the Romans had discovered the cave, smashed the jars and torn the fragments. The tiny scraps found just underneath the soil of the cave are a minute percentage of what once was there. The mere existence of an Exodus fragment, for example, tells us there had to be scrolls of all five books of the *Torah*, or even one complete *Torah* scroll. It was – and is – inconceivable that a group of Jews could collect single books of the *Torah* to the exclusion of the others. But what about Baruch 6, the apocryphal Letter of Jeremiah? And what are these odd fragments of 7Q 1 and 7Q 2? Are they really Exodus 28:4–7 and Baruch 6:43–44 as we know them from our editions of the Greek Bible?

Readers of the Bible today know the phenomenon: a group of people meets for Bible study, and they all bring their own Bibles. Here is a New International Version, over there a New Revised Standard Version; unmoved by the spirit of the times, someone has brought the Authorized Version. The New Jerusalem Bible, the Revised English Bible, the Good News Bible and a few others – they are all there. The group decides to begin by reading the passage which will be studied, and everyone reads a verse or two in turn. After the first instalment, embarrassed silence: the end of the first verse in the first translation and the beginning of the second verse in the next one do not match. And so it goes on. Surely a mistake? But no, the reason is obvious: every translation follows a different pattern. The vocabulary, the idiom, the sentence structure, the rhythm – they are meant to be different, because every one of these translations aims at a specific type of readers. No one would want to claim that only one of them can be correct, or inspired, or acceptable for Bible study. It is true that in the Church of England, the Authorized Version or King James Bible has a traditionally sacrosanct status, mainly because of its use in the Book of Common Prayer services, where all additional readings are taken from it. But this is certainly no longer reflected in everyday practice. The Alternative Service Book, introduced in 1980, made this unmistakably obvious when it took the Sunday readings from a number of different modern translations, often from two or three different ones for Old Testament, epistle and gospel on one and the same Sunday, thereby confusing the fun of variety with the need for cohesion.

At the beginning of the first century, and increasingly so in the

131

second and third centuries, the same situation was faced by readers of the Old Testament in Greek. As mentioned above, the 'official' text of the Septuagint was constantly revised, and, eventually, rival translations appeared on the market. From the second century onwards, Jews often refused to use the Septuagint, because it had become the Bible of the Christians. Much like the Greek fragments from Cave 4, the two Greek papyrus fragments found in Cave 7, from the *Torah* and from the Apocrypha, illustrate the early stages of this multifaceted scene.

Here is the text of the first fragment, Exodus 28:4–7, according to the English translation of the New Revised Standard Version:

> *These are the vestments that they shall make: a breastplate, an ephod, a robe, a chequered tunic, a turban and a sash. When they make these sacred vestments for your brother Aaron and his sons to serve me as priests, they shall use gold, blue, purple and crimson yarns, and fine linen. They shall make the ephod of gold, of blue, purple and crimson yarns, and of fine twisted linen, skilfully worked. It shall have two shoulder-pieces attached to its two edges, so that it may be joined together.*

This is of course translated from the Hebrew, following the text of the Masoretes. Most modern English translations have the turban in verse 4, evoking images of some pious Sikhs, rather than of Aaronitic priests. The Authorized Version has a mitre instead. This in turn looks like a bishop's headgear to modern readers, but at least it reminds one of priestly status, which the odd turban certainly does not. And what has changed when we look at the standard Greek text of the Septuagint? Apart from minute differences in style, the actual description is identical. Unlike some of the other biblical books, the five books of the *Torah* were treated with faithful reverence by the translators at every stage – a common opinion which appears to be justified by this comparison. But the differences are interesting. For example, in verse 4, the Septuagint omits the words 'for your brother' before 'Aaron'. And now for the papyrus fragment from Cave 7.

In verse 4, it has 'for your brother' before 'Aaron' and thus agrees with the commonly accepted Hebrew text against the Septuagint. Immediately afterwards, in the following line, 7Q 1 has the Greek word αυτου, which is not in the Septuagint. Conversely, 7Q 1 omits the two Greek words (εις το) at the beginning of this line, whereas they can be found in the Septuagint.

We have hardly begun, and yet the subtle differences are there right from the beginning of the fragment. Apart from the addition of 'his brothers', these variants concern style and syntax rather than statements or clarifications of content. But whatever the reason for and degree of these nuances, they tell us that the scribe of 7Q 1 did not follow a standard edition of the Septuagint. If a textual critic today had to identify 7Q 1 on the basis of the accepted edition of the Greek Old Testament, he would have to admit it is not *the* Greek Old Testament, but a variation on a theme, as it were – closer to the Hebrew than to other known Greek models. And so it goes on.

At the beginning of verse 5, fragment 7Q 1 has 'scarlet/purple' as one of the colours, but it omits the word 'spun/woven' (or 'fine twisted', according to the NRSV) (κεκλωσμενον, from κλητω, 'to spin'), which would have to be here if the translator had strictly followed a standard Hebrew text. He offers us 'spun' in the following verse, however – against the Septuagint, but this time with the standard Hebrew text. In verse 7, he has the two shoulder pieces 'joined together' and only then fastened to the two sides, a variant of the Septuagint, but against the Hebrew text of the Masoretes. All in all, we can count ten variations from the previously known Greek, the Hebrew or from both, on eleven damaged, incomplete lines preserved on two scraps of papyrus. The only *complete* words on 7Q 1 are the Greek και, 'and', which occurs twice, the article το, 'the', which also appears twice, and χρυσιον, 'gold', just once. Certainly not much to go on, but with some of the incomplete words that can be reconstructed, it makes sense to identify this passage as a form of Exodus 28:4–7, in spite of the textual variations. What sounds complicated and very specialized in this brief description is the daily bread and butter of papyrologists working with ancient papyri; most of them have survived as tattered fragments. It is the art of the scholar to reconstruct and identify them. With the Old Testament, or indeed with the New Testament, this is – comparatively speaking! – an easy task. There are always versions to compare them to – in Hebrew, from one of the Greek translations, from the important but often underestimated Samaritan Pentateuch,[12] or even from later Syriac, Armenian or Latin translations which may give us valuable information about different textual traditions throughout the Roman empire. But remember, many of the finds from the Dead Sea caves are previously unknown writings – commentaries, treatises, and so forth – with no complete edition preserved anywhere else. It should be obvious by now how excruciatingly difficult it is to make sense of fragments from such texts.

A scribe called Baruch

Occasionally, even biblical texts are challenging enough. Take the second Greek fragment from Cave 7, 7Q 2. In the first edition of 1962, it was identified with the apocryphal Letter of Jeremiah, also called Baruch 6, of which just two verses survived in Cave 7, 6:43–44. In the Revised English Bible, this reads:

> *When one of them is led off by one of the passers-by and is taken to bed by him, she derides the woman next to her, because she was not as attractive as herself and her cord was not broken. Whatever is done for these idols is false. Why then must anyone think that they are gods, or call them gods?*

The women in verse 43 are servants of pagan gods of the Chaldeans, sitting along the passageways of the Temple precinct, and burning bran for incense. The whole Letter of Jeremiah is introduced as 'a copy of the letter which Jeremiah sent to those about to be led captive to Babylon by the King of the Babylonians, to tell them what he had been commanded by God.'

The complete book of Baruch, a collection of writings, was composed – according to its introduction, Baruch 1:1–14 – by Baruch, Jeremiah's secretary, after the deportation of the Jewish elite to Babylon. Baruch, of course, was the very man who put documents in an earthenware jar to preserve them 'for a long time' – the reference point for the Qumranites' practice (Jeremiah 32:13–14). As the introduction was originally written in Greek, whereas the prayers, poems and apologetics were written in Hebrew, we may assume this collection was put together by a Greek-writing group who regarded these texts as 'Baruchian' in style and nature and arranged for a Greek translation of all elements to be added to the Septuagint. In the days when Baruch 6 was added, towards the beginning of the first century BC, it was not regarded as an integral part of the book of Baruch, but separated from it by the Lamentations of Jeremiah the Prophet. Only the Latin Vulgate of the fifth century AD,[13] and translations such as the English Authorized Version, included it as a sixth chapter of the composite book of Baruch. There was a reason for the separation: chapter 6 deals with Babylonian/Chaldean idolatry, both polemically and apologetically. But since it belongs to the collection of anti-Babylonian literature, referring to Isaiah 44:9–20 and Jeremiah 10:1–16, it also made sense to add it to the apocryphal 'Baruch' writings – as Jerome with his Latin Vulgate, and those who followed him, decided to do.

In any case, however, Baruch 6 or the Letter of Jeremiah was not merely an obscure addition to a Greek biblical collection. 2 Maccabees 2:1–3 refers to it – in other words, it was taken seriously by Jews who defended their political and religious independence in a time of crisis. And the letter has a central message which appealed to the first Christian generation. The outspoken, harsh refusal to accept the presence, or even the toleration of idols, is summed up in the last verse (73) of Baruch 6: 'Better, therefore, is someone upright who has no idols; such a person will be far above reproach.' Compare this to 1 Corinthians 10:14: 'Therefore, my dear friends, flee from the worship of idols,' and 1 John 5:21: 'Little children, keep yourselves from idols.' Strikingly, this admonition comes at the very end of both the first letter of John and the letter of Baruch. To put it differently, if Paul in 1 Corinthians and John in his first letter wanted a scriptural authority, known to fellow Jews, they found it in Baruch 6/Letter of Jeremiah 73. And in the letter of John, this is the very punchline, as it is in Baruch. The parallels are anything but accidental. When the Letter of Jeremiah was composed, the threat of pagan idols was an everyday reality, and so it was when the first Jewish Christians encountered their pagan 'target groups' in the Roman empire. Such observations may eventually help us to answer an open question: why, if this document has not been preserved in its Hebrew original in any of the caves, was it found in Greek in the extraordinary Greek papyrus collection of Cave 7?

Before we try to answer this question, we have to tackle the problem of the text itself: Is it really the Letter of Jeremiah 6:43–44? A mere five lines have survived, with twenty letters, perhaps (including a very damaged trace) twenty-one, five of which are incomplete. Furthermore, only two rather common Greek words are extant in full, ουν, 'then/therefore' in line 3, and, in line 4, αυτους, a determinative pronoun, 'self', (also used as the emphatic 'he/she/it', etc., and often left untranslated). By any standard, this is not much, and, theoretically, there should be countless Greek texts which would fit these distinguishing marks. But then, of course, some of the fragmentary letters can be reconstructed to yield complete words, and if the full lines tentatively reconstructed with these words result in a legible, consecutive text which makes sense as something resembling a known writing, those countless options disappear, and an identification can be suggested with some confidence. This is what happened in 1962, when the scrap called 7Q 2 was identified with Letter of Jeremiah 6:43–44. But, again, what was it really? Does the text resemble the received version of the letter as we know it?

The basis on which the identification was built occurs in lines 3 and 4, where we read]ως ουν νο[and]αυτους θ[. The right-hand curvature of the *theta*, θ, has disappeared on the fragment; thus, it could also be an *epsilon, ε*. The brackets,] and [, are used to indicate that lost letters or words existed before and after them. It is the art of the papyrologist to operate with tentative completions, going through the different possibilities offered by the Greek language, and then to check them against remnants in other lines. Fortunately, the two complete words occur in consecutive lines, and the αυτους in line 4 is obviously the beginning of the line. This is of enormous importance in any attempt to work out the complete text. A yardstick which has to be taken into account is the approximate length of the original lines. It helps to know of at least one line how it began. For the Greek papyri in Cave 7, it turns out that the average number of letters per line is twenty-two. There is, of course, no 'spacing' between words and sentences in ancient Greek writing; there are no punctuation marks, and the letters on literary papyri are capitals. Thus, ως ουν νο looks like ωCOYNNO, and αυτους θ looks like AYTOYCΘ. In quite a few cases, this makes a deciphering difficult or controversial, for there can be different ways of dividing consecutive letters into separate words. An English example would be the following sequence: GODISNOWHERE. This could be understood as 'God is nowhere', or as 'God is now here'. As we shall see in the next chapter, the problem is even more acute in Hebrew, which has no vowels in its written alphabet. Our little sentence would then be GDSNWHR. 'Good sin,

137

whore!' perhaps? To decide what it means, the context is often of vital importance. But what if you have not got a context, because your manuscript is a badly damaged fragment of unknown provenance? Quite a few unsolved controversies among scholars who work with fragments revolve around such problems. 7Q 2 is not as intractable as that. The first editors decided to try out Greek Bible passages where the extant words and letters occur in close proximity. A concordance – these days, it would of course be a computer concordance – facilitates the first steps.]ωCOYNNO[can be traced as [π]ως ουν νο[μιστεον], which occurs in Baruch 6:44 and means, 'How can it then be thought...?' In the next line, the Septuagint has only one word with a θ, ΘΕΟΥC, θεους, 'gods'. Thus, it makes sense to reconstruct]αυτους θ[as αυτους θ[εους]. And so the work continues step by step.

However, anyone who may have been curious enough to open a Greek Bible at this stage will have noticed several severe problems: Beautiful and somehow meaningful as this reconstruction is, it does not even come anywhere near the standard text of the Septuagint. In the Septuagint, the αυτους does not appear before θεους, but after it. The word before θεους is ως, which means 'as/just as/like as', etc. Depending on the sentence, it can also be the adverbial form of the relative pronoun ος (who, which, that, what). But whatever it is or means, it does not occur anywhere in the reconstruction of papyrus 7Q 2. Another word is definitely missing, the εν, 'among/in', for it would have to be between γε][νομε]να and αυ[τοις], in lines 2–3. But this is not the place to go into all the philological details, fascinating as they may be to the specialists.

Summing up, all one should say is this: this text is a fragmented passage of the Letter of Jeremiah only if a wide range of allowances is made for missing words, and a completely different sentence structure. Furthermore, of a maximum of twenty-one visible letters on these five lines, two – in the last line – are sheer guesswork, and three others are damaged to such an extent that they could be reconstructed as completely different letters, unless of course the suggested identification, step B, is taken as the yardstick for their reconstruction, step A. This is a legitimate procedure, needless to say, within the standard method of papyrological work – as long as everyone is aware of it and is not led to assume all letters are clear enough to leave no room for doubt or alternative readings.

It takes some courage to suggest this really is the Letter of Jeremiah as we know it. But no one has protested or seriously offered different identifications. After all, why not accept such a text at Qumran, for want of a better alternative, and why not take into account that some later translations, the Syriac and the Latin, appear to suggest at least a partial relationship with this Greek version? In a nutshell then, and accepting that it is a fragment of this letter, we would have further evidence for our intermediate conclusion: the Greek text of the Bible – with the Apocrypha, it seems – was anything but consolidated at the time of the Qumran library. The identification is allowed to stand as a variation on a theme. Everyone, it seems, agrees: 7Q 2 appears in all lists of fragments of the Greek Bible.

The nineteenth hole: creation and the scriptures?

Do we sense something unusual, out of the ordinary? One book of the *Torah* (Exodus), and one apocryphal writing (Baruch 6/Letter of Jeremiah): in spite of the exclusive nature of Greek papyri, the 'system' of Cave 7 so far looks like that of any other Qumran cave, even though the text of 7Q 2 itself is a find without parallel at Qumran. But there are nineteen fragments altogether which were found in this cave. To put it into perspective again, it may look like a meagre harvest, compared with the fragments from 575 texts in Cave 4, or to the seventy-nine of Cave 1, even to the thirty-three of Cave 2. But in Cave 3, only fifteen were found, twenty-five in Cave 5, thirty-one in Cave 6, just five in Cave 8, only one in Cave 9, no more than one again in Cave 10, and twenty-three in Cave 11. In 1962, the editors treated all seventeen fragments after 7Q 1 and 7Q 2, that is 7Q 3–7Q 19, as unidentifiable. This was remarkable, for there are some fragments which are larger than 7Q 2: 7Q 3 has thirty-one letters on four lines (a count which includes damaged letters, as it did in 7Q 1 and 7Q 2); 7Q 4 preserves twenty-two letters on seven lines of two scraps; 7Q 5 shows twenty letters on five lines; and 7Q 19, the reverse image imprint of a papyrus on hardened soil – another unique Qumran phenomenon – has thirty-five letters on six lines, which makes it the second largest of the Cave 7 discoveries after 7Q 1/Exodus 28:4–7. Why, if 7Q 2, a fragment smaller than most of these, could be identified, did the first editors fail to make sense of any of them?

7Q 3 was attributed to a type of writing very similar to, if not identical with, 7Q 2. And yet the fragment does not belong to the Letter of Jeremiah. All attempts to link the one complete word which can be deciphered, και, 'and', in line 2, to a biblical passage which would also accommodate the remnants of other words and letters on the fragment have failed. Even so, the text is quite specific: before the word και, there are the letters ακειμ (akeim) which may belong to a personal name with this frequent male ending, like Ainakeim, Eliakeim, Iakeim, Iôakeim, Enakeim, Sousakeim, and others. One suggestion, based on the sequence of an –ακειμ name and a και, has been Jeremiah 43:28–29.[14] Here, the name Joakeim (Ιωακειμ) is indeed followed, in the Greek text, by a και. In translation, the passage reads, 'and write all the words which were on the scroll, which was burnt by King Joakeim, and you shall say...' Unfortunately though only the wildest contortions of Greek sentence structure could force the rest of fragment 7Q 3 into any conceivable variant of Jeremiah 43:28–29. And therefore, when the papyrologist José O'Callaghan, who had himself thought of the Jeremiah passage when he prepared an annotated list of Greek biblical papyri, analysed all options once again, he admitted, like Baillet before him, that the fragment could not be identified.[15]

Even so, in view of the contents of other caves, this result is not as negative as it sounds. If we say a fragment cannot be identified, we usually mean it cannot be identified with any known, surviving text. But only a minute percentage of classical literature, biblical or otherwise, has survived. By not being able to identify something, we just imply it cannot be given a name or title which has already been 'registered'. If a fragment makes sense on its own, like many of the scroll fragments from other Qumran caves, we would not call them 'unidentified' or 'unidentifiable', but would give them new names of their own – such as 'Son of God fragment' for 4Q 246, or 'New Jerusalem fragment' for 11Q 18, and so forth. Only fragments which lack any distinctive word(s) or (half) sentences should therefore be called 'unidentified' or 'unidentifiable'. In fact, the last category should be avoided. Again and again, different new methods of analysis – some of which will be described in Chapter VIII – have been applied, and the tiniest of scraps have been shown to belong to other small fragments, thereby yielding a larger, more comprehensible whole. 7Q 3, unfortunately, lacks distinctive characteristics. And the one complete word, the 'and', και, is unremarkably ordinary. As we shall see in fragment 7Q 5, even a και can be meaningful if it comes after a distinctive gap of a few letters' width. Such gaps signal new paragraphs, and therefore also the beginning of a new sentence. When they occur on tiny fragments, they are an important help to papyrologists; the text they are looking for, the complete text to which the fragment belongs, must begin with a paragraph change, the end of one story and the beginning of a new one. But in 7Q 3, the και follows after the –ακειμ without a noticeable gap. The small space may just indicate that the scribe knew he was about to begin a new word and used the opportunity to lift his stylus and dip it into ink before he continued his sentence. As a rule, 7Q 3 and all the other Greek fragments from Cave 7 follow the ancient Greek custom of continuous writing, *scriptio continua*, where words and sentences are not separated. Thus, every single exception to this rule is important. Now obviously, if 7Q 3 is the Jeremiah passage, a gap before the και would be wrong, because there is no new story after the naming of Joakeim – it is one single sentence. But then again, there are countless sentences with such an indistinctive 'and' in the middle; it just is not enough for an alternative identification. It would be tempting to do something with it, of course – after all, the hypothetical Jeremiah passage mentions scrolls. However, even calling 7Q 3 the 'Joakeim scroll fragment' would be too much. After all, the word 'scroll' is part of the hypothetical, invisible text, and the name Joakeim is anything but certain. In other words, 7Q 3 is a solid example of unidentified text.

Far more peculiar than 7Q 3 is another fragment from this cave, and once more, it is a unique find – not just at Qumran, but anywhere in the world of classical papyrology: 7Q 19, a papyrus which does not exist anymore – but which is still there to be read. At some stage, probably when the roof of the cave had collapsed and slid down into the wadi underneath, one of the papyrus scrolls, which were no longer protected by the broken jar(s), got wet, and when the soil of the marl cave hardened, the papyrus had dissolved, but its fragmentary text survived as a reverse-image imprint on the now solid bit of earth.[16] For decades, no one took this fragment seriously. Even José O'Callaghan, who published the most thorough analysis of Cave 7 in 1974,[17] hardly even mentioned it. The reasons for this silence are difficult to understand. Reading the reversed fragment was and is no problem. There are two photographs in the first edition of 1962, one of which mirror-imaged the text, so it can be read 'the right way round'. When the author of this book first worked with the original many years ago, he took a colour slide and just turned it round. For study purposes, the 'stone' is almost as good as the original fragment would have been. And what is more, 7Q 19 preserves thirty-five letters (five of which are severely damaged) on six lines. As we noted above, this makes it easily the second largest fragment in Cave 7. More importantly, unlike 7Q 3, it has two lines with complete and fragmentary words which make sense.

Line 4 speaks 'of creation', τ]ης κτισεως. And line 5 preserves 'in the writings', εν ταις γραφα[ις. Even in line 3, remnants are left which include one and a half complete Greek words – not meaningful enough on their own, but useful as additional material in an attempt at identifying the fragment – the words απο το[υ, 'of the/in relation to the'. Line 3 as it has survived reads,]κται απο το[υ. And the]κται can be understood as the perfect passive of a verb. In spite of all these characteristics, the first editors were not very interested in this piece of reverse-image literature. 'The few words which one can get hold of make one think of a text of a theological nature,' is all they had to say.[18] But even the few words in lines 4 and 5 tell us what the writing was about: it discussed aspects of the creation in relation to 'the scriptures', a formula which at a place like this, a Qumran cave, can be expected to refer to holy scripture, the Bible. And this very expression also warns us that we should not expect to find the text in the Greek Old Testament itself, but rather in a writing about an Old Testament book – such as a commentary on Genesis or the *Torah*. In fact, this is exactly what research has established: a text as we have it on 7Q 19 cannot be traced in the Greek Bible, nor in any other known apocryphal text, nor in Greek literature as a whole. It is, like so many texts found in the Qumran caves, an unknown writing of an exegetical type, a commentary perhaps. Like similar partly recognizable Qumran writings, we may now give it a name, and call it 7Q 19 Creation. But can we find out more about its context? Who wrote about creation and the scriptures in a text which was thought important enough to be collected in a Qumran library cave?

A clue may be 'hidden' in the way the fragment speaks about something 'in the writings', εν ταις γραφαις. If we look at Jewish literature in Greek, written before the Qumran caves were left – in other words, before AD 68 – we discover a peculiarity: whenever biblical texts are referred to as 'scriptures', they are explicitly called 'holy', and the Greek attribute ιερος (*hieros*) is set before the plural word 'scriptures'.[19] It may well have been the customary thing to do; even Josephus writes like this, almost half a century later.[20] Thus, if we continue to assume that the 'writings' in line 5 of our fragment are biblical writings about aspects of creation, it seems very unlikely that the text can have been written by a Jewish author accustomed to the way Jewish-Greek texts used to refer to the Bible as 'holy scriptures'. Strikingly, though, there is one exception: first-century Jewish texts written by followers of the Messiah Jesus never use the attribute 'holy' when they refer to the Bible as 'writings/scriptures'. A good example which shows how difficult this usage can be is 2 Peter 3:16. Here, Peter speaks about some letters by Paul and links them to 'the other writings' τας λοιπας γραφας (*tas loipas graphas*). Those who prefer to think Peter was not Peter at all, but a pseudonymous author of this letter, who knew an edited collection of Paul's epistles which he already regarded as on a par with the 'holy scriptures' of the Old Testament, interpret 'the other writings' as though it said 'the other *holy* writings' which, obviously, it does not say. And whether it *means* 'holy scriptures' – without saying so – is far from certain. The only exception to this New Testament way of omitting 'holy', whether the object is holy scripture or not, comes from Paul himself: in Romans 1:2, he talks about God's promise through the prophets 'in the holy writings'. But the Greek 'holy' follows after 'scriptures'; it does not, as in other Jewish literature of the period, precede it: εν γραφαις αγιαις (*en graphais hagiais*).

Six chapters later (8:19), Paul's letter to the Romans discusses creation, much like 7Q 19: 'For the anxious longing of the creation expects the revealing of the sons of God,' (*hê gar apokaradokia tês ktiseôs*). Thus, we have found one Jewish (messianic) document, Paul's letter to the Romans, which predates, by some thirteen years, the end of the Qumran settlement, and refers to the creation with the same genitive clause as 7Q 19 and offers even one further avenue: if this was Paul's way of mentioning holy scriptures, placing the 'holy' after 'scriptures', then our fragment 7Q 19 would give us the space to reconstruct it in this manner; nothing prevents us from assuming that line 5 once read εν ταις γραφα[ις ἁγιαις. Now obviously, even if this is an accurate reconstruction, which we cannot know any more, fragment 7Q 19 is *not* from Paul's letter to the Romans. But then again, this type of reference to the scriptures cannot be found anywhere in extant Greek Jewish literature of the first century and before, with the exception of Romans, a letter which also happens to talk about the creation. Should we be allowed to follow the usual practice of Qumranologists in their attributions of unknown texts, using what circumstantial evidence we have at our disposal? If so, we would see in 7Q 19 a writing of a Jewish Pauline circle, a *pesher* or commentary on Romans perhaps. And indeed why not? Regardless of the nature of the whole cave – and we shall look into the disputed Christian fragments 7Q 4 and 7Q 5 in a moment – there was a sizeable Jewish community in Rome – up to 60,000 people[21] – and some of the addressees of Paul's letter 'to the Romans' were among them: Jewish Christians who still kept their own, separate house churches, according to the list of greetings at the end of the letter. It should not have been difficult for them to send a copy of the letter,[22] with their comments, to their brothers and sisters in Roman Palestine. And the contents of the jar in Cave 7 very probably came from Rome, as we saw in a previous chapter.

The great debate: Christian scrolls in Qumran?

Cave 7 was discovered in 1956. In 1962, the fragments were edited. In 1972, the Spanish papyrologist José O'Callaghan, a highly respected specialist in Greek papyri, editor of the journal *Studia Papyrologica* and professor of papyrology at the Biblicum in Rome, suggested that some of these fragments can be identified with texts from the New

Testament.[23] Twenty-eight years later, the debate is still going strong. Many arguments have been proffered for and against O'Callaghan's suggestions. In the first years of the controversy, the technical aspects appeared to be balanced. Concentrating on 7Q 4/1 Timothy 3:16 – 4:1, 3 and 7Q 5/Mark 6:52–53, O'Callaghan had explained his reasons, his reconstruction of damaged letters and his solutions to text-critical problems. All this had been done on the basis of the typology of 7Q 1 and 7Q 2, the two fragments which had been identified in 1962: scribal characteristics, average number of letters per line, and so forth. But while this side of the argument – to which we shall return – led to a stimulating, constructive dialogue among scholars, one line of reasoning against the identifications came from a completely different direction: O'Callaghan was told by many New Testament scholars that his identifications were impossible, anyway. Since the caves at Qumran were abandoned in AD 68, all scrolls found at the site must have been written earlier. And it is common knowledge – or so it was argued – that neither Mark, nor, above all, 1 Timothy, could have been written in time for copies of them to reach Qumran by AD 68. And what is more, it must be ruled out by definition that Christian texts, the writings of the New Testament, could have been collected by the Qumran Essenes. Both assumptions are wrong.

If there is one lesson we have learnt over the past years of Jewish and Jewish-Christian studies, it is the one which has been the groundwork of this book: the very first Christians, and the authors of the New Testament writings, were all Jews.[24] The missionary strategy of reaching out to the Gentiles, which was first practised by Philip (baptizing the Ethiopian minister of finance) and Peter (baptizing the Roman centurion Cornelius with his whole household – the first indirect but unequivocal reference to the baptism of children in New Testament times), and which was later developed by Barnabas and Paul, was initiated by Jews. And Paul in particular targeted the Gentiles where he knew they would be open for a messianic message:

his first non-Jewish addressees were the 'Godfearers' who attended the synagogues. These were the people who had not converted, but felt so close to the monotheistic God of the Jewish faith, the teaching of the *Torah* and the Prophets, and to the Jewish way of life, that they attended the weekly services at the synagogues, read the books in the synagogue libraries, met at the community centres and generally followed Jewish rites and customs. In every city Paul visited, he first went to the synagogue where Jews and God-fearing Gentiles would be found together. In other words, even the Gentile mission came from within Judaism. And Greek cultural influence, noticeable as it was, could not be regarded as an alien import. Since the times of Alexander the Great, hellenistic culture, and the Greek language, had permeated Jewish culture, in the diaspora but also 'at home', sometimes with ease, sometimes against resistance. Jews who spoke and wrote about the Jew Jesus in Greek were understood by practically all fellow Jews. And for those who wanted to reach the Jews who had not acquired fluent Hebrew – in Egypt, for example, but also in Jerusalem, where we read about the 'Hellenists' who had their own synagogues in the city[25] – the choice of Greek was unavoidable, anyway. To put it differently, the Greek of the first Christian texts was not a sign of a late, 'post-Jewish' stage, in the 70s and 80s of the first century. It was not a reaction to the increasing separation of Jews and Christians, which may have begun after Nero's Roman persecution from the summer of AD 64 to emperor's death in AD 68, or, in a parallel development, after the Jewish revolt which started in AD 66 and culminated in the destruction of Jerusalem and the Temple in AD 70. In other words, it cannot be explained by the practical demands of a period when the mission to the Gentiles had almost completely superseded inner-Jewish activities. On the contrary, it was a strategic necessity of the inner-Jewish mission itself, from its very earliest stages.

The Christians' use of language was inconspicuous in Jewish

circles, and their origins as Jews made them members of the same family of God, the house of Israel. There was, in those early decades, no Christianity as an established, organized religion, and there certainly was no 'church' as we know it. The Jews who recognized Jesus as the promised Messiah formed communities, in Jerusalem, in Caesarea, in Antioch, Rome, Athens and elsewhere, and they saw themselves as the one community based on the faith in the suffering and victorious Messiah, as Jesus had proclaimed it at Caesarea Philippi (Matthew 16:18). But the word which Jesus used in Matthew's Greek version, *ekklesia*, corresponds to the Aramaic *qahal*, a common term not least in the Dead Sea Scrolls: like the Greek word it just means 'community'. The messianic community of the first Christian generation must not be judged by the standards and structures of the established church two or three centuries later. Thus, groups of Jews who claimed that the Messiah had come, and that he was Jesus of Nazareth, did not separate themselves from Judaism merely by doing so. On the contrary, they would claim – as Paul and others put it – that the age-old Jewish messianic hope had reached the stage of its true fulfilment. Even the tendency to reach beyond the confines of Judaism and to target Gentiles was not truly un-Jewish; there had always been moments in Jewish history when 'proselytizing' was encouraged and seen as the will of God for the nations.[26]

This then is our scenario: there was a fast-growing movement of messianic Jews who had become convinced, by eyewitness experience, that Jesus, *Yeshua*, was the Messiah, suffering according to Isaiah 53, triumphant through suffering according to Psalm 22, victorious according to Isaiah 11. They wrote about him, told his story in scrolls which were to be known as gospels, explained and defended the consequences and practicalities in letters, soon had a first history of their community and even developed their own revealed, 'apocalyptic' view of the future. These Jews wrote for Jewish readers, occasionally for 'mixed' communities, never exclusively for 'Gentiles'. The Messiah had come, the messianic age had arrived. Could their fellow Jews ignore the message? They could not, and they did not. Many become followers of the Way (see Acts 2:41; 3:4; 6:7, etc.). Some remained sceptical but open-minded (see Acts 4:13–22; 5:34–40, etc.). Many refused point-blank and reacted violently (see Acts 7:54 – 8:1; 9:1–2; 12:1–3; 21:27–36, etc.). Whatever they did, they took on the challenge – all the more so as it came from within Judaism, not from outside. Between the first public proclamation of the Christian message at Shavuot/Pentecost in AD 30, and the 'closure' of Qumran in AD 68, some thirty-eight years or almost one and a half generations (in terms of adult life expectancy in those days) went by. It goes without saying that the Qumran Essenes heard about the new, personified messianic message during those decades. After all, they even had an outpost in Jerusalem, on the south-west hill which today is called Mount Zion, not far from the local community centre of the followers of Jesus. To put it bluntly, if there is any place where we must expect to find the first writings of these Jesus People, it is the study library of that other vibrant messianic and eschatological movement, the Essenes. They, probably more than anyone else beyond the immediate target groups, had a natural, keen interest in the writings of such a Jewish group. After all, they were rivals, opponents, perhaps even enemies. It is quite unlikely that any Essene would have read a letter of that former Pharisee called Paul, or Mark's Gospel, with the express desire to be converted to the new eschatology. But, as any good strategist knows, one has to study the thoughts and moves of one's potential adversary – now, not later. When the Qumran scholars who debated the origins of Cave 7, during a panel discussion at the Notre Dame Centre, Jerusalem, in January 1999, agreed that Qumran was a self-evident place for the first Jewish-Christian writings, they merely confirmed and substantiated the obvious – as they all realized.[27] The punchline, after all, can surprise only those who refuse to realize that these writings are Jewish. If the collection of Cave 7 came from a group which believed in the Nazarene Jew, Jesus, one could of course look at them from an established Christian position and claim them for a 'first New Testament'. But, above all, they add to the Jewish literature of the late Second Temple period. Like the writings of the Essenes, and the sources behind the Talmud, they represent the multifaceted, often polemical, highly charged climate of a period in political, sociological and religious turmoil. Much later, the New Testament became the basis for the new state religion of the Roman empire, and the Old Testament was interpreted from its vantage point. But before the separation of Jews and Jewish Christians – a development which was initiated by the killing of the leader of the Jewish-Christian community in Jerusalem, James, 'the brother of the Lord', in AD 62,[28] continued in the Neronian persecution from AD 64 to AD 68 in which Jews and Christians were kept apart by the Roman authorities for the first time, and ended in the destruction of the Temple in Jerusalem in AD 70, when the last place of common worship was taken away – before all this happened, the oldest Christian statements and writings were treated as messianic and eschatological literature within Judaism. And this is how we should understand them again today – certainly not with the aim to deny their importance for all humanity, or the role they acquired in the later history of the churches, but to regain the perspective of the first listeners and readers.

For the question of Judeo-Christian writings at Qumran, this means, quite simply, that we have to expect their existence in this library before AD 68, even if not a single shred should have survived.[29] The Qumranites could have ordered their copies from Jerusalem, or they could have preferred to avoid any semblance of over-eager contact with the Jerusalem evangelists by getting their first scrolls from the place where they had been written and published, and where the orthodox Jewish community included – as we saw in a previous chapter – at least a few Essenes: from Rome. It took about a fortnight, if not less, for a message to reach Rome from Qumran, by land to and from the harbours, and on a mediterranean trading ship from Yafo or Caesarea to Rome's harbour Ostia. Another fortnight for the return journey, and perhaps a day or two to pack the parcel, another week or so if the scrolls had to be copied 'to order'. Amazing as it sounds, and probably surpassing modern experiences with postal services between Israel and Italy, in less than a month after the dispatch of their order, the Qumran librarians would have received the delivery with the 'Christian' texts, and placed them in jars which they inscribed with the name of the place they had come from: 'Roma'.

Mark, Paul and the Great Debate

THE CASE OF 7Q 4 AND 7Q 5

Few Dead Sea Scrolls have provoked a controversy as heated and long-lasting as the one about fragments 7Q 4 and 7Q 5. In 1972, these tiny papyrus scraps were identified with 1 Timothy 3:16 – 4:1, 3 and Mark 6:52–53. Ever since, enthusiastic supporters among leading papyrologists and classical scholars, and equally vociferous opponents among other papyrologists and New Testament scholars have joined the fray. Both 'wings' have attracted others who use these identifications – or their purported rejection – in theological debates for and against the nature and origins of the gospels. After some twenty-eight years of an occasionally fascinating debate, where are we now? What do we really know about these fragments and their importance?

Timothy and a penchant for Enoch

There is a recent dialogue between Jewish and Christian Bible scholars about the Jewishness of the New Testament. The detailed investigations portrayed in the previous chapter are part of this new and intensifying dialogue. We are witnessing an encouraging and stimulating process. The public debate about the papyri from Cave 7 has not reached that stage yet, it seems; the layers of controversy and polemic about the actual fragments themselves have not been penetrated. The fragments should not be 'instrumentalized' by either side, neither by those who are convinced that these are fragments from Mark and Timothy, nor by those convinced that they may be anything, provided they are not from the 'New Testament'. Words and exact terminology count for much – and common ground can easily be found if one agrees there was no New Testament as we know it, and no Christian church, before AD 68 – and therefore, these fragments cannot, and should not, be defended or rejected as parts of the church's New Testament.

At that time, there were, as we have seen and shall see again, Jewish writings about a Jewish Messiah, written by Jews who believed that Jesus of Nazareth was the Son of God and Saviour prophesied of old. But to some, it is apparently still easier to use 7Q 4 and 7Q 5 as tools of anti-liberal apologetics or conversely as sledgehammers against superficial 'fundamentalists'. As the Cave 7 literature shows, both attitudes have been all too common. The jubilant reaction of those who thought Christian texts at Qumran, of necessity older than AD 68, would put an end to decades of destructive New Testament studies, was met by those who saw themselves at the receiving end and accused their opponents of being ignorant simpletons living in a world of fiction and fantasy. The so-called evangelical wing, however, soon lost interest in an exchange of below-the-belt diatribes. The case was stated, leading papyrologists had agreed, and above all, the apologetical sting had disappeared. Four years after O'Callaghan's identifications, John A.T. Robinson had shown that it was possible to argue for apostolic, pre-AD 70 dates for *all* New Testament writings without a single papyrus.[1] Here was (and is) an avenue to be pursued, a paradigm shift in its own right, with more circumstantial evidence than a mere two papyrus fragments to rely on. Papyri will always be important witnesses to the beginnings of textual history; they are the tangible pieces of evidence, but they must be understood as stones in a complex mosaic, not as the mosaic itself.

Amazingly, however, the old guard of the traditional school continued to attack the philologists and papyrologists who had written in favour of 7Q 4 as 1 Timothy and 7Q 5 as Mark. The high (or low) point was reached in 1995, when a French scholarly journal, the *Revue Biblique*, published a three-pronged attack by Émile Puech, Marie-Émile Boismard and Pierre Grelot, which culminated in the description of O'Callaghan's supporters, among them world-famous papyrologists such as Sergio Daris (Trieste), Herbert Hunger (Vienna), Heikki Koskenniemi (Turku) and Orsolina Montevecchi (Milan); Old Testament scholars such as Karl Jaroš (Vienna/Linz); classical scholars such as Ulrich Victor (Berlin); epistemologists such as Claude Tresmontant (Paris); and even eminent New Testament scholars with papyrological training such as Harald Riesenfeld (Uppsala) and Giuseppe Ghiberti (Turin), as 'journalists'.[2] Needless to say, such desperate means of unscholarly mud-slinging have failed to convince. It is, however, far from difficult to state and understand the basis for any attempt at identifying these fragments. All it takes is a willingness to look at the Greek text. Admittedly, the following few paragraphs may, therefore, test the patience of readers who are not keen to follow specialized arguments – but the results of the investigation will be summed up in less technical language.

The first edition of 1962 had treated fragment 7Q 4 as two separate pieces written by the same scribe – papyrus, ink, style of handwriting (formation of letters, etc.) are identical. The two pieces had been placed on the plate in such a way that the larger one came first. And there is a rare source of joy for papyrologists who have to identify small fragments: the larger piece is obviously the top right-hand corner of the leaf or column, with a horizontal margin of 4 cm on top, and a vertical margin of 2.2 cm to the right. In other words, we know how the text ended in the first five surviving lines of the 'page'. It is this fact which has led scholars to observe that the identification of 7Q 4 with 1 Timothy 3:16 – 4:1, 3 is even more certain than that of

the twenty-one letters, five of them incomplete or inferred rather than visible, on merely five lines, which were thought to be entirely sufficient for the identification of 7Q 2 with Baruch 6:43–44, or the fourteen letters on one line sufficient to identify and reconstruct the hexameter of Virgil's *Aeneid* 4:9 on the Latin papyrus fragment 721a discovered on the fortress of Masada.³ When José O'Callaghan analysed 7Q 4, his aim was not to find a New Testament text. All fragments in Cave 7 were part of his project of an annotated list of extant Greek Bible manuscripts not merely at Qumran; since 7Q 1 and 7Q 2 had already been identified as such texts, he hoped to find more by studying the originals and specially provided infrared photographs. And as the infrared photo, double-checked against the original, clearly shows, the first surviving letter in line 5 is not a *gamma* followed by an *iota*, but one single letter, an *eta*, η.⁴ In capital letters, as they were always used in ancient literary papyri, the difference is that between a ΓΙ (*gamma* + *iota*) and an H (*eta*). This H, with its beautifully straight horizontal bar in the middle, is so unmistakable on the infrared photo that all attempts to identify the fragment must incorporate it instead of the *gamma* + *iota* suggested by the first edition. O'Callaghan did not find a single text in the whole Greek Bible, nor in the Apocrypha or Pseudepigrapha, which fits the extant letters. The breakthrough came when he realized that Greek-Jewish literature of the time before the end of Qumran in AD 68 could include writings of the New Testament-to-be. Suddenly, the two big fragments 7Q 4 and 7Q 5 were identifiable as known texts of Greek literature. It was not a 'cure-all', of course. As we saw above, other fragments such as the equally substantial 7Q 3 and 7Q 19 remained 'unknown', although they have since been analysed and described beyond the limited scope of the first edition. But in any case, the inclusion of the Greek New Testament, against the vast majority of New Testament scholarship which excluded Christian texts before AD 68 (with the exception of the 'authentic' letters of Paul), was the decision of a papyrologist who was not convinced that the changing fashions of lower biblical criticism should get in the way of the papyri themselves. And when he began to work on the 7Q papyri, he did not know that he was about to identify a gospel and a controversial pastoral epistle like 1 Timothy. Had it been, say, 1 Corinthians and Romans instead, the international reaction would have been much less agitated.

7Q 4 was identified with 1 Timothy 3:16 – 4:1, 3, and we give the text in a Greek transcription which does not imitate the uninterrupted sequence of capital letters on the papyrus:

Prose	*Letters per line*
[... σιν, επιστευθη εν κοσμω, ανελημφθ]η	28
[εν δοξη. Το δε πνευμα ρη]των	21/28 (*gap of up to 7 letters' length*)
[λεγ(ε)ι. υστεροις καιροις αποστησ]ονται	31 (*or 32, if the reading was* λεγει)
[τινες της πιστεως προσεχοντες]πνευ–	30
[μασιν πλανης και διδασκαλιαις δ]ημο–	31
[νιων, εν υποκρισει ψευδολογ– ων, κε–]	27
[καυστηριασμενων την ιδιαν συνει–]	28
[δησιν, κωλυο]ντ[ων γαμειν, απεχεσται]	29
[βρωματων α]ο θε[ος εκτισεν εις μετα–]	28

*[pag]ans, believed in throughout the world, raised to glory. The
Spirit warns us expressly: in times to come, some will forsake the
faith by paying attention to deceitful spirits and the teaching of
demons, through the hypocrisy of liars whose consciences have
been branded with a hot iron. They forbid marriage and demand
abstinence from food which God created to be received...*

The regularity of the number of letters per line, between twenty-
seven and thirty-one, is an important yardstick for the 'workability' of
any identification; in the case of 7Q 4, it helps to understand the
length of the gap ('spatium'),[5] after 3:16, and to bridge the missing bit
between the end of line 5 and the tiny fragment 7Q 4_2, where the
specks of ink in the first line can now be read as *nu + tau*, ντ – printed,
in the textual edition, with dots underneath to explain that they are
practically illegible, but have been reconstructed from the context. For
the identification as a whole, it is equally important that O'Callaghan
managed to find a text which includes both fragments, 7Q 4_1 and 7Q 4_2,
with merely two lines of lost text between them.

Only one proper variant over against the edited standard Greek of
1 Timothy was noted by O'Callaghan: in line 3, the standard Greek text
is λεγει οτι εν υστεροις, whereas O'Callaghan reconstructs λεγει.
υστεροις, 'dropping' the two middle words οτι εν (*hoti en*) and
supposing a so-called 'high point', ·, after the word λεγει. Such a high
point is used to mark the beginning of a quotation or direct speech, a
kind of colon, although it is not absolutely necessary to insert it. This is
a variant on the same level as those encountered in 7Q 1 and 7Q 2. In
fact, it is less remarkable, since it is no scribal error, nor does it change
the structure or the meaning of the sentence(s). Apart from this
variant, there are spelling differences: in line 2, we read ρη]των instead
of ρη]τως. It is a normal shift from final *sigma* to final *nu* in many
papyri, and in the New Testament in general. This is the straightforward
explanation.[6] In fact, any papyrologist who intends to make sense of an

unidentified manuscript has to take into account – and to know about – a whole range of spelling variations, including such an ordinary shift from 'αι' (*alpha + iota*) to 'η' (*eta*) as we find it in 7Q 4. A papyrus which happens to conform to the classical rules and the typology of modern editions is the rare exception, not the rule. In line 5, we have δ]ημο– instead of δαιμο–.[7] But this is a normal 'itacism', caused by the identical pronunciation of 'η' and 'αι'. The gap in line 2 is equally unremarkable; it is a common occurrence in Greek papyri, separating 'paragraphs', chapters, etc. – which is of course the case if 7Q 4 is 1 Timothy 3:16 – 4:1, 3. Immediately before the beginning of a new paragraph in 4:1, such a gap is eminently sensible in an ancient Greek manuscript which otherwise does not separate words or sentences, let alone 'chapters' (it is of course only accidental that this happens to coincide with our modern chapter division which did not exist in those days).

As we saw in Chapter VI, the variants in 7Q 2 over against the text of Exodus 6:43–44 cannot be explained on the basis of any known text of these two verses; they constitute a new version. Even so, no papyrologist has so far rejected the identification or suggested a different text from a biblical or non-biblical writing. Conversely, the one variant of 7Q 4 over against the 'standard' text of 1 Timothy 3:16 – 4:1, 3 can be explained without stretching the limits of documented and admissible nuances: οτι εν (*hoti en*), which means 'that in', is surplus to requirements. 'The Spirit expressly says: During the time to come, some will forsake the faith...' Although we have, so far, no further manuscript of 1 Timothy which omits these words, this variant is far less noteworthy than all those which result in contorted new readings as they are presupposed by the first editors' identification of 7Q 2 with Baruch 6:43–44, the Letter of Jeremiah. In the first fragment from Cave 7, 7Q 1 (Exodus 28:4–7), one such omission was noted by the first editors: in verse 4, εις is missing before ιερατευειν. In 7Q 2, four words are missing between a word of which only the first two letters have survived and another word which is not even on the papyrus, but has been reconstructed from the supposed length of the line as it once was.[8]

If we judge all papyri from Cave 7 by the same yardstick, the apparent omission of the words οτι εν (*hoti en*), 'that in', from 7Q 4/ 1 Timothy 3:16 – 4:1, 3, and of the three words *epi tên gên* ('on[to]/in[to] the land') from 7Q 5/Mark 6:52–53, to which we shall return later, are as newsworthy as the information that a papyrus consists of papyrus. And, if we consider the evidence outside Qumran, we find commonly accepted New Testament papyri which offer similar peculiarities. For example, one of the oldest papyri of the book of Acts, the late second-century P91 with Acts 2:30–37 and 2:46 – 3:2, drops the decisive words 'of the Christ', του Χριστου, in 2:31. It is the only manuscript of Acts to do so, and yet no one bats an eyelid.[9] To put it in a nutshell, if 7Q 1, 7Q 2 and P91 can be identified with their omissions, alterations and variants, so can 7Q 4 and 7Q 5 which have far fewer of them. It is a pity that such self-evident facts have to be stated at all, but particularly in the debate about 7Q 5, the Markan fragment, too much printer's ink has been wasted about the importance of missing words. It helps to remember that a text has to be understood in its context. And the context of the textual characteristics of 7Q 4 and 7Q 5 is, first and foremost, the state of the matter in 7Q 1 and 7Q 2, the first two fragments for which accepted identifications had been suggested back in 1962. If papyri from other discoveries strengthen this analysis, so much the better. Thus, 7Q 4 can be regarded as safely identified – unless, that is, someone suggests a different text which operates with the very same letters. Sixteen years after O'Callaghan's thesis that 7Q 4 is 1 Timothy 3:16 – 4:1, 3, a German scholar, G.-Wilhelm Nebe, left the depth of non-constructive polemics against the identification and proposed a different biblical writing: 7Q 4 is, or so he wrote, Enoch 103:3f.[10] This was soon refuted as papyrologically and textually impossible,[11] but it somehow left a mark on the fantasy of other scholars, and a few years ago, two of them returned to Enoch: Ernest A. Muro, Jr, suggested Enoch 103:3–4, 7–8;[12] and Émile Puech thought of

Enoch 103:3–4; 105:1.[13] In other words, all three of them, Nebe, Muro and Puech, favoured more or less the same passage, Enoch 103:3f. At long last, a fair and constructive comparison was possible.

For those who are certain, like these three authors, that 1 Timothy could not have been written before the closure of Qumran in AD 68 anyway, Enoch is irresistibly attractive. It is a writing which was – as we saw in a previous chapter – very popular among first-century Jews, although it did not belong to the 'canon', and the Qumran discoveries provided the first evidence for its Hebrew/Aramaic text. Unfortunately, though, the very fact that the Cave 7 fragments are *Greek*, not Aramaic or Hebrew, militates against the identification. There is no shred of evidence for the existence of a *Greek* Enoch in the first century. Papyrologically, the earliest trace is the Chester Beatty Papyrus of the fourth century AD. If Enoch is supposed to be an improvement on 1 Timothy because the pastoral epistles are deemed to be later than the Qumran dates, the effort has already failed: chronologically, the case for a Greek Enoch is considerably weaker than that for 1 Timothy.[14] But what about the surviving letters and their reconstruction?

Nebe, who disregarded the smaller fragment 7Q 4$_2$, based his study on C. Bonner's reconstructed edition of Enoch in the Chester Beatty Papyrus[15] and suggested the following reading:

[... και εγγεγραπται τ]η

[ς ψυχαις των αποθανον]των

ευσεβων και χαρησο]νται

[και ου μη απολωνται τα]πνευ

[ματα αυτων ουδε το μν]ημο

[συνον απο προσωπου του με]

[γαλου...   ]

Strikingly, Nebe accepts O'Callaghan's improved decipherment of the papyrus in line 5: no longer]γιμο, as in the first edition, but]ημο; the H has replaced the Γ. Thus, it looks as though there are now two suggested identifications for 7Q 4 which are of equal value, and one would have to admit that the fragment is too small to permit certainty. But this is not the case. Nebe's attempt fails because he has to operate with a variant which – unlike those investigated by O'Callaghan – does not exist in Greek papyri: a separation of the word της (*tês*) in lines 1–2, after the *eta*, η. A monosyllable like *tês*, in Nebe's reconstruction, could – theoretically – be separated on inscriptions where almost anything is possible, but not in literary papyri. There is no need, anyway, to separate such a word before the final letter; the average number of letters per line would have left room for one more. But the problem is that Nebe's identification *depends* on this useless and meaningless procedure. In the same context, he assumes a stupid or at least inconsistent scribe who forgets his own way of doing things from one word to the next. As Nebe realizes, της (*tês*) should really be ταις (*tais*), since it is the article which belongs to *psychais* in the next line. Fair enough – a vowel change from αι (*ai*) to η (*ê*) was presupposed by O'Callaghan in his own identification. But O'Callaghan's change from '*daimonion*' to '*dêmonion*' is quite common in Greek papyri, wheras Nebe's suggested change of the dative plural article, from '*tais*' to '*tês*', is extremely unusual in literary papyri. Even so, it may be accepted, for the sake of the argument; but in this case, the scribe would have written a 'wrong' *tês* followed immediately by a 'correct' *psych*ais – surely too much of a good thing. No such inconsistencies are demanded by the identification of 7Q 4 with 1 Timothy 3:16 – 4:1, 3.

In his footnote 12, Nebe turns to the tiny scrap 7Q 4_2 after all. Only Enoch 98:11 is conceivable, he says, if 7Q 4 is from this writing. And it is obvious from this admission that O'Callaghan's proposal is far superior: for him, 7Q 4_2 belongs to the same passage, following on from 7Q 4_1 after a gap of just two lines. But in his note 26, Nebe goes on to suppose that another fragment from Cave 7 could also belong to Enoch – 7Q 8 as Enoch 103:7f.[16] Apart from the fact that it cannot be substantiated in this case, this idea of seeing other tiny 7Q fragments as parts of one and the same former scroll is certainly thought-provoking. It was taken up by Muro and Puech. Did they fare better? Muro suggested that 7Q 4 (but only piece 1), 7Q 8 and 7Q 12 originally belonged to one and the same scroll, since they were written by the same scribe on the same type of papyrus, and he further suggested a 'grid' into which he could place all three fragments. It is immediately obvious, before going into any details, why this must fail: in order to achieve his reconstruction, he has to discard the one tiny piece which truly does belong to the same scribe and papyrus – 7Q 4_2. Furthermore, the nature of a papyrus and the characteristics of a scribal hand cannot be ascertained by looking at photographs; one has to work with the originals. O'Callaghan and the author of this book did so, the latter by further analysing these originals under a confocal laser scanning microscope. And this microscopal analysis confirms what even the photo produced with Muro's article makes visible: 7Q 12 cannot be placed underneath 7Q 4 – as he requires for his theory. The fibres do not match.

Much more important, however, and the decisive argument against Muro's attempt, is an inescapable observation: Of the three (!) letters visible in 7Q 12, *omicron*, o, *upsilon*, υ, and *epsilon*, ε, only the *omicron*, which is not always a particularly characteristic letter, looks somewhat similar to the *omicron* on 7Q 4_1 and on 7Q 8. The *epsilon* is pretty similar on 7Q 4_1 and 7Q 12, with its top curvature sharply bent downwards, but it is worlds apart from the *epsilon* on 7Q 8, which is simple with straight upper and lower ends, and where the median stroke does not touch the left-hand curvature, which it does on 7Q 4_1 (the left-hand part of this letter is missing on 7Q 12). Thus, it is an inescapable conclusion that 7Q 4_1, 7Q 8 and 7Q 12 cannot all belong to the same papyrus – even less so as Muro assumes that 7Q 12 is not a distant, separate piece of the scroll, which, theoretically, could have been written by a different scribe continuing the same 'Enoch' scroll, but a column immediately to the right of the 7Q 4_1 column. But let us look at the link between 7Q 4_1 and 7Q 12 from a different angle.

Since 7Q 12 must be placed immediately underneath 7Q 4_1 in his reconstruction, we might be positively impressed by the similarity of the *epsilon* here and in 7Q 4_1 (apart from the above-mentioned technical fact the fibres do not match). But even this is only a first impression. For, at second sight, and under the microscope, it looks as though the damaged *epsilon* on 7Q 12 may not be an *epsilon* at all, but a *theta*, θ. The top curvature bends down so far it almost touches the remaining part of the lower curvature bent upwards. After all, a Greek capital *epsilon* is – simply put – nothing but a *theta* with the right-hand half circle 'missing'. In other words, it is an open question – *epsilon* or *theta*? The certain identity of the two letters on these two fragments has become questionable, and therefore Muro's reading of 7Q 12 has disappeared as well. He needs (1) Enoch 103:4, and this passage depends on an *epsilon* in line 2. With a *theta* instead, 7Q 12 – consisting of only three letters, after all – cannot be Enoch 103:4 any more.

However, even if we accept the *epsilon*, which in all fairness we may, it is visibly certain that 7Q 4_1 and 7Q 12 did not come from the same scribe, for another reason: the third letter on the 7Q 12 scrap is an *upsilon*. There is also such a letter on 7Q 4_1. But while the 7Q 4_1 *upsilon* is straight, unembellished, with just a hint at a bottom-left serif, the 7Q 12 *upsilon* is thick, with a horizontal bar linked to the vertical stroke, and two serifs at the top right and top left of the letter. They are not the *upsilons* of the same scribe. And this is the end of the story. Having pursued every avenue of palaeographical analysis, we realize that 7Q 4_1, 7Q 8 and 7Q 12 do not belong together and they therefore do not constitute parts of an Enoch scroll. This indictment is further corroborated by our previous observation that the one fragment which clearly does belong to 7Q 4_1,[17] the three-letter piece 7Q 4_2, had to be 'deleted' from the calculation by Muro, whereas it makes perfect sense in O'Callaghan's reconstruction of 1 Timothy. One question remains: does Émile Puech's attempt manage to prove the case for Enoch?

Disappointingly, however, he does not improve on the position taken by Nebe and Muro. Repeating their erroneous reconstructions and quoting from his own earlier essay of 1996,[18] he spends valuable space trying to show why 7Q 8 cannot be James 1:23–24 – an identification which no one has ever *seriously* suggested.[19] He then repeats the arguments of Muro in favour of three pieces of Enoch, adding four non-existent letters invented in a 'line' above the first real line of 7Q 4_1, two speculative letters underneath the second line of 7Q 12 (to the credit of Muro, it must be said that he resisted the temptation of seeing such letters where the context of the piece itself does not suggest or demand them on 7Q 12) and another equally non-existent one above the first visible line of 7Q 8; and he provides a drawing to show the fragments next to each other. This drawing, in Puech's own hand, cleverly glosses over the evident differences between individual letters which we analysed above. To the gullible reader, it looks convincing enough, but as we already know, it is not. The problem here is a general problem of the debate about Cave 7: those who are convinced that there must not be and cannot have been 'Christian' texts at Qumran stoop to a polemical approach which includes a palpable misleading of non-specialist readers. One wonders why this should be necessary. The motives are apparently not strictly papyrological. But at the present state of the Jewish-Christian debate about the nature of the first Christian writings as inner-Jewish, messianic and eschatological literature, no harm is done to anyone's faith, nor to the historical context as such, if 7Q 4 is finally accepted as 1 Timothy and 7Q 5 as Mark.

Puech does attempt something new at the end of his paper: he takes yet another tiny scrap, 7Q 14, consisting of two half-letters which may be *omega* and *nu*, and a complete *epsilon* underneath them, to complete Enoch 103:3–4. Unrelated to the 'reconstructed' context of Enoch 103:3–4, 7–8, he finally proceeds to interpret two further minute scraps, 7Q 11, with four letters on two lines, and 7Q 13, with three letters on one line, as bits and pieces elsewhere in Enoch (100:12 and 103:15 respectively). Like Muro, he ignores fragment 7Q 4_2, the only piece which everyone has agreed since 1962 does belong to the same scribal hand and to the same type of papyrus, and which fits beautifully to 7Q 4_1 in O'Callaghan's reconstruction. As he should know, and as O'Callaghan did know when he looked at the minute pieces of 7Q 11 to 7Q 14 for which he did not offer any tentative identifications, the context may prove to be decisive. It is therefore highly suspicious when the proponents of Enoch fail to place the one fragment which, as far as anyone can see, does belong to the bigger piece of 7Q 4_1. Conversely, we can easily play Puech's game and 'demonstrate' that there are three further fragments of 1 Timothy in Cave 7.

Find a text of Greek literature, including the New Testament, where the sequence *nu, tau, omicron* (or perhaps *omega*) on 7Q 13 occurs – just for the fun of it, what about 1 Timothy 3:15 ζωντος (*zontos*)? Or, with *omega*, 1 Timothy 4:10 παντων (*pantôn*)? Shall we claim we have found additional proof for the existence of 1 Timothy in Cave 7, because 7Q 13 is 1 Timothy 3:15? The one speck of ink left in the line underneath, conjectured by Puech as υ and ν, not because these are the undoubtedly visible letters, but because they fit his Enoch theory, could equally well be reconstructed as the α and ι of the και – the first word of 1 Timothy 3:16, fitting perfectly underneath *zontos* of 3:15, within the 7Q 4/1 Timothy length of lines. Or take 7Q 14, with the letters *omega* and *nu*, and underneath them, *epsilon*. Rather than Enoch 103:4, should it be 1 Timothy 3:7, των...εμπεση (*tôn...empesê*)? Or 7Q 12, with *omicron* and *upsilon*, and, according to Puech, with an *epsilon* underneath (or perhaps rather a *theta*)? Why should it be a part of Enoch 103? Why not, for example, 1 Timothy 3:1–2 – εργου...ανεπιλημπτον (*ergou...anepilêmpton*)? Finally, 7Q 11: Puech reads four letters on two lines, two each at the end of their respective lines, *omega* + *iota* (as 'iota adscript'), and *sigma* + *iota*. The penultimate letter in the second line can hardly be a *sigma*, however: it is too small and too low for it. It does look like the surviving bottom half of an *epsilon*, though – where the lower half has exactly the same curvature as a *sigma*. What Puech took for the top curvature of his *sigma* is, in reality, the pretty straight median of an *epsilon*. And for this combination of four end-letters, we suggest a fitting passage: 1 Timothy 2:15 – 3:1, αγιασμωι...Ει (*agiasmôi...Ei*). All four passages fit the number of letters per line based on 7Q 4 for 1 Timothy perfectly. And thus, employing Puech's own procedure, we could easily 'prove' that there are at least six fragments of 1 Timothy in Cave 7: 7Q 4_1 and 7Q 4_2 anyway, but now 7Q 11, 7Q 12, 7Q 13 and 7Q 14 as well.

And so we could go on. But the purpose and effect of this counter-exercise should be clear: it is neither useful nor convincing to operate with the tiniest of fragments. Puech, unfortunately, gives the impression that he has succeeded in placing no fewer than seven fragments from Cave 7 in the (Greek) book of Enoch. The sober fact, without a shadow of the smallest doubt left, simply is that neither he nor Nebe and Muro has identified a single one of them as Enochic. We are back at the beginning: O'Callaghan's identification of 7Q 4 as 1 Timothy 3:16 – 4:1, 3, with both pieces of the fragment (and – hypothetically, applying Puech's own method! – with 7Q 11, 7Q 12, 7Q 13 and 7Q 14 now added), remains the best option available. There is no text in Greek literature as we have it which conforms to the actual letters on these fragments better than 1 Timothy, within the commonly known and accepted framework of Greek papyrology and palaeography. And again: why should this be a problem? Why should a letter attributed to the Pharisee Paul, a Jewish writer who played a major and public role in the inner-Jewish debate about the true Messiah – why should such a letter not have been collected in a Qumran cave? Is it because current scholarship has decreed, by a sizeable majority, that the letter was not written by Paul, and not before AD 68? We asked this question before, and we have to ask it again, at the end of this analysis. Should the changing results of Pauline studies and the mainstream dating of the pastoral epistles predetermine what a papyrus is allowed to contain? If one accepts that 7Q 4 truly is a fragment of 1 Timothy, this would indeed mean that the letter was written in AD 68 at the very latest.[20] No one, least of all a community of open-minded New Testament scholars, has to be afraid of such a conclusion.

A Jewish account of a Jewish hero in a Jewish library?

The controversy about 7Q 4 has been a mild summer breeze compared with the often embittered, unrestrained polemics fielded against the identification of 7Q 5 with Mark 6:52–53. There must not be a gospel fragment at Qumran – for a long time, this was a foregone conclusion. And although Jewish and Christian scholars alike have ceased to envisage a fixed, post-Jewish New Testament canon with four established gospels when they discuss the origin and existence of Judeo-Christian texts about Jesus (as we saw at the beginning of this chapter), there are still those who prefer to fight from the old, abandoned trenches: 'The identification with Mark 6:52–53 is based, as one knows, on... impossibilities of the history of the composition of the gospel books', Émile Puech wrote in 1997.[21] In recent years, some specialists in Greek papyrology have gone to the other end of the spectrum. Orsolina Montevecchi, author of the standard handbook on papyrology,[22] stated that 7Q 5 must be given a 'P' number in the semi-official Gregory–Aland list of New Testament papyri,[23] and the doyen of papyrus reconstructions and papyrological philology, Heikki Koskenniemi, compared the importance of the, to him, watertight identification of 7Q 5 as Mark 6:52–53 with the importance of the decipherment of 'Linear B'.[24] A Jewish scholar, Ory Mazar, son of the archaeologist Benjamin Mazar who had helped to rescue the first Dead Sea Scrolls, studied the fragments in Jerusalem and recently expressed an equally positive assessment of 7Q 5/Mark 6:52–53.[25]

Conversely, the Dead Sea Scroll scholar Geza Vermes, like Émile Puech an expert in Hebrew and Aramaic rather than Greek palaeography, simply wrote in 1999, 'the claim that some tiny fragments from Cave 7 represent the New Testament is unsound'[26] – as if anyone today, in 2000, after years of constant development in Judeo-Christian studies, would make that claim. It cannot be stated strongly enough and often enough that there was no New Testament to be represented when Jews whom we know as Mark and Paul wrote their texts, and that no Essene, nor any Pharisee for that matter, would have read these Jewish messianic writings as documents of a new canonical collection, let alone of a new faith or religion. These writings are highly significant for New Testament studies, since they can be recognized as the groundwork of the first Christian library, the later New Testament. But prior to AD 70, they are not yet New Testament writings, nor do they represent the New Testament.[27] Vermes displays the characteristic double standards when he generously admits, later in the same book, 'tiny scraps, containing a letter or two, may belong to' the book of Esther otherwise undocumented at Qumran.[28] One could not wish for greater clarity: comparably large fragments such as 7Q 4 and 7Q 5 with twenty or more letters are merely 'some tiny fragments' used for an unsound claim, but if Esther is concerned, far from the Judeo-Christian literature which Vermes does not want to see at Qumran, then of course even scraps of 'a letter or two' could turn out to be identifiable. Geza Vermes is undoubtedly one of the great Qumran scholars of the first generation, a brilliant and stimulatingly controversial mind. It is a pity he cannot disentangle himself from the bias with which Cave 7 has been treated in some quarters. But then again, the controversies about Cave 7 may look particularly heated to those who study the *Christian* aspects of the Qumran heritage – in Dead Sea Scroll studies as a whole, they only confirm the old adage that two Qumran scholars have at least three different opinions.

We shall resist the temptation to unfold twenty-eight years of 7Q 5 debates. For the period until 1998, the state of the matter is summarized in books and articles which are easily available.[29] The paper published in 1998 by Joan Vernet is particularly remarkable: Professor Vernet, who teaches at the International Theological Institute 'Cremisan' near Bethlehem, used his access to the archives at the John-Rockefeller-Museum in Jerusalem, where the 7Q 5 fragments are kept, to study the originals, and the literature about them, with his students. Diploma dissertations were written, all of them corroborating the Markan identification, and finally Vernet himself published his own results. They can permit, he wrote, 'a positive approach with respect to the identification of 7Q 5 with the Gospel of Mark.'[30] We could rest our case with this verdict, but even so, it helps to know what exactly is at stake in those five lines with their twenty-one letters, and why the Markan identification has been controversial at all – not just because of its consequences for the dating of Mark's Gospel and early Jewish Christianity at Qumran, but also because of doubts about the correct understanding of the extant letters on the papyrus on palaeographical grounds, and because of other tentative identifications. This last aspect is the least problematic one: even Émile Puech, perhaps the most emphatic opponent of anything looking Christian at Qumran, admitted that not a single attempt at identifying 7Q 5 with a text other than Mark 6:52–53 has succeeded.[31] This then is the papyrus as it was first published in 1962:

].[

]. τω α.[

]η και τω[

εγε]ννησ[εν

]θησσ[

It was a remarkable piece of guesswork. The editors noted one letter in the first line and a first and last letter in the second line which they could not reconstruct even tentatively; they placed dots under eight further letters to mark the provisional nature of their readings;[32] but even so, they felt confident enough to complete a whole word in line 4, of which – according to their own decipherment – only the two middle letters, *nu* and *eta*, νη, were certain: εγε]ννησ[εν, 'were born'. And on the strength of this, they suggested that 7Q 5 might be regarded as a kind of genealogy.[33]

The technical nature of any reconstruction of such a damaged papyrus may not look very attractive, but we have to do it. More often than not, the critique levelled against Mark 6:52–53 was based on the smallest of details. The first editors of 7Q 5 worked with numerous approximations. For the one dot in line 1, a footnote indicates that it could be an *epsilon, theta, omicron* or *sigma*. This is a useful observation, as it lists all letters which in Greek capitals have a bottom curvature bent upwards – and of such a curvature, a remnant is indeed left. This means, in other words, that any successful identification of 7Q 5 has to have one of these letters at exactly this place. If, for example, someone were to suggest a text which necessitates an *alpha* or an *omega* at this spot, it could be ruled out straightaway. Surprisingly, the editors decided to read the letter after the clear *omega*, ω, in line 2 as

171

a so-called *iota adscript*, that is an ι linked to the preceding letter and therefore printed, in the edition, not separately, but as a tiny *iota* underneath the *omega*.

This was surprising for a simple reason: the letter does not look like the indubitable *iota* of the και in the following line, with its straight horizontal serif to the top left. Given a certain scope for varying the same letters on the same papyrus – as this scribe did with his N and his H (the Greek capitals for *nu*, ν, and *eta*, η)– such a vertical stroke could perhaps tentatively be interpreted as an I (the Greek capital for *iota*, ι). But reading it as an *iota adscript* goes too far; the editors should at the very least have marked their suggestion with the dot of uncertainty underneath, which they failed to do. Identifying the next letter in line 2 as an *alpha*, albeit with such a dot underneath, was inventive guesswork: there is no *alpha* anywhere in Greek papyri which looks even remotely like the traces left on the papyrus. A further surprise came at the end of line 3, where the last letter, after the *tau*, was read as an *omega*, ω, and in a footnote alternatively as an *omicron*, ο. Both letters need a curvature. However, the one line which has remained of the letter is straight. It is slightly inclined towards the right, but, within this inclination, it is a perfectly straight line, as the original, the UV photograph and the laser scanning demonstrate without a shadow of doubt. The only excuse, so to speak, for those who saw an *omega* or *omicron* in this letter, is the erroneous impression of a minute 'bent' caused by a tiny, missing trace of ink which has flaked off just underneath the long horizontal top bar of the *tau*.

Why did the editors think of a genealogical word in line 4? *Nu, nu, eta, sigma,*]ννησ[, is a comparatively rare combination of letters in Greek. Their guess, εγε]ννησ[εν, is one of the few possibilities. And writings about genealogies were common in Jewish literature, including Qumran – so much so, in fact, that the Jewish author Paul of Tarsus warned his readers, 'do not pay any attention to the myths and the never-ending genealogies, which only cause quarrels instead of serving the saving plan of God in faith' (1 Timothy 1:4). The genealogical idea, however, attractive as it looks, did not help the first editors to identify the text with any known writing of Greek literature. Thousands of Dead Sea Scroll fragments were unedited in the 1960s; it is quite understandable that no one felt inspired to look at these Greek papyri again: there were other, more important things to do. And even José O'Callaghan may not have taken them seriously, had it not been for his work, mentioned above, on an annotated list of Greek Old Testament papyri – of which, after all, two had already been identified in Cave 7: 7Q 1 and 7Q 2. He soon confirmed the negative result of the first edition – 7Q 5 could not be identified with any text of the Septuagint. But as with 7Q 4, he did not feel constrained by lower criticism and searched that other part of the Greek Bible, the one we have come to know as the New Testament. Again, the result was negative – on the basis of the reconstructed letters published by the first editors. But perhaps]ννησ[was not εγε]ννησ[εν after all? And if not, what else could it be?

Once that door was opened, fresh light was shed on the fragment. There is a Greek word with the]ννησ[(*]nnês[*) combination: Gennesaret, or, in the Greek spelling, Γε]ννησ[αρετ (*Ge]nnês[aret*). It is not frequent, and, as O'Callaghan realized when he double-checked the Greek Old Testament, the Septuagint has different names and spellings for that lake, none of which is *Gennêsaret*. However, this is precisely how it occurs in Mark's Gospel. And not only that: the sentence where it is written in this orthography, Mark 6:53, begins with a καί, 'and'. As anyone can see, and as the first editors acknowledged themselves, the one complete word on 7Q 5 is such a καί, and it occurs visibly at the beginning of a sentence. Before it, there is a gap of several letters' width, the so-called 'spatium' or 'paragraphus' marking the beginning of a new 'paragraph', chapter or story, which we already encountered in 7Q 4.

Strikingly, this is exactly what happens in Mark 6:53. After the feeding of the 5,000 and Jesus stilling the storm (6:32–44, 45–52), the boat reaches Gennesaret, where a new sequence of events begins.

What about the other letters on 7Q 5? Starting with the identification so far, and operating with a regular number of letters per line, the following reading can be established:

Prose	Letters per line
[συνηκαν]επ[ι τοις αρτοις	20
[αλλ'ην α]υτων η[καρδια πεπωρω–]	23
[μεν]η και τι[απερασαντες]	20 (plus 'spatium')
[ηλθον εις Γε]ννησ[αρετ και]	21
[προσωρμισ]θησα[ν και εξελ–]	21

> ... *understood about the loaves; their hearts were hardened.*
> *And when they had crossed over, they landed at Gennesaret*
> *and anchored there. And when they got...*

Palaeographically, this reading is unspectacular. In line 1, the *epsilon*, necessitated by the word επι, of Mark 6:52, was always one of the options. In fact, a renewed microscopal analysis has shown that next to the now visible horizontal median bar of the *epsilon* (which excludes the previously possible alternatives *sigma* and *omicron*), a vertical stroke is visible which can now be understood as part of the *pi*, π, of the word επι. In line 2, the vertical stroke which the first editors misread as an *iota*, and the following remnants which they felt inclined to visualize as an *alpha*, are now reconstructed as one letter, a *nu*, ν, or, since it is a capital letter, N. Herbert Hunger of Vienna, a papyrologist with a worldwide reputation, had demonstrated that this was the only conceivable reconstruction on the basis of all types of Ns in Greek papyri, at a Qumran Congress in 1991, even before the letter was analysed under an electronic stereo microscope in Jerusalem, where the previously invisible diagonal stroke which is needed to link the left vertical bar with the right vertical bar in any N, was rediscovered and photographed.[34] Hunger's masterly reconstruction was further supported by a comparison of letters on papyrus 7Q 5: the fragment has two complete *etas* (H) in lines 4 and 5, which, although undoubtedly the same letters, are different in width and 'straightness' – the right vertical stroke of the second H bends towards the right, whereas it is perfectly straight in the first H. And measuring the extremities in width, one finds that the first and the second H differ from 3.0 mm to 3.5 mm. These variations are precisely those which we see between the N in line 2 and the traces in line 4: 3.0 mm to 3.5 mm, and a 'bending' stroke linking the two vertical bars in the first N, instead of a straight one as in the second N. Hunger and the microscopal analysis conclusively settled the last remaining palaeographical question of 7Q 5: this decisive letter, which in Mark 6:52 must belong to the Greek word αυτων, is an N and nothing else. The *iota* + *alpha* of the first edition have disappeared for good; instead, another letter has been firmly established after the N.

Following a hole in the papyrus, which was probably the result of a wilful attempt to destroy the scroll in antiquity (by the Romans in AD 68?), the right-hand part of an *eta*, H, which was overlooked by the first editors, is clearly visible and was inserted in O'Callaghan's reconstruction of the papyrus. Furthermore, the last letter in line 3, previously misread as an *omega* or *omicron*, is now correctly seen as an *iota*. In line 5, the last two extant letters, read as *epsilon* and *sigma* by the first editors, are now reconstructed as *sigma* and *alpha*. The *sigma* is straightforward enough: the first editors misread a speck of ink as the horizontal bar of an *epsilon*, for which, however, it is far too high, anyway. At the end of the line, practically nothing is left of what Boismard in 1962 interpreted as a *sigma*, and O'Callaghan in 1972 as an *alpha*. In the Markan identification, it must be an *alpha*, and whatever is left on the papyrus could, of course, be such a Greek letter. But it would be fair to say there is just not enough ink left to identify (or reject) it with any degree of certainty. The reconstruction of the papyrus should stop with the preceding letter, the *sigma*. In a reconstruction of 7Q 5, the final *alpha* can be legitimately printed, with a dot underneath, only because the indecipherable traces must once have been such a letter, on the basis of the assured decipherment of the whole papyrus. Such a procedure is of course standard practice in papyrology.

7Q 5, identified with Mark 6:52–53, does not differ from the other papyri identified in Cave 7. Like 7Q1, 7Q2 and 7Q4, its text is not fully identical to that of the 'standard' Greek edition. There are two variants, a minimal number in view of the numerous deviations in 7Q2/Baruch 4:43–44 over against the Greek Old Testament, or those of 7Q 1 over against the standard text of Exodus 28:4–7; but even so, they have to be analysed and explained. The first variant is immediately obvious: in all editions of the Greek New Testament, the word for 'having crossed over' in Mark 6:53, διαπερασαντες, is written with a *delta*, δ, at the beginning. But in 7Q 5, the letter is a *tau*, τ. At first glance, this looks odd. In reality, however, it is a variant which cannot merely be explained; it can even be expected on such a papyrus.

One of the so-called 'hard facts' concerning language and spelling in Palestine at the time of Jesus is an inscription which was displayed at the Temple in Jerusalem. It forbade non-Jewish foreigners entrance to the Temple courts, on pain of death. Two copies were found; one – fragmentary – is on display at the John-Rockefeller-Museum, Jerusalem; another – complete – can be seen at the Turkish National Museum in Istanbul.[35] The summary death sentence pronounced on this inscription plays a role in early Christian history:

Paul and Trophimus were arrested by a group of Jews who were trying to kill the apostle under the pretext that he had taken the uncircumcised Greek Trophimus into the Temple (Acts 21:27–36). Two details are remarkable. First, the inscription is in Greek – and only in Greek. Jews coming to the Temple with their visitors, and the visitors themselves, were expected to understand the warning. Since everyone knew Greek, worshipping Jews included, there was no need for Hebrew or Aramaic – Greek would do. And second, the word for 'barrier', δρυφακτος, is spelt with an initial τ, rather than a δ: τρυφακτος. A Jerusalemite was regularly confronted with this variant spelling, which may have been a true variant (for which pre-Christian evidence exists even outside Palestine), or the result of a peculiar regional pronunciation (hard τ (*t*) instead of soft δ (*d*)); but whatever the reason, here was contemporary evidence that the shift from *delta* to *tau* was part of an official, public text in Palestine.[36] It may be argued that the gospel story originated in Palestine, but was not written there. Whatever such a change of topography may have meant for the spelling, the change from δ to τ is documented elsewhere in the Roman empire,[37] and what is more, there is even dated evidence (AD 42!) for the shift from δ to τ before the vowel ι, exactly as it occurs in 7Q 5.[38]

The second variant in 7Q 5 is equally interesting. On the basis of a regular stichometry (that is the number of letters per line), the number is between twenty and twenty-three. A reconstruction which takes this stichometry seriously has to drop three words – the words immediately after *tiaperásantes*: επι την γην (*epi tên gên*), 'on(to)/in(to) the land' in Mark 6:53. Compared with the changes and omissions in 7Q 2, or in the papyrus of Acts – P91 – discussed above, it is a negligible variant. And unlike those in P91, where Christ himself was deleted, or those in 7Q 2 which create a new text, this omission turns out to be corroborative evidence for a very early text. Anyone who reads the Greek text in our standard editions should be aware of the inelegant, unnecessarily contorted form of the addition of *epi tên gên* after *tiaperásantes* and before *êlthon eis Gennêsaret*. It looks plainly like an afterthought, a tautology or pleonasm: *eis*, followed by the name of the locality, already means 'on(to)/in(to) the land'. Thus, the Greek sentence *kai tiaperásantes êlthon eis Gennêsaret*, without *epi tên gên*, reads, 'And having crossed over, they arrived in the land Gennesaret'. This is a perfectly sufficient statement, since there was a land Gennesaret, independently documented by Josephus (*War* 3:10, 7). The three words *epi tên gên* are, for the sparse, down-to-earth Greek of Mark's Gospel, an uncharacteristically convoluted insertion, surplus to requirements. Obviously, since there was no Greek manuscript evidence to make New Testament scholars think about this peculiarity, it was left uncommented on.[39] It comes as a relief that there is now a scroll fragment of this gospel which corrects the impression. The latest possible date of 7Q 5 is certain, as we saw above: it must be older than AD 68, and the repeated, comparative palaeographical analysis has shown, time and again, that it was written around AD 50. Thus, we have to ask: why were these three words added after AD 68, during the second 'generation' of Markan copies, and why was the first stage of the better, shorter text discontinued?

Archaeology has paved the way towards an answer. The inhabited place called 'Gennesaret' existed until the first revolt against the Romans who destroyed it in c. AD 68. Teams of European and Israeli archaeologists excavated it in the late 1980s and early 1990s. It was an old settlement, going back to the Iron Age. Jesus and the disciples could see it from Capernaum, below today's Tell Kinnereth. Thus, the original text of Mark 6:53 was based on first-hand knowledge of the area. Someone who crossed the lake in that direction would reach a settlement area called Gennesaret. Everyone up there knew it; even Josephus, the Jewish historian, mentions it. However, there was no such inhabited place after AD 68: the Romans had destroyed it; only some 1,900 years later would archaeologists rediscover its ruins. And this is where an editor or scribe could have come in: By adding *epi tên gên*, he would have explained to the readers of the gospel text that there was once indeed a piece of land (*gê*) called Gennesaret, reached by Jesus and the disciples. In a way, it was a well-meant insertion: no reader should think that Mark had stupidly mixed up the lake (still called Gennesaret) with the land, where no 'Gennesaret' was left any more to anyone's knowledge. But scribes and 'correctors' are seldom of the author's calibre. They leave their marks. And those of the person who inelegantly added *epi tên gên* are obvious enough. The manuscript tradition of Mark 6:53 shows many variations; apparently, there were always 'editors' who did not feel all that happy about a text with *epi tên gên* and tried to find alternative positions for the words in this verse, and so forth. The radical and original solution, which purifies the later form of the text conclusively and helps to reconstruct the original, is the one which has been preserved in the oldest papyrus of Mark's Gospel, 7Q 5.

The Judeo-Christian fragments from Cave 7 are the visible, tangible background to a new understanding of the Jewish origins of Christianity. They strengthen the case, made by Jewish and Christian scholars alike – and independently of these papyri – for the beginnings of a Judeo-Christian literature at the end of the Second Temple period. From a Jewish perspective, these papyri and the writings which they represent can be added to the Jewish literature of this late period. Even the format, scrolls rather than codices, confirms the inner-Jewish context. It was always rather obvious that the first followers of Jesus knew and used scrolls rather than codices – internal and external evidence points in that direction – but apart from a very few exceptions, there was no papyrus of a gospel or an epistle to show for it.[40] After AD 70, radical changes took place. In the aftermath of the loss of the Temple and of Jerusalem, Judaism reasserted itself, of necessity, and did so not least by defining its identity. The so-called rabbinic council of Jamnia, in the 80s, began the process of

179

establishing the oral teaching in written form; the two Talmuds, the Talmud Yerushalmi and the Talmud Bavli (Babylonian Talmud) are the lasting result. Those who did not adhere to the law and its corollaries in a strictly defined sense were excluded from the synagogues – and this included the followers of Jesus. An addition to the Eighteen Prayers, the so-called Birkat ha-Minim, delivers them to eternal judgment in what could be perceived as a final, irrevocable curse. The followers of Jesus, in turn, were increasingly moving towards non-Jewish 'target groups'. They, too, were suffering from the loss of the Temple where the Jerusalem community had continued to worship until their flight from Jerusalem to Pella, before the onset of the first suicidal Jewish revolt against the Romans in AD 66, which they, like many other Jews in fact, did not support. Outside the Holy Land, in the 'diaspora', the separation between Jews and Jewish Christians left the latter in an increasingly difficult position. Opposed by their fellow Jews and sidelined by the growing majority of non-Jewish Christians, they soon lost their influence on the budding church. Internal and external elements of a common tradition were neglected; a very early aspect of this shift was the change from scroll to codex which began in the 60s of the first century. Existing models like the parchment notebook (2 Timothy 4:13) could be developed into the more practical, space-saving, cheaper codex, at a time when the new format was highly fashionable among the Romans.[41] In a word, it was no longer necessary to show consideration for common Jewish traditions; the Christian strategists had cast their eyes on different pastures. In view of this separation, which led to despicable consequences in the anti-Jewish history of the churches, it is all the more important to realize that the origins of Christian literature belong to a period which was marked by shared traditions and values.

Another positive side-effect of this insight is the termination of all 'politically correct' talk about anti-Semitism (or anti-Judaism) in the New Testament. These twenty-seven Jewish-Christian writings can no longer be held responsible for the extremes of a later, manipulative anti-Jewish exegesis and its inexcusable, horrific results. Jewish and Christian scholars have demonstrated that the language of these texts was that of an inner-Jewish 'family conflict' – with much at stake, after all. And they have shown that the crass vocabulary, which one does find occasionally, is caressingly mild if compared with the vocabulary employed against fellow Jews by the authors of some of the Hebrew and Aramaic texts found at Qumran.[42] It was the way they did it, in those days – incomprehensible as we today may find it, post-enlightened, meek and mild and unpolemical as we, of course, always are. At the Cave 7 panel discussion in Jerusalem, held at the Notre Dame Centre on 3 January 1999, James Charlesworth of Princeton University stated that all major Christian developments happened before AD 70, and this includes the origins of the gospels, 'even' of the purportedly anti-Semitic John which, according to Charlesworth, may be as old as c. AD 50. To avoid terminological confusion, he suggested that the followers of Jesus in first-century Palestine should not (yet) be called 'Christians', which was a name given to them by non-Jews at Antioch (Acts 11:26). Charlesworth prefers to use their inner-Jewish designation as 'Nazarenes', the followers of the Messiah, Jesus of Nazareth. The texts from Cave 7 help us to understand this historical context. As Paul put it in his letter to the Galatians (2:14): 'We ourselves are Jews by birth.'

VIII

How Shall We Then Live?

THE CASE OF GODLY WAYS OF LIFE
AND MESSIANIC EXPECTATIONS AMONG
FIRST-CENTURY JEWS

What are the similarities between Jesus and the Qumran movement, between certain New Testament events and allusions and the life of the Dead Sea communities? How much did the first Christians know about the Essene movement? How much did the Essenes know about the first Christians? Was John the Baptist an Essene? Did Jesus celebrate the Last Supper in an Essene guesthouse? Was the organization of the first Jewish-Christian community based on an Essene model?

Most Jews at the time of Jesus were filled with messianic expectations and eschatological desire. The end would come 'like a thief in the night'. But who was the Messiah they expected? The Dead Sea Scrolls present different role models. A 'Son of God' and 'Son of the Most High' appear in a scroll (4Q 246) and highlight the political realities of the times, with Roman emperors such as Augustus and Tiberius who were called 'Sons of God'. A fragment of the War Scroll may even talk about a suffering, pierced Messiah. Essenes would have been among those who understood why Jesus quoted the messianic Psalm 22 on the cross. And the eschatological writings found in the caves underline that a Jewish group expecting the end of times with the coming of the Messiah in the immediate future wrote and distributed their writings immediately, eagerly, widely and extensively (and at Qumran, only the 'archive copies' were found). Was this a model for the first Christians who did not wait until the second or third generation before they began to write?

The last days and the first days

On 7 November 1999, *The Sunday Times* had a 'World News' headline: 'Scroll names Jesus as sect member'.[1] Once again, the excitement did not match up to the facts. Weeks before the news reached *The Times*, scholars in Israel and worldwide had begun to discuss and to dismiss the alleged sensation, after a first account published in the *Jerusalem Report* magazine.[2] Everyone realized immediately that it was yet another attempt to link Jesus with the Essenes at Qumran, to belittle the origins of Christianity while throwing in a bit of pseudo-Muslim teaching for good measure: all religions in one scroll, politically correct to the utmost. A caption in *The Times* saw yet another angle: 'The Angel Scroll challenges accepted Christian perceptions of Jesus' teachings as unique, suggesting he could have been just one of many similar philosophers within the Essene sect.' This sounds intriguing – philosophers at Qumran, and Jesus among them, would give us a completely new terminology for Jewish messianism and godliness. No longing for a deeper knowledge of God or 'theo-logy' any more, just love for wisdom, 'philo-sophy': good riddance to 3,000 years or so of Jewish thought!

Joking apart, a sober perusal of the few excerpts of the Angel Scroll which have been made available so far (at the time of writing, no papyrologist has seen photos, let alone the 'original') leads to much more sobering conclusions. Nothing which has been quoted is earlier than any of the texts already known, and the story of the discovery of the scroll has more holes than a Swiss cheese. The Benedictine monk who allegedly bought the scroll 'armed with huge sums of Benedictine money' does not exist. Bargil Pixner, a world-famous expert in Essenism and Dead Sea studies and himself a Benedictine who knows well the 'monastery somewhere near the

German-Austrian border' where the scroll is supposed 'to be studied by a team of monks who had taken a vow of silence', was the first to debunk the story – with regrets perhaps, since Pixner has always believed there were close contacts between the Essene communities outside Qumran, Jesus and his followers. It was probably the decisive mistake of the people who invented the 'scroll' to link it with Benedictines who were in the best possible position to refute the story. In fact, anyone who knows Pixner's research or that of others who have investigated the similarities and differences between Jesus and those of his fellow Jews who happened to be of an Essene persuasion could have made up such a text. As Magen Broshi, former director of the Shrine of the Book in Jerusalem, and an acknowledged Dead Sea expert, told *The Times*, 'The whole thing is so strange and I think, if I were about to commit a forgery, this is what I would have done.' The Hebrew and Aramaic words which occur in the 'transcripts' are so common in the published Dead Sea Scrolls that anyone could have copied them since 1947, and the Greek which also appears in the 'scroll' seems to come from passages in the writings of the Jewish historian Josephus, who wrote in the last third of the first century. If a 'scroll' like this were composed in antiquity, it cannot have been earlier than the beginning of the Muslim period in the Holy Land, in the seventh century, when contacts between Jews, Christians and Muslims were intense and fruitful before Islam decided to go its own way, the way of the Koran. But it seems that the whole story is just an elaborate practical joke. Even so, the claims that the origins of Christianity are overshadowed and put into question by this alleged discovery are characteristic of a debate which continues to fascinate many people: what did Jesus and the people of the Dead Sea Scrolls have in common? Did the Essenes influence the development of early Christianity? And if so, what of it?

Since the people of the Dead Sea Scrolls and the Jews who believed in Jesus shared the same basic texts – the *Torah*, the

Prophets, and so forth, and since both groups adhered to a messianic and eschatological concept of the world, similarities should be expected. We have encountered many examples in previous chapters. It is fascinating to see, however, that these similarities never reach the stage of identity. At the profoundest level, the Jewish followers of Jesus added a dimension which was new and troubling to the others. There was obviously more to it than just accepting Jesus as the Messiah. And one central element of this new dimension was the Judeo-Christian form of belief in the last days, the 'eschatology'. We can see it, for example, in the use of the Greek letters *alpha* and *omega*, the A and Ω, the beginning and the end of the Greek alphabet. They have come to symbolize the all-encompassing presence and power of Jesus the Messiah. John's Revelation, the last book of the New Testament,[3] used this image for the first time in Judeo-Christian literature. And its introduction by the Jewish author of Revelation is all the more remarkable as the apocalyptic and visionary models which had shaped Jewish eschatological language before him – in particular in the book of Daniel – did not use such symbols. It is true, of course, that Daniel was not written in Greek. But needless to say, there are equivalent first and last letters in the Hebrew alphabet (*aleph* and *tau*). Alphabetical symbols for God and the power he holds over the beginning and the end of his world could easily have been expressed in Hebrew, by the same means. But it was not done before the book of Revelation. '"I am the Alpha and the Omega", says the Lord God, "who is and who was and who is to come, the Almighty"' (Revelation 1:8). 'And the one who was seated on the throne said, "See, I am making all things new." Also he said: "Write this, for these words are trustworthy and true." Then he said to me, "It is done! I am the Alpha and the Omega, the beginning and the end"' (Revelation 21:5–6). 'See, I am coming soon; my reward is with me, to repay according to everyone's work. I am the Alpha and the Omega, the first and the last, the beginning and the end' (Revelation 22:12–13). God and the Christ are one. The decisive second coming of the Messiah will be, yet again, an incarnation.

Throughout the Jewish writings which became the New Testament, this wholeness of the creator God and the Son of God, the Messiah, is maintained. In 1 Corinthians 16:22, Paul writes an Aramaic phrase: *Maranatha*. It can be read as *Maran atha*, 'Our Lord has come,' or as *Marana tha*, 'Our Lord come!' In the Greek script of the papyri, the Aramaic words are written in capital letters, and like the Greek, in continuous script. In other words, we cannot see where Paul himself wanted the syllables to be separated. But this is precisely the point: MARANATHA does mean both things to the believers. Beginning and end are in one hand: the Lord has come, and he will come again. This was and is a very Jewish statement, poignantly written in Aramaic, and it was a new paradigm at that: there is no parallel in the old common scriptures, nor in the Dead Sea Scrolls. Only at a later stage, in the rabbinic period, was the Hebrew alphabet used to express comparable ideas: Abraham kept the law from *aleph* to *tau*; the Lord has blessed his people Israel from *aleph* to *tau*. A later Midrash explains Isaiah 44:6 ('I am the first and I am the last, apart from me, there is no God.') with the first and last letters of the Hebrew alphabet.[4] But comparable as they are, these rabbinic images are literal; they do not imply the far-reaching perspective of a creator God who acts through the Messiah, his Son.

In Christian art, the symbolism of *alpha* and *omega* was often turned round – we find inscriptions, particularly on tombstones and lead baptismal basins, where the order is inverted: first the *omega*, then the *alpha*. The end is the beginning: there is a new life after the old one (through baptism in Christ), and there is life after death (through resurrection in Christ). In both cases, as A and Ω, and as Ω and A, this idea of an eschatological renewal was linear, not cyclical – and this means it contradicted the popular Graeco-Roman philosophy of creation, blossoming, decay, catastrophic destruction and new creation as a continuous repetition.[5] We can see that John's and early Christianity's vision is Jewish, not far from Isaiah, but we can also see where it leaves behind the realm of traditional Judaism (carefully developed and faithfully continued by the later rabbis), and reaches out into a wider world of thought which cannot have been easy to digest – neither for the 'pagans', nor for the Jews themselves. This was certainly aggravated by the undeniable historical fact that the Messiah/Son of God had been crucified as a royal pretender ('The King of the Jews', it said on the inscription above Jesus' head on the cross) by the Romans according to Roman law. How could it possibly be accepted by anyone that salvation should come through the suffering and death of an outcast?

To the Jews, scriptural evidence was paramount. A tell-tale example occurs in the book of Acts, where the Jews at Berea listened to Paul and Silas 'and examined the scriptures every day to see whether these things were so' (Acts 17:11). The world of this new messianic message was deeply couched in history: No contemporary Jew, not even the fiercest opponent of Jesus, doubted that he had performed his miracles, that he had made his messianic claims, that he had died on the cross, and that his tomb was empty on the third day. But could it be squared with scripture? Could the eschatological proclamation of Jesus' first followers be seen to come straight from the *Torah* and the Prophets? If it could not, there was not much chance that any Jew would be convinced. The old chestnut of the alleged lack of originality in Christianity, recently rehashed in the debate about the so-called Angel Scroll, and in the old and spurious axiom of some New Testament scholarship that only those sayings of Jesus which cannot be derived from Judaism (or, for that matter, from paganism) can be deemed authentic, are wide of the mark. The closer to the mutual sources, the more authentic – and the evidence of the Dead Sea Scrolls is not the only clue to this inner-Jewish closeness. The example of the *alpha/omega* image, with its new eschatological and messianic emphasis, is clear enough: we can see how a prophet like Isaiah prepared the ground, we can see how later rabbis took it up, and we can see how between them, a man such as the author of Revelation found his own mode of expression, and all of this without any additional trace in the scrolls from Qumran to provide further links. The artistry, the virtuosity of the Judeo-Christian proclamation in the first decades depended on fellow Jews recognizing the common background – and having done so, realizing how a novel, but certainly not alien concept of messiahship and the last days could come from this.

Revelation apart, Peter's speech in Jerusalem at Pentecost (Acts 2:14–40) is the first outstanding example of this strategy, and there is no historical reason whatsoever to doubt its success (2:41–47). Peter, a man who must not be underestimated as a simple fisherman any more,[6] demonstrates his technique again when he talks about the end of this world, in his second letter.[7] 'But do not forget this one thing, dear friends: With the Lord, a day is like a thousand years, and a thousand years like a day. The Lord is not slow in keeping his promise, as some understand slowness. He is patient with you, not wanting anyone to perish, but everyone to come to repentance' (2 Peter 3:8–9). Facing an historical situation which was shared by the Essenes at Qumran, who had been expecting the coming of the end towards 160 BC but patiently went on waiting, writing and collecting other messianic literature for more than a century, Peter refers to a psalm. In Psalm 90:4, we read, 'For a thousand years in your sight are like a day that has just gone by, or like a watch in the night.' It is obvious that Peter wants his readers to understand the context. Once more, this is not cheap solace, but solid teaching: his impatient readers could have known long ago, if only they had read and understood Psalm 90.[8] And Peter operates with a subtle variation. He begins with the day, whereas the psalm begins with the years, and unlike the psalm, he emphasizes the teaching by repeating it, now in inverse

the Sadducees and Pharisees. Then again, in other areas, the first followers of the Christ Jesus are closer to the Pharisees than to the Essenes – and so forth. No movement lived a solitary life, and as we saw in previous chapters, not even the Essenes who stayed in touch with developments throughout the Roman empire. They knew of each other, they learnt from each other, they rejected each other, giving and taking all the time. No Jesus, no Paul, no John the Baptist had to live at Qumran to hear about the Essene way of life or to read their scrolls. Even the Baptist, a favourite candidate for the theory of Essene links, cannot be directly associated with Qumran. His years in the wilderness before his appearance in public (Luke 1:80) do not justify the connection with Qumran; in fact, the early church located his desert abode in a valley five miles west of Hebron, and even saw one of his baptismal sites nearby, at a place still called Ain el-Ma'mudiyyeh ('Spring of Baptism').[10] John's act of baptism itself, a complete purification, once and for all, through an immersion by another person, does not bear any resemblance to the Essene practice of daily, repeated, ritual self-purification (1QS 3:9; CD 10:11, etc.)[11]. The only undeniable connection between Essene self-'baptism' and John is the use of water and the evident fact that water as such has a cleaning effect. John the Baptist was the first person in Jewish history who immersed fellow Jews in an act of repentance and purification. However, some scholars have suggested that the early Christian baptismal rite, initiated by Jesus (Matthew 28:19) and first described in Acts 2:38, bears a certain resemblance to the Essene initiation rite, and that traces can even be found in Hippolytus' early third-century description of admission to baptism.[12] But this is an unwarranted interpretation of the evidence which exaggerates the obvious similarities anyone will always find when different communities go about their business of arranging ceremonies and 'initiations'. No Christian needed Essene models to give shape to a ceremony, and the decisive elements are as different as they could be. After all, the baptism formula proclaimed by Peter is quite unprecedented: 'Repent, and be baptized every one of you in the name of Jesus Christ so that your sins may be forgiven; and you will receive the gift of the Holy Spirit. For the promise is for you, for your children, and for all who are far away, everyone whom the Lord our God calls to him' (2:38).

Other alleged links are equally weak. The Community Rule (1QS) mentions twelve men and three priests to guide the council of the community (1QS 8:1–2). This has often been understood as the model of the twelve disciples and apostles, happily overlooking the fact that 1QS also mentions three priests which make no appearance on early Christian boards of governors.[13] The model, of course, was common to both Essenes and Jesus: the twelve tribes of Israel which play such an important role in apostolic parlance (cf. Acts 26:7; James 1:1; and Revelation 21:12–21) and are a prototype which reappears in several gospel contexts. In the twelve baskets after the feeding of the 5,000 (Mark 6:43), for example, or in the reference to the twelve patriarchs (Acts 7:8). Another such alleged Essene link is the Last Supper. The Community Rule mentions a priest who blesses the food and the wine (1QS 6:4–5) at the common meal, and the so-called Rule of the Congregation talks about a meal over which two Messiahs will preside (1QSa 2:17–21). It is, of course, quite unreasonable to infer that the Last Supper of Jesus is prefigured by these Essene meals. The Qumran scroll merely mentions a blessing of the firstfruits of bread and wine, and after the two Messiahs, all members of the congregation will speak a blessing, 'according to their order of dignity'. Not only does the Last Supper of Jesus – one Messiah only – refrain from incorporating blessings by the disciples, there is no order of dignity, either. Jesus was adamant that everyone, including the disciples, was of equal rank 'at the banquets' and among the followers of the Messiah (Matthew 23:6–12; Mark 9:33–35). If anything, Jesus explicitly contradicts Essene teaching in this matter. And if we do need a model of an eschatological meal, it is provided, once again, by common Jewish prophecy of old – Isaiah 25:6–12. Time and again, we must look at the common prophecies before we even think Essenes may have influenced Jesus and early Christianity directly. The New Covenant, for example, is part of Jesus' proclamation (Luke 22:20) and is claimed by the Essenes (Damascus Document CD 6:19, 8:21, etc.). Both independently refer to Jeremiah 31:31–34, but the last verse of this passage, 34, was fulfilled in the Son of God alone: 'The days are surely coming, says the Lord, when I will make a new covenant with the House of Israel and the House of Judah... I will forgive their iniquity, and remember their sin no more.'[14] In brief, the question of the Dead Sea Scrolls and their direct link with the Jewish origins of Christianity does not demand an unreservedly affirmative answer. There are Jewish origins of Christianity outside and beyond the scrolls. And there are things Jesus and his first followers did which were new, as well. It is with this in mind that we can look into these scrolls again, to find out where they do help us to understand the background of early Christianity.

Expecting the Messiah among the sons of God

Jesus was proclaimed the Messiah. Simon Peter was the first to say it, quite spontaneously, without being asked (John 6:69), and again after the first opinion poll in early Christian history (Matthew 16:13–14) in reply to Jesus' question at Caesarea Philippi (Matthew 16:16). Others, such as the blind man at Jericho (Luke 18:38) and Martha of Bethany, confirmed it (John 11:27). Jesus himself said it in his own words (Mark 9:41; John 10:24–25).[15] If we want to judge messianic expectations by the yardstick of the Dead Sea Scrolls, we encounter a colourful picture. On the one hand, there is the Messiah from the line of David. Because of this forefather, he is a royal Messiah, and he is victorious and triumphant (4Q 161; 4Q 285). But on the other hand, there is also a priestly Messiah, and accordingly, he is not Davidic, but Aaronitic. This 'Messiah of Aaron' is the superior one: the Messiah of

David has to consult him, and to accept his precedence. The Aaronitic Messiah is the last one of perhaps up to three (Dead Sea Scrolls scholars are not unanimous) who are referred to in the scrolls, and he is the truly eschatological one, for, as it says in the Damascus Document, 'he will teach righteousness at the end of the days' (CD 6:11). If a third Messiah can be identified, he is the so-called 'Prophet'. The Community Rule mentions him once (1QS 9:11) and specifies that he will come together with the Messiah of Aaron. But it looks as though this person is a prophet of the Messiah (or a messianic prophet) rather than a Prophet–Messiah himself. It is easy enough to recognize him in someone like John the Baptist, or to see him as an Elijah *redivivus*, as a divinely inspired prophet, in fact even as a new Moses. Thus, this widespread expectant mood among the Jews was mirrored precisely by the opinion poll near Caesarea Philippi. When the disciples had asked the people who they thought Jesus was, they reported back to him: 'Some say John the Baptist, but others Elijah, and still others Jeremiah or one of the prophets' (Matthew 16:12). In other words, at that time, not long after the beginning of his ministry in Galilee, Jesus was already acknowledged as an eschatological figure, but not as the Messiah himself. And the separation between the messianic priest and the true Messiah is obvious from Simon Peter's reply to Jesus: '*You* are *the* Messiah, the Son of the living God.'

The scene of the transfiguration of Jesus, 'on a high mountain', in the following chapter of Matthew's Gospel (see also the parallel account in Mark 8:27 – 9:13) underlines this new perspective. Elijah and Moses appear to Jesus, Peter, James and John, and in their presence, a voice from heaven is heard to say, 'This is my Son, the Beloved; with him I am well pleased; listen to him!' (Matthew 17:5). God himself decides. And Jesus explains it, when the disciples ask him why Elijah had to come first – he has indeed to come before the Messiah, but he has already come, in John the Baptist (17:10–13). And the priestly writing of the New Testament, the letter to the

Hebrews, brings Moses into the picture, who stood next to Christ when the voice from heaven spoke. 'Jesus is worthy of more glory than Moses,' the Jewish author of the letter to the Hebrews states after a praise of faithful Moses, 'just as the builder of a house has more honour than the house itself. For every house is built by someone, but the builder of all things is God. Now Moses was faithful in all God's house as a servant, to testify the things that would be spoken later. Christ [i.e., in Hebrew and Aramaic, the Messiah], was faithful over God's house as a son' (Hebrews 3:3–6).

Peter considered the event on the mountain of the transfiguration so pivotal that he used it as the only direct reference to a personal experience with Jesus in his second letter (2 Peter 1:16–18). Not only that, it also serves as the decisive argument against those who think the Jesus story was based on myths: he, the eyewitness, can guarantee its authenticity.[16] If Jesus supersedes the idea of a prophetic Messiah (or messianic prophet), what about the other two Messiahs? The two family trees in Matthew and Luke, with their different approaches to genealogy, agree in one vital point: Jesus is of Davidic descent. This means the Messiah whom Peter proclaimed at Caesarea Philippi, and the others later on, cannot be the Messiah of Aaron, the final, eschatological Messiah of the Dead Sea Scrolls. And if this is so, we are faced with a profound difference between the messianic interpretation of the last days in the Dead Sea Scrolls, and that in early Jewish Christianity. But this should not surprise us: the notion of a Messiah of Aaron was peculiar to the Essene communities. As far as we can tell, other Jews and Jewish movements at the time thought of the Messiah as Davidic. And even some Dead Sea Scrolls do so, as we saw above. In other words, one cannot speak of a uniform messianic concept in the texts found at Qumran. While the emphasis on the Aaronitic, priestly Messiah makes sense among a priestly community, the triumphant Messiah of David is accepted as an alternative projection, not necessarily always as a subservient one. A sceptic might say the people at the time were just playing safe. Better be prepared for more than one Messiah than for none at all. This opened the field to the proclamation of Jesus as *the* Messiah, and on the basis of his genealogy, as the Davidic one.

However, and there was almost complete unanimity at the time, the Davidic Messiah was triumphant, he was victorious. He was the Messiah of Isaiah 11, of 4Q 161, 4Q 285, and perhaps even of the famous War Scroll 1QM. He was also the Messiah of Peter who refused to accept a suffering and executed Christ (Matthew 16:21–23; 26:51–54 with John 18:10–11). But he most certainly was not the Messiah of Jesus himself, who had insisted, from early on, that he would suffer, would be killed, and would be raised again (Matthew 16:21; 17:9, 12; Mark 10:45; 14:22–24, etc.). How could such a provocatively different interpretation, one which was alien to practically everyone at the time, including the disciples who still saw reason enough to believe he had given proof of his messiahship more than once – how could it be reconciled with scripture? Did not Paul, writing with the benefit of hindsight, after crucifixion and resurrection, state quite unmistakably that the proclamation of Christ crucified is 'a stumbling block to Jews and foolishness to Gentiles' (1 Corinthians 1:23)? Did not the *Torah*, the collection of the Mosaic writings, condemn those who were crucified, indeed even curse them? 'When someone is convicted of a crime punishable by death and is executed and you hang him on a tree, his corpse must not remain all night on the tree; you shall bury him that same day, for anyone hung on a tree is under God's curse' (Deuteronomy 21:22–23).[17] One Qumran fragment has fascinated many readers who have been looking for a clue. It appears to be a fragment of the War Scroll (1QM), 4Q 285 fr. 5. Six lines have survived, and even they are not complete. A reconstruction reads as follows:

> *Isaiah the Prophet: 'The forest thickets fall beneath the axe, and the Lebanon falls to the blows of a Mighty One. A shoot will*

> spring from the stock of Jesse... the branch of David, and they will
> take to court the... and the prince of the community, the br[anch
> of David (?)] will be killed/will kill him... by strokes and by
> wounds... and dancers, and the... priest will command... corpses
> of the Kittim...'

The beginning of the fragment is straightforward enough. Isaiah is
mentioned, and chapters 10:34 and 11:1 of his book are quoted. God
will help his people, it seems, against an alien invader and oppressor.
So much for part 1. For the second quotation, the scene shifts.
Although only the first few words have remained, a look at the full
text of Isaiah 11:1 and the following verses explain the message: 'The
shoot from the stock of Jesse will bring peace, he will be a signal for
the peoples' (11:10). The language of the whole chapter is clearly
messianic. Here we have the famous, proverbial line 'the wolf shall
live with the lamb, the leopard shall lie down with the kid, the calf
and the lion and the fatling together, and a little child shall lead them'
(11:6). Peace on earth, messianic peace – this was not least how Paul,
the Jewish writer of Romans 15:12, understood the prophetic praise of
the shoot from the stock of Jesse. But our Qumran fragment suddenly
introduces a new topic. There seems to be a reference to a court case,
to a legal judgment. Who will sentence whom, and why? We read
about the 'prince of the community', and in the Dead Sea Scrolls, he
is a messianic figure (Damascus Document CD 7:20; War Scroll 1QM
5:1). If the few words behind this title can be correctly reconstructed
as 'the branch of David', we would know that the prince of the
community is seen as the Davidic Messiah. This Messiah is
triumphant, as we already know. Is he the object or the subject of the
court case? Our natural assumption is, of course, to see him as the
judge, not as the accused. And thus, it is easy to suppose the following
sentence mentions an action of the messianic prince of the
community: he will kill the enemy.

Some of the first commentators immediately after the publication of the fragment in 1991 saw a different solution, however. They vocalized the Hebrew letters *hmtw* to read 'wehemitu', which means that the enemies will kill the prince of the community (i.e. he is the object of the sentence), instead of 'wehemito', which means the prince will kill his opponent. The Hebrew consonants allow both possibilities. The suggestion that 4Q 285 (fr. 5) could be the first and so far only known Qumran text to refer explicitly to a killed Messiah was treated as a sensation. In fact, the controversial scholar John Allegro had talked to the press about this fragment a quarter of a century before its publication.[18] The suggested reading of a 'crucifixion' was rejected even then.[19] And the reference to the *kittim* in the last line may indicate that they, the oppressors, will be killed by the prince of the community. But the context of the word 'corpses' is guesswork: it could refer to the slain Romans, but it could also mean those slain by the Romans – i.e. the many Jews killed by these *kittim* – even before Jesus was crucified by them. The apocalyptic language of the Dead Sea Scrolls is ambiguous, and this was no accident. From the mid-second century onwards, many Jews lived with the urgent hope and expectancy that theirs was the end of times, the last days, but unlike some modern sects such as Jehovah's Witnesses, the Essenes and other Jewish movements never set exact dates. And there are only very few personal names in the scrolls to guide us chronologically – for example, 'Yohanan' in 4Q 448, perhaps to be identified with John Hyrcanus who ruled from 143 BC to 104 BC. Others interpret it as a prayer which mentions a certain King Jonathan who may be identified with Alexander Jannaeus (103 BC–76 BC); we have a general of Pompeii called Aemilius Scaurus in 4Q 323 who was one of the Romans/*kittim* involved in the capture of Jerusalem in 63 BC; Queen Shlomzion (i.e. Salome Alexandra, 76 BC–67 BC) with her son Hyrcanus, both mentioned in 4Q 324. Some of these names are fragmentary and therefore uncertain, but although all evidence is

As in the War Scroll fragment 4Q 285, the reader is longing for more. What war are they talking about? Will the ruler proclaim himself Son of God, or will others proclaim him? In any case, the apocalyptic imagery involves two real kingdoms, Assyria and Egypt, and broadly speaking, both belonged to the Roman empire at the time of writing, just before the turn of the century, some time during the reign of Emperor Augustus (44 BC–AD 14). If one assumes that the text is looking back at real kings, one might think of someone such as Alexander Balas, a Syrian (Seleucid) ruler, or of the Syrian tyrant, Antiochus IV, who persecuted the Jews between 170 and 164 BC. He used the byname 'Epiphanes', appealing to godlike 'appearance'. But all this was past history when the text was written, and the final battle, supported by God himself, evokes the present plight, under the Romans, the *'kittim'*, rulers over the province of Syria (to which the Jewish homelands belonged at the time) and neighbouring Egypt. Whatever one's preference, it is obvious enough that this Son of God, this Son of the Most High, is a negative 'Messiah', an usurper, one who claims (or has others claim on his behalf) that he is someone who he plainly – in God's judgment – is not. And this was precisely the situation at the time of our text. Emperor Augustus had deified his adoptive father Julius Caesar, with the help of the Senate. Henceforth, he himself was a 'Son of God'. Other emperors with natural or adoptive fathers who could be deified in the same manner, followed Augustus' example – Tiberius, for example. Thus, Jesus was born under an emperor and crucified under an emperor, both of whom claimed to be 'Sons of God'. Inscriptions and coins provide ample evidence for this usage, in Greek and Latin. Temples to emperors were built; three of those dedicated to Augustus have been excavated in the Holy Land, at the two Caesareas, and at Samaria-Sebaste, and one dedicated to Tiberius can be inferred from Pontius Pilate's inscription which was found at Caesarea Maritima, where the prefect had apparently erected a 'Tiberieum', a temple to Tiberius.

199

solidly based on biblical precedents. God condemns the usurpers –
Isaiah 14:12–21 comes to mind, and Ezekiel 28:1–10. The most telling
basis for the Aramaic 'Son of God' scroll, however, is Psalm 82:6–8:
'I had thought: "Are you gods, are you all sons of the Most High? No!
you will die as human beings do. As one man, princes, you will fall."'
Arise, God, judge the world, for all nations belong to you.' We can see
how the Dead Sea Scroll 4Q 246 interprets this psalm. False, self-
appointed sons of God fall under God's own verdict; he will arise and
help his faithful people in the final, messianic battle. The Romans,
those whose emperors were blasphemously called 'Sons of God', will
fall, and their princes, the emperors, will die like any ordinary man.
We cannot read the conclusion to this scroll any more, but seeing it in
the context of the War Scroll, we may assume that the true Messiah,
the true Son of God, will have been mentioned in the apocalyptic
vision at the end. Jesus the Messiah had to reckon with fellow Jews
who were fully aware of Psalm 82, and the other passages mentioned
above, even of 4Q 246. It is with such knowledge in mind that we can
understand his rejection by those who thought he was not the true,
but yet another false, Messiah. John 10:33 protocols the authentic
voice of this opposition: 'It is not for a good work that we are going to
stone you, but for blasphemy, because you, though only a human
being, are making yourself God.' It took Easter to understand how
history had come full circle, from the angelic annunciation in Luke
1:32–35 to the resurrection of the messianic Son. Or, as Paul put it,
'This is the gospel concerning His Son, who, in terms of human
nature, was descended from David and who, in terms of the Spirit and
of holiness, was declared to be Son of God in power by resurrection
from the dead, Jesus Christ our Lord' (Romans 1:3–4).

And again, returning to that other messianic Qumran text, the
War Scroll fragment 4Q 285, we realize how some questions can only
be answered in the context of the times, the hopes and expectations,
and the solid knowledge of scripture among practically all Jews. But

even the search for the proper context demands discernment. Could a Jew expect a suffering, crucified Messiah? Most scholars assume the wider context provides the answer, and this sounds plausible: the other Dead Sea Scrolls do not know such a suffering, killed Messiah. And in a fragment like 1Q 28b 5:20–26, the very same Isaiah quote which introduces the fragmentary passage 4Q 285 is used to interpret the Messiah as the one who will triumph over the godless enemies.[22] When 4Q 285, fr. 5 was sent to exhibitions in Washington, Glasgow, Cologne and St Gallen between 1993 and 1999, the catalogue and the panels opted for the 'active' version of a killing prince, but explicitly mentioned the alternative and quoted an article in its favour.[23] Funnily enough, the 'passive' solution has been used as an argument against Christianity: if there was a pierced, slain or otherwise killed Messiah in a Dead Sea Scroll, the uniqueness of the Christian faith appeared to be questioned.[24] Thus it came as no surprise that defensive Christian scholars were the first to reject the interpretation of a killed Messiah. But this was based on a misunderstanding.

Paul does indeed call the message of 'Christ crucified' a stumbling block to Jews, and yet he does not say that such a stumbling block was a final hindrance, nor does he say that all Jews stumbled. And how could a killed Messiah in a Dead Sea Scroll be surprising in the first place, if Isaiah 53 describes precisely such a Messiah? The argument that the fragment begins with Isaiah 11, which is about a triumphant Messiah of peace, does not hold water in this context: Isaiah 11 was used as a prefiguration of Jesus the Christ by the same Jew Paul (Romans 15:11) who also used Isaiah 53 (Romans 4:25). These two chapters of the same prophetic book are not mutually exclusive. Because they are in one and the same book, it cannot be ruled out that there were Jews, readers of Isaiah, with at least an inkling of a suffering Messiah who would be redeemed in triumphant glory – very much the picture of Psalm 22 which combines these elements and which was spoken by Jesus on the cross. If the theory of

Bargil Pixner and other scholars is correct – that a number of Essene priests became Jewish Christians in the early years of the Jerusalem 'church',[25] with some of them remaining members of their communities (much as Paul remained a Pharisee after his conversion) – it could have been a text like 4Q 285, linked to the words of Isaiah himself, which may have persuaded some Essene priests to find out more about the new Jesus movement, and to realize that this group of Jews was preaching a Messiah whom they could recognize. Having reached that point, they could – and some did – become 'obedient to the faith' (Acts 6:7).

To us, the riddle of this fragment carries the same challenge which the complete scroll may have held for its readers at the time of Jesus. For a long time, for many centuries perhaps, the image of the triumphant Messiah overshadowed all other messianic models. The crowds in Jerusalem who shouted, 'Hosanna to the Son of David!' on Palm Sunday expected this victorious Messiah; the crowds who shouted, 'Let him be crucified!' five days later were disappointed; they felt let down, betrayed. There is no trait of 'anti-Semitism' in the gospel accounts about the people encouraging Pilate to crucify Jesus. On the contrary, it is a credible and understandable scenario. Jesus was, to them, a false Messiah. Away with him – but let the Romans do it! These Jews had been permeated by a messianic expectancy which excluded a prisoner, helplessly tortured by the oppressors. After Easter, the followers of Jesus suddenly saw what they had not seen before, like all the others: this Messiah Jesus was triumphant after all; he had won his victory through suffering and death. He truly was the Messiah of Isaiah's prophecy, bringing the images of chapters 11 and 53 together in one person for the first time. Now, but only now, was it obvious why he prayed Psalm 22 on the cross (the first verse, needless to say, representing the whole psalm), from 'My God, my God, why have you forsaken me?' to 'He did not despise or abhor the affliction of the afflicted; he did not hide his face from me, but heard when I cried to him. From you comes my praise in the great congregation; my vows I will pay before those who fear him. The poor shall eat and be satisfied; those who seek him shall praise the Lord. May your hearts live for ever!' Finally, 'To him indeed shall all who sleep in the earth bow down; before him shall bow all who go down to the dust, and I shall live for him.' And, with the last two verses: 'Posterity will serve him; future generations will be told about the Lord, and proclaim his deliverance to a people yet unborn, saying that he has done it.' With Easter, with Psalm 22 and with Isaiah, the first believers in the risen Messiah could turn to their Essene fellow Jews, telling them that the messianic question of the War Scroll was answered. Jesus was both the suffering and the triumphant Messiah. The apparent contradiction was solved. And the fragment of 4Q 285, in its present state, symbolizes the messianic questions asked, but unanswered before the crucifixion and resurrection of Jesus.

The resurrection and the Dead Sea Scrolls

A crucified Messiah was controversial enough. A Messiah risen from the dead was hardly less provocative. For those Jews who saw the *Meshiach/Christos* as a triumphant appearance, the concept of his resurrection was as unnecessary, even meaningless, if not downright offensive, as his preceding death on a Roman cross. There were influential groups, such as the ruling class of Sadducean Temple priests, who ruled out a bodily resurrection – anyone's bodily resurrection – to begin with. In the account of their clash with Jesus, they are explicitly introduced as those 'who do not believe in a resurrection' (Matthew 22:23; Mark 12:18; Luke 20:27; Acts 23:8, where the Pharisees are contrasted as those who do believe in a resurrection).[26] In his reply, Jesus reminds them of the story of Moses at the burning bush (Exodus 3:6) – the highest and earliest authority for the necessity of a general resurrection faith, regardless even of the specific case of Jesus himself. Perhaps even more importantly, Jesus uses the resurrection as one of the messianic proofs in his answer to the messengers of John the Baptist: 'Are you the one who is to come?' (Matthew 11:2–5; Luke 7:18–23). The Baptist was in a desperate situation, imprisoned by Herod on the fortress of Machaerus,[27] on the eastern side of the Dead Sea, soon to be executed – and Jesus still had not acted with the commonly expected display of messianic power, rescuing people like John himself, nor had he begun to baptize himself. How would Jesus reply? He referred to his miracles, closely echoing Isaiah 26:19, 29:18, and 35:5–6; and thus, he revealed himself as the true Messiah and Son of God, doing what only God himself had been predicted to do. 'Your dead shall live, their corpses shall rise' (Isaiah 26:19), fulfilled twice by Jesus even before his own resurrection: 'The dead are raised,' he says (Luke 7:22), and we have the raising of the widow's son at Nain (Luke 7:11–17) immediately before John's question, and the raising of Lazarus in Bethany (John 11:28–44).

Do the Dead Sea Scrolls take sides in the tension between resurrection believers and opponents? Three texts appear to be specific enough. There are the famous Thanksgiving Hymns, 1QH, one of the seven great scrolls on display in the Shrine of the Book at the Israel Museum, Jerusalem, published as early as 1954. Fragments 2 and 3 of 4Q 385 comment on the 'dry bones' passage from Ezekiel 37:1–14 – a particularly important discovery, as an Ezekiel scroll fragment with the resurrection of the dry bones was found in the library of the synagogue on Masada, just behind the wall with the 'Aaron ha-Kodesh', the niche for the *Torah* Scroll. And there is a more recent publication, the two fragments of 4Q 521, which has been dubbed the 'Resurrection fragment', and has been dated to the first century BC. All of them confirm what Hippolytus of Rome (c. 170 AD – c. 236 AD) wrote about the Essenes in his treatise *Against All Heresies*, mentioned at the beginning of this book: the teaching of the resurrection, Hippolytus said, had found support among the Essenes, 'for they acknowledge both that the flesh will rise again, and that it will be immortal'.[28] 4Q 521, fragment 2 reads:

> [For the heav]ens and the earth will listen to His Messiah, [and
> all w]hich is in them will not turn away from the commandments
> of the holy ones. Strengthen yourselves, you who seek the Lord,
> in His service. All you who are hopeful in your hearts, will you
> not find the Lord in this? For the Lord will seek the pious and
> call the righteous by name. Over the poor [the humble] His spirit
> will hover and will renew the faithful in His strength. And He will
> honour the pious on the throne of His eternal kingdom. He will
> set prisoners free, opening the eyes of the blind, raising up those
> who are bo[wed down]. And f[or]ever shall I (?) hold fast [to the
> h]opeful and pious... And the fr[uit?] will not be delayed. And the
> Lord shall do glorious things which have never been achieved, [just
> as He promised]. For He shall heal the wounded/pierced, He shall
> revive the dead, and bring good news to the poor [the afflicted].
> He will... He shall lead the uprooted, and knowledge (?) and...

This text is full of allusions to Old Testament prophecy and to the psalms, and several New Testament passages share its theology. Isaiah 61:1 is present: 'The spirit of the Lord God is upon me, because the Lord has anointed me; he has sent me to bring good news to the oppressed, to bind up the broken-hearted, to proclaim liberty to the captives, and release to the prisoners.' So is Psalm 146:5–8: 'the Lord their God who made heaven and earth, the sea and all that is in them, who keeps faith for ever, who executes justice for the oppressed, who gives food to the hungry. The Lord sets the prisoners free, the Lord opens the eyes of the blind, the Lord lifts up those who are bowed down, the Lord loves the righteous.' And in Daniel 12:2 we read, 'Many of those who sleep in the dust of the earth shall awake, some to everlasting life, and some to everlasting shame and contempt.'

Fragment 7 of 4Q 521 reiterates the teaching of a resurrection: 'He [the Lord] who revives the dead of His people', and this is particularly close to the word of Jesus in his defence of resurrection against the Sadducees, in Matthew 22:32 (and parallels): 'He is the God not of the dead, but of the living.' In fact, we should read the whole reply of Jesus to John the Baptist's messengers: 'Go and tell John what you have seen and heard: The blind receive their sight, the lame walk, the lepers are cleansed, the deaf hear, the dead are raised, the poor have good news brought to them.' Those who knew Isaiah and the psalms, those who shared the Jewish expectancy of 4Q 521, would have understood that metaphorical or symbolic interpretations of the old biblical passages were no longer sufficient. Jesus was the real-life fulfilment of these prophecies – he did it, raising others, and after his death, people would realize that he, too, had risen, according to scripture. Peter tells his audience in Jerusalem that the Davidic Psalm 15 (16) had predicted it: 'Therefore my heart is glad and my soul rejoices, my body also rests secure. For you do not give me up to Hades [Sheol], or let your faithful one see the pit' (Acts 2:27).[29]

The Thanksgiving Hymns at Qumran point in the same general direction: 'You [the Lord] have purified man from sin, so that he may be made holy for you, with no abominable uncleanness and no guilty wickedness, so that he may be one with the children of your truth and share in the lot of your holy ones, so that bodies gnawed by worms may be raised from the dust, to the counsel of your truth' (1QH 19 [11]:10–14). Finally, the Talmud, published centuries after the rise of Christianity, but based, in parts at least, on pre-Christian oral teaching, emphasizes a bodily resurrection. We find it explicitly in Shabbat 88b, using a reference to Psalm 68:9 as scriptural evidence. In Sanhedrin 90b, 91a/b, it comes with an unequivocal rebuttal of those who claim that the resurrection cannot be derived directly from the *Torah*, combined with a quotation from Deuteronomy 32:39: 'See now that I, even I, am He, there is no God besides me. I kill and I make

THE DEAD SEA SCROLLS

alive, I wound and I heal, and no one can deliver from my hand.' Taanit 2a/2b quotes and interprets Ezekiel 37:13, from the prophecy of the dry bones, as proof of a physical resurrection: 'And you shall know that I am the Lord, when I open your graves, and bring you up from your graves, O my people.' Chagiga 12b speaks of a future resurrection of the dead, again quoting Psalm 68:9. And Ketubboth 111b compares the rising bodies to grain which is 'buried' naked, but will rise clad in splendour.[30]

But as much as we can detect similarities between the Old Testament, in the Dead Sea Scrolls and in rabbinical teaching, a decisive fact remains: the Jews who had seen and who taught that Jesus himself had risen from the dead did not simply claim that certain prophecies and, for example, Essene tenets, had finally been fulfilled in one historical person. The crucified and risen Messiah, proclaimed by Jews like Simon Peter and Sha'ul/Paul, could be understood on the basis of certain passages in scripture, but as a whole, it was a new revelation – not just fulfilment, but much more than that. As Gordon D. Fee put it, commenting on the Messiah's death for our sins and the prophecy of Isaiah 53:

> *Since Judaism did not interpret this passage [Isaiah 53:4–12]*
> *messianically, at least not in terms of a personal Messiah, and*
> *since there is no immediate connection between the death of Jesus*
> *and the idea that his death was 'for our sins', it is fair to say that*
> *whoever made that connection is the 'founder of Christianity'. All*
> *the evidence points to Jesus himself, especially at the last supper*
> *with his interpretation of his death in the language of Isaiah 53.[31]*

This messianic combination of death and resurrection (Mark 14:28 and parallels), which was once again – and for the last time – announced by Jesus at his Last Supper and on the way to the Mount of Olives, is the unparalleled cornerstone of the new faith. Paul finalized this teaching in his first letter to the Corinthians when he combined the death and the resurrection of Jesus as saving, eschatological truth for all humanity (1 Corinthians 15:12–28).

Godly ways

Many books have been written about traces of the Dead Sea Scrolls in the gospels, in Paul's letters and in other New Testament writings. And, as we saw above, there are good reasons for such traces. It is not their presence which should surprise us, but their absence. Every single scroll and scrap is available to scholars, and with a handful of exceptions, they have all been edited and – as far as possible, given their very fragmentary state – translated into English and other languages. The future work of scholars will not be about new discoveries, but about a proper understanding of the existing material. Positions which have been taken for granted will be reinvestigated, and surprising new insights may result. To give just one very recent example, not directly related to Christian questions, the question of celibacy among the Essenes, discussed in a previous chapter, was given a new twist in November 1999, when the Israeli anthropologist and archaeologist Joseph Zias provided unexpected evidence. Zias analysed the famous cemetery near the settlement at Qumran, where burials of women and children had been found next to those of men. These burials had convinced many Qumran scholars that the Qumran Essenes could not have been celibate, and auxiliary explanations such as that of certain exceptions at Qumran, of families of 'tertiaries' or families of employees living at the oasis of En Feshkha next door had been offered, to save the concept of general Essene celibacy, including the main settlement at Qumran. Zias, however, established that these women and children were not Essenes at all: their skeletons are no more than 300 years old; the women had beads around their ankles; their anthropological characteristics (such as average height) do not conform to those of any known Jewish burials of antiquity; all are directed towards Mecca – they belong to Muslim Bedouins. For centuries, Bedouin tribes from the Bethlehem area have been travelling south, as they still do, through the Wadi Qumran, to stay in the preferable climate of the Dead Sea area during the winter months. The Qumran plateau, not far from what was not visible any more as a former Jewish settlement and Roman barracks, provided them with a perfect burial site. And thus, a highly controversial 'fact' of Qumran archaeology has disappeared overnight. The so-called Essene family graves have turned out to be a burial site of a Bedouin tribe of the modern era.[32]

The fascination with dead people is, of course, common among archaeologists and anthropologists, although ultra-orthodox Jewish movements have made the life of those who dig for bones in Israel excruciatingly difficult. Disturbing a burial site is anathema to the very religious, and quite a few archaeologists have received phone calls with curses and death threats in the middle of the night. Even so, it is a well-known case of a 'sudden death' and burial which provides us with one of the real, rather than imagined, links between the Dead Sea Scrolls and the first Christians. At the beginning of the fifth chapter of Luke's Acts of the Apostles, we read the story of Ananias and Sapphira who had lied 'not to us men', as Peter put it, 'but to God', about their property and the percentage of the proceeds which they had donated to the community. Peter did not pronounce any sentence, let alone the death sentence, but when Ananias heard the apostle accuse him of his lie, 'he fell down and died. And great fear seized all who heard of it. The young men came and wrapped up his body, then carried him out and buried him' (Acts 5:5–6). Three hours later, Sapphira, the wife of Ananias, 'not knowing what had happened', appears on the scene, repeats the lie, hears Peter telling her the fate of her husband, falls down at the apostle's feet, dies and is buried next to her husband (5:10). The Essenes had a kind of property-sharing community, and a new candidate gave his property on a provisional basis at first; after a year, it passed into the community's keeping, but not into its possession.[33] This is precisely the scenario of Acts 5:4. Peter insists that the property of Ananias and Sapphira remained 'in their power', even though they had given it to the community for shared use. In other words, there was no reason to withhold anything. The community would exercise the trust of looking after this property until the day when the candidate would either become a full member or decide to leave. No legal change of ownership occurred, but truthfulness was of the essence. And the penalty for a lie in this matter was severe enough: 'If one of them has lied deliberately, he shall be excluded from the pure meal of the congregation for one year and shall do penance by being deprived of one quarter of his food ration' (Community Rule, 1QS 6:20–25, here 6:24–25).

Needless to say, ritual exclusion and temporary starvation are not lethal. The death of Ananias and Sapphira surpassed Essene punishment by far. However, Josephus points out that the Essene punishment could easily lead to the same deadly consequences: 'The outcast often perishes most miserably, for, bound by oaths and commitments, he cannot accept nourishment from strangers. Living on herbs, he starves, loses his strength, and perishes.'[34] In any case, it may be suggested that the incident of Ananias and Sapphira served a purpose: since the first Christian community on the south-west hill of Jerusalem, today's Mount Zion, and the Jerusalem Essenes behind the 'Essene Gate' were next-door neighbours, as we saw in a previous chapter,[35] the Jewish Christians could only hope to convince their neighbours of the veracity and viability of their message if their own standards of godly life were at least as strict and uncompromising as those of the Essenes. Ananias and Sapphira did not die because Peter had sentenced them, but die they did. And this was more than good enough to convince the Essenes next door that their rules and regulations of community life, and their strictness of discipline before God were anyone's match. In fact, it is difficult to imagine how the first Jewish Christian community on that hill could have lived a less committed, leisurely life even without 'peer pressure'. These were formative years. Deceit could not be tolerated, the eighth commandment was an inflexible yardstick, and Paul later emphasized that believers are 'God's temple, and God dwells in you. If anyone destroys God's temple, God will destroy that person. For God's temple is holy, and you are that temple' (1 Corinthians 3:16–17).

The Community Rule (1QS), which specifies how people who lied about their property should be punished, was one of the standard texts of the Essene way of life. Any Judeo-Christian group keen on convincing Essenes that Jesus was the promised Messiah and that a new community of the faithful was developing in his name had to know this text, just as Essene Jews would have been eager to read the first literary products of the new messianic, eschatological movement of Jesus followers. The sizeable success of the Christian message among Essene priests, reflected in Acts 6:7,[36] is as unsurprising as the traces of Essene influence on certain Christian community regulations. The Essenes who became 'obedient to the faith' did not come empty handed; in a fledgling movement which was beginning to shape its own structures, their expertise and traditions were as welcome as (for example) hellenistic elements provided by the circle of Stephen, or pharisaic learning which came with Paul. And yet, nothing was merely copied. The first Christian communities were no epigones. As we have seen again and again, vital ingredients cannot be traced to any Essene source whatsoever; sometimes, as with Ananias and Sapphira, the 'model' was surpassed; sometimes, much less was said or done.[37] Details of parables in the gospels which were anything but mysterious to contemporary hearers and readers can be understood more fully because of scroll fragments which tell us how Jews at the time of Jesus interpreted ancient prophecies or observations of daily life. And technical terms, misunderstood or misdated for a long time, can be seen in their true light.

One particularly important example is the office of *episcopos*, the 'overseer' of the community, which etymologically is the origin of the term 'bishop'. It has been interpreted as a comparatively late title of office in the 'church' (Philippians 1:1; 1 Timothy 3:1; Titus 1:7), yet its model is anything but late: it can be traced back to the Essene *mebaqqer* or 'guardian' of the Damascus Document.[38] One of the most pious Jews in the early Jerusalem community, James the brother of the Lord, who was killed in AD 62, was the first example of such a *mebaqqer–episcopos*, at least in the twenty years after the departure of Peter from Jerusalem in AD 41. And it was a famous Protestant scholar, not a Roman Catholic, who asked whether James was perhaps the first 'pope' – in the sense of a monarchic episcopate which originated in Jerusalem and spread via the Jewish-Christian communities.[39] Suggestions such as these may be controversial, but they open new avenues: suddenly, supposedly late Christian developments, second- or third-generation structures and hierarchical orders begin to look ancient and Jewish, part and parcel of the Jewish roots of Christianity. We know from the history of the church that the Jewish Christian 'wing' eventually lost its influence and authority throughout the Roman empire, and the rivalry between different bishoprics became a constant and lasting source of irritation; even in the fourth century, Emperor Constantine could not rely on any 'first among equals', let alone a pope in the medieval and modern sense, when he convened the Council of Nicea. But it was not least the strength of the position held by the local or regional bishop, the *mebaqqer–episcopos*, which led to such tensions. One community's Jerusalem was another community's Antioch, or Athens, or Rome. Neither the Damascus Document, nor Paul in his letters, nor James claimed that there was one bishop above all other bishops.

These overseers were in charge of 'camps', or branches of the overall community; in the hierarchical structure of the Essenes, one such 'guardian' was set over a camp, with other men, from highest to lowest rank, in charge of special tasks and duties. If, for the sake of the argument, we regard the Christian community in a city like Philippi as a 'camp', we recognize a difference over against the similarities: an Essene camp has one *mebaqqer*, but Paul speaks of more than one *episcopos* at Philippi (Philippians 1:1). Thus, once again, even a useful form of hierarchical structure was not simply imitated by the Christians. It was applied and adjusted according to their specific needs. The hierarchical structure reappears in 1 Timothy: there is a hierarchy of bishops above deacons, but again, there is no hierarchy among the bishops. Remarkably, though, bishops are supposed to be married with children, which conforms to the traditional image of a rabbi, or indeed any Jew for that matter, but conflicts with the special, celibate status of the Essene priestly hierarchy, Jesus and Paul himself.

As for James, who was married (1 Corinthians 9:5), he exercised his authority beyond Jerusalem, but did not act entirely on his own. The so-called Apostolic Council in Jerusalem, which paved the way for a concentrated mission among non-Jews (Acts 15:1–30) was teamwork and would have been impossible without Peter's decisive opening address – a speech which is a remarkable case of early Christian leadership and diplomacy (15:7–11). James in turn quotes Amos 9:11–12, and he does so in a form which is close to two Qumran texts: 4Q Florilegium (4Q 174) 1:10–12 and the Damascus Document, CD 7:16. And like these two Qumran fragments, James links the prophecy of Amos with another prophecy, 2 Samuel 7:13.[40] The most remarkable aspect of this rare use of Amos is its strategy: James does not reject the 'pagans'; on the contrary, he invites them into the fold, under the promise given to the house of David, of which of course he, like Jesus, was a member by direct lineage:

> *After this I will return, and I will rebuild the tent of David, which has fallen; from its ruins I will rebuild it, and I will set it up, so*

that all peoples may seek the Lord, even all the Gentiles over
whom my name has been called. Thus says the Lord, who has
been making these things known from long ago.

(Acts 15:16–17)

And, 'He shall build a house for my name, and I will establish the throne of his kingdom forever. I will be a father to him, and he shall be a son to me' (2 Samuel 7:13–14). Compare this to 4Q 174:10–12:

The Lord declares to you that he will build a house for you. 'I will
raise up your seed after you, I will establish the throne of his kingdom
forever. I will be his father and he shall be my son. He is the branch
of David… I will raise up the tent of David, which has fallen. That is
to say, the fallen tent of David is he who shall arise to save Israel.'

In a separate incident, even Paul had to understand the authority of James was that of a true 'overseer' who relied on trusted colleagues: concerned that Paul was doing too much too soon at Antioch, disrupting the sensitive equilibrium of Jewish and Gentile believers, he sent messengers to Peter who took swift action and reassured the Jewish-Christian community by eating with them rather than with the Gentiles (Galatians 2:11–14).[41] Paul himself, at the receiving end of these measures, was less than pleased, and his depiction of the scene is as frank as it is understandably one-sided. Even so, Paul admitted that Barnabas, the experienced diplomat of the early church who knew Antioch well, sided with Peter (2:13), and in a later letter, Paul himself pronounced the careful balance maintained by James, Peter and Barnabas:

To the Jews I became as a Jew, in order to win Jews. To those under
the law I became as one under the law (though I myself am not
under the law) so that I might win those under the law. To those

outside the law I became as one outside the law (though I am not free from God's law but am under Christ's law) so that I might win those outside the law.

(1 Corinthians 9:20–21)

No less a theologian than Tertullian (c. AD 180 – AD 220) was the first to see that Paul had learnt from the Antioch incident:[42] in the end, the 'overseer's' message and Peter's action had been beneficial to all concerned, a far-reaching example of the *mebaqqer–episcopos* structure at work during the early stages of Jewish and Gentile mission, before the death of James in AD 62 and the destruction of Jerusalem in AD 70. Adding to these credentials, the New Testament letter of James has recently been reattributed to the historical apostle, after decades of doubts about its authorship and date.[43] With the authority of someone who is confident enough to address all 'twelve tribes in the diaspora' (James 1:1), James admonishes and strengthens his readers and he does so in a language which is often reminiscent of the Community Scroll, 1QS. If James reckoned with people among the recipients of his epistle who knew the message of the 1QS document, his parallels would have been particularly poignant.[44]

James and the followers of Jesus in Jerusalem, like so many other Jews, knew about the writings and teachings of the Essenes, as they also knew about those of other Jewish groups of their time. And they not only knew the teachings, they knew the people themselves. As we saw before, Essenes, Pharisees, Sadducees, zealots and the others did not live in convents. They could be met almost everywhere. And one passage in the book of Acts may indicate that Essene priests even joined the first Christian community in Jerusalem. Conversions from one distinctive Jewish group to another were not unheard of: Paul was perhaps the most famous example – the Pharisee who became a follower of Jesus Christ. Other Pharisees became Jewish

Christians before and after Paul (Acts 15:5). Acts 6:7 mentions 'a great many of the priests who became obedient to the faith'. It is obvious that these many priests cannot have been Sadducees, members of the 'priestly' movement who refused (as we saw above) the basic starting point of a debate about Jesus as the crucified and risen Christ – the belief in a resurrection. The Pharisees did not even have a sizeable priesthood from which many priests could have converted. This leaves us with the Essenes, that messianic, eschatological and priestly community.[45] Essene converts – still Essenes by training, as much as the Pharisaic followers of Jesus did not join a new religion or 'church', but an inner-Jewish messianic movement, to begin with – could have helped to get the scrolls which were found in Cave 7 to the study library of Qumran; but conversely, they would have shared their knowledge and interpretation of scripture, and some of their scrolls, with the other messianic Jews. The allusions to Essene thought in James' speech of Acts 15, and in chapter 3 of his letter, could easily have been inspired by this very specific new target group.

In fact, a particularly intriguing 'present' which the Essene Christians would have brought with them was the combination of a fervent, immediate messianic hope and the urge to write about it. Some New Testament scholars think the first Christians did not write about Jesus until the second generation or so, in the 70s and 80s of the first century, when Jesus still had not returned. But the Qumran evidence tells us that the opposite scenario is true: a fervently messianic, eschatological Jewish movement does not meditate quietly until the final day dawns, or disappointment sets in and writing becomes a kind of therapy. On the contrary, they write, immediately, fast and efficiently, so that other Jews can share in their beliefs before it is too late. The first Jewish Christians would not have survived long, among such Jews, if they had not followed suit, put pen to paper and told others about Jesus. The origins of this literary tradition are not late; they are, of necessity, very early indeed, and parallel the oral tradition itself. Even the strategy of preserving the message of one's teacher – not just the community's interpretation of biblical prophecies, etc. – was part of this approach. At Qumran, six, perhaps more, different copies of 4Q MMT (Miqsat Ma'ase ha-Torah, 4Q 394–99, the Letter of the Teacher of Righteousness) have been found. Given such an example virtually next door, it is inconceivable that the messianic, eschatologically minded followers of the teacher Jesus would have left his words and deeds to the literary endeavours of later communities, a generation or two after their own time.

Peter, first among equals and James' supporter at the Apostolic Council, and the other original twelve disciples, had been aware of real-life Essenes before James joined the believers. Some scholars are even convinced that the Last Supper took place in an Essene guesthouse. The characteristics are striking: Jesus tells Peter and John to prepare the paschal lamb in a room which they shall find by following a man with a jar of water (Luke 22:8–13). Water in jars was carried by women. If men carried water, they were, as a rule, slaves who transported it in skins. Here, however, is a man who carried a jar. This appears to suggest that he belonged to a community without slaves and without women. Only one Jewish community in Jerusalem met these criteria: the Essenes.[46] An Essene guesthouse in Jerusalem would not be surprising, and the possibility that Jesus used it looks sound and practical; no one who stays at a Ramadan Hotel today is by definition a Muslim, nor are all guests of the popular YMCA hotel in Jerusalem Christians. Practical considerations abound, and the use of the Essene solar calendar (later developed into a solar-lunar one) rather than that of the lunar calendar of Pharisees and Sadducees may have been another of these down-to-earth decisions. The Essenes at Qumran even had their own subtle sundial, only recently discovered among the finds kept by the Israel Antiquities Authority in Jerusalem.[47] Today, the analysis of the different calendar systems in use at the time of Jesus may help us to synchronize the different chronologies of the Passover Week and the

Last Supper,[48] but even this does not turn Jesus or a gospel author into followers of the Essenes. Israel's leading English-language newspaper, *The Jerusalem Post*, has three dates on its front-page: first(!) the Christian date, then the Jewish date and finally the Islamic date. But no one doubts that it is a Jewish newspaper published by Jews in Israel, and the date as such is the same.

The great connection does not exist. The first Christians were no Essenes, and the Essenes did not all of a sudden mutate to Christians. James was not the Teacher of Righteousness, John the Baptist was no Essene, Paul was no Roman secret agent chasing the Essene Christians. The coding and conspiracy theories of authors such as Robert Eisenman (whose considerable contributions towards speeding up the publication of the scroll fragments must not be forgotten), Barbara Thiering or, outside the world of academe, Michael Baigent and Richard Leigh (whose *Dead Sea Scrolls Deception* has done more harm than any other publication to the public understanding of the scrolls) have created a world of their own which is not that of Judaism during the late Second Temple period. Real progress is most tangible in those many unspectacular cases where words or idioms suddenly illuminate a saying, or an action acquires a meaningful context thanks to Hebrew or Aramaic usage in a Dead Sea Scroll. The examples of *qahal* and its Greek equivalent *ekklesia* for a structured community, highlighting the fact that the historical Jesus could easily have spoken about a 'church' (to use the modern etymological derivative) in Matthew 16:18, was one such example; the *mebaqqer–episcopos* for the overseer of the community was another. Sometimes, a whole verse loses its 'mystique'. Generations of Christians have been brought up with the angels' message to the shepherds in the nativity story: 'Glory to God in the highest and on earth peace, good will towards men' (Luke 2:14, Authorized Version). Others, in the Roman-Catholic tradition, heard about 'peace to men of good will' (based on the Latin Vulgate) or 'peace on earth and [God's] favour towards men' (based on certain manuscripts and favoured, since Luther's translation, among the Reformers). The Thanksgiving Hymns from Qumran Cave 1 know the Hebrew expression as 'men of God's good pleasure' (1QH 4:32–33; 11:9).[49] These people are the object of divine predilection, and Luke can best be understood in this sense: 'Peace upon earth among men of his good will'. It would be too much to claim that Greek-writing Luke copied a Hebrew Essene idiom; but what the Qumran scroll does achieve is a textual clarification: it was like this that Jews at the time of Jesus could speak about God's will for his faithful. Insights of this kind will result in the years to come, when all the scrolls, including the smallest fragments, will be scrutinized for their language, vocabulary, style and idiom.

Saving the Scrolls: An Epilogue

THE CASE OF THE HIDDEN FUNGI

What is left, and what will be left? Latest techniques of restoring, preserving and reconstructing the scrolls and their fragments for the next generation of readers have furthered research into the texts themselves. And here, the scene is set for the next acts. When the Essenes fled Qumran in AD 68, what happened to them? Are there any traces of their writings or their thought and lifestyle after the collapse of traditional Judaism through the destruction of the Temple in AD 70? Will scholars respond to rumours that Essene traces can be discerned in early Christian writings outside the New Testament? Is there an 'Essene heritage' today?

Letters without ink

The Dead Sea Scrolls have been rediscovered 'by accident'. They could also be lost again by accident, if the fragments are left untreated. Ideally, damage detection and the search for further letters on damaged fragments should go hand in hand with the analysis of isolated scraps with a view to joining them together again. And first results are promising. Often enough, this is achieved by the time-honoured approach of trial and error, on the scholar's desk. But recently, a new technique was established which may reach the parts other microscopes cannot reach.

Ancient manuscripts on leather, parchment and papyrus challenge our patience and our ingenuity. More often than not, the traditional methods and even the latest 'state-of-the-art' techniques have come up against limiting factors. A fragment with missing letters or indecipherable remnants of ink is problem enough, but sometimes the very conditions under which such manuscripts are preserved are another. The most important of these is the protective glazing between which most ancient manuscripts are kept. It may indeed protect the manuscript from the acidic sweat of human fingers, but it may also conserve earlier organic damage – from tiny spiders, fungi and others. For the analyst who wants to decipher what is there, under a traditional or even an electronic microscope, glazing causes image degradation which may be so subtle that it is not even noticed, but which tends to influence, occasionally even to falsify, the reading, all the more so if the angle of the natural and artificial light – from a lamp next to the microscope, for example – creates shadows. Then again, many manuscripts are placed on a black surface. Average microscopes, and photographs produced with their help, turn a simple hole in the papyrus into a black spot or even a whole letter. Accidental specks of ink are identified as punctuation marks or letters, diagonal but straight lines are interpreted as curvatures, and so forth. A simple warning to scholars follows from such observations: never rely on a photo alone, unless you have taken it yourself, or it was taken in your presence, or the printed photograph is accompanied by a description of the process. Conversely, if the analysis of a manuscript is based on photos without the possibility of a detailed comparison with the original, this should be stated. If examining a manuscript through glass is difficult, the next step, if it includes the removal of the protective glazing, could be fraught with danger.

Damaged, loosened particles of letters have been kept in place merely by the pressure of the glazing. Active fungi, for example, have an appetite for papyrus fibres and ink. They eat the papyrus and detach the ink from the surface. Such particles will fall off when the glazing is removed. Leaving the glass where it is, however, does not really help, either. There are highly developed multi-spectral imaging

(MSI) techniques which manage to penetrate layers of dirt underneath the surface of the glass, or between glass and writing surface, but they are unable to produce a precise enough differentiation between particles of dirt, fibres (papyrus) or treated animal skin (leather, parchment), remnants of ink, and traces left by the writing instrument. And as the going gets tough, those who are not interested in the technicalities should skip the next three paragraphs!

Experiments with high-resolution X-ray radiography and Computer-Aided Tomography (CAT) have helped to overcome some of these problems. However, only materials with good density value differences are suitable for such high-resolution X-ray CAT detection. And, more importantly, a disadvantage of this technique for manuscript analysis is the fact that high-energy electromagnetic rays and X-rays can cause changes in the chemical composition – such as the severing of polymeric chains and the formation of free radicals, etc. And if this sounds complicated, so it is. Such changes, even if minute, may provoke lasting damage. In fact, we can be certain that some of the 'harmless' traditional methods of manuscript analysis have damaged the ink and the material. Jet propulsion infrared techniques, developed for space laboratories and cloud-penetrating spying cameras, may be less risky; in any case, they have achieved remarkable results:[1] in one case alone, some 900 new, i.e. previously illegible, words became visible in the Genesis Apocryphon (1Q 20).[2]

Since G.H. Bearman and his team began their work, a new application method of confocal scanning optical microscopy (CSOM) has been developed by the author of this book and the biologist Georg Masuch of Paderborn, which overcomes all the above-mentioned problems. Thanks to the capacity for direct, non-invasive serial optical sectioning of the manuscripts, and because of a significant improvement in lateral resolution, the organic writing material (papyrus, leather and parchment, or wood) can be analysed where it is: under glass, plexiglass, etc., of even more than 1 cm, which is twice the usual thickness of protective glazing. The manuscript is scanned by a diffraction-limited spot of laser light, and light transmitted or reflected by the in-focus illuminated volume element (so-called voxel) of the specimen, or by the fluorescence emission excited within it by the incidental light. It is then focused onto a photodetector. As the illuminating spot is scanned across the specimen, the electrical output of the detector is displayed on a TV monitor at the appropriate spatial position. And thus it builds up a two-dimensional image. Finally, a series of digitized two-dimensional images is able to provide high-resolution digitized data sets of three-dimensional distribution. This is suitable for subsequent image processing (colour or black-and-white print-outs and ektachromes or 'slides'). And they can be read with simple green-red 3D glasses for two a penny.

Depending on the individual substratum on which a text was written, and depending on the type and amount of information required, the analyst will have to apply different laser sources with separate excitation wavelengths, varying between 360 and 648 nanometres (nm) – and a nanometre is one thousand-millionth of a metre. The specimen can be analysed sequence by sequence, in different depths, both horizontally and vertically, in up to ninety individual micrometre layers – a micrometre (μm) is one millionth of a metre. Traces of ink, which have disappeared from the surface and cannot be detected by any of the traditional microscopal methods, and the indentation of the writing instrument will be rediscovered by the laser beam which detects ink in lower layers of the material and measures the impression of the stylus in micrometres, thereby indicating depth and direction of a letter.

In other words, missing letters become legible, whole words can be reconstructed and doubts can be removed by analysing and describing the way the letter was shaped. And a 'library' of scribal hands can be established, since all writers write differently. This means we will eventually accumulate an archive of scribal hands. It will enable scholars to reassemble the tiniest fragments written by the same scribe.

All of this is accessible straightaway: the up to ninety layers and their characteristics can be visualized separately or simultaneously on the computer screen as well as on a video print-out or slide. This results in the unequivocal reconstruction of letters and provides us with details about letter shapes. Scholars can see and study at leisure – thanks to the print-outs – a scribe's individual manner of beginning and ending a letter, and his or her preference for its formation. And since the results are immediately available, disputes about a correct reading can be solved without delay, and for good.

Thousands of tiny fragments of Dead Sea Scrolls have been put together by patient scholars since 1947, but there are still numerous pieces where certainty has remained elusive. Identifying scribal hands is one of the steps towards a reliable placing of fragments – all the more so as many different scribes were employed in the writing process of the Dead Sea Scrolls, often for one and the same scroll. The identification of the scribe may therefore tell us not only which scroll the fragments once belonged to, but also to which part of that scroll. The new confocal laser scanning analysis supplements, and may perhaps replace, a very costly and time-consuming technique developed at Brigham Young University: the DNA/DNS identification of the animal skin used for the leather scrolls. The identification of an animal's genetic code means that dislocated fragments can be put together if they came from the skin of the same sheep or goat, calf or antelope. As a rule, no animal has enough skin for more than one scroll, and on this basis, one may assume that fragments of skin which came from the same animal also belong to the same scroll. It is not foolproof, but one of many steps forward.

Everyone who works with ancient manuscripts has heard about 'palimpsests'. These are papyri (or documents on leather or parchment) where the first, original text has been washed or scraped off to make space for a new text. For the process of rescuing the original layer of the first text, traditional methods, among them ultraviolet microscopy, have been quite sufficient. The Dead Sea Scrolls and the Herculaneum discoveries in Italy before them have presented scholars with a related, but different problem, however: because of some nineteen centuries of pressure from soil (or lava, etc.), several manuscripts have been compressed in such a way that the once separate layers can no longer be clearly distinguished under the usual microscopes. Since the confocal laser scanning analysis is able to differentiate between up to ninety individual micrometre layers, it can separate even the most densely compressed manuscripts under the microscope and on the print-outs. It does not have to be done any more by mechanical means, with all the risks of damage to the original material. Such laser scanning 'separations' will be among the forthcoming projects on behalf of the Israel Antiquities Authority Jerusalem.[3]

A common and lasting heritage

While the reconstruction of ancient texts is of paramount importance to classical scholars, museum curators often have other priorities. As we saw above, ancient manuscripts tend to be affected by organic damage. Fungi, mycelia and other organisms live happily on the organic texture of ancient writing material. Humidity and temperature affect 'breeding' conditions. Confocal laser scanning microscopy identifies them, and differentiates between living and collapsed forms. For example, we found living fungi on the oldest extant papyrus of the biblical book of Esther, a Greek papyrus of the late second century AD.[4] And we traced collapsed mycelia on the oldest surviving Latin papyrus of Virgil's *Aeneid*, found on the Dead Sea fortress of Masada and dated to AD 73/74.[5] In the latter case, a relative humidity above fifty per cent is to be avoided at all costs, and in the former case, the papyrus must be treated urgently by methods tested in biochemical experiments.

A summary of damage-detection work so far suggests that ancient manuscripts of outstanding cultural, literary or theological importance should be analysed sooner rather than later – and this may be one of the most important challenges faced by scholars. After all, remaining questions of an Essene heritage will fascinate future generations. But even the question of whether the majority of Essenes who had not become Jewish Christians disappeared without trace after the destruction of Qumran in AD 68, Jerusalem in AD 70 and Masada in AD 73/74, or whether they found shelter among a movement like the Ebionites, who in turn later helped pave the way for Islam,[6] can only be tackled as long as the manuscripts remain well preserved, with increasing rather than decreasing legibility. In this sense, 'manuscripts' means of course all manuscripts of antiquity, not just those found near the Dead Sea. Unique as the Dead Sea Scrolls are, they are part of our common heritage.

Having said as much, we are faced with a dilemma. If Essenism, unlike other forms of Judaism, disappeared from the stage of world history in or around AD 70, perhaps – or perhaps not – seeping into the Ebionite movement which then ceased to exist in the early Middle Ages, scholarly endeavours may appear to be merely antiquarian, safeguarding and describing an ingredient of our heritage which has become defunct. Not least for this reason, the present book has resisted the temptation to speculate about underlying streams of Essene presence in modern Judaism and Christianity. It is a book about the Dead Sea Scrolls, not about Essenism, and it cannot be emphasized too strongly that the scrolls and the Essenes are not one and the same thing. The Babata archive, the Greek and Hebrew scrolls from the wadis and nahals south of Qumran, even many of the Qumran texts themselves, have different and independent pedigrees.

Seen like this, elements of Essene community structures,

exegesis and messianic fervour, as we find them in Qumran scrolls, have contributed to a fascinating mosaic, but there are many other stones besides. Early Christianity survived and developed into the leading religion of the Roman empire precisely because it treated Essene models and examples, like so many other Jewish traditions, as part and parcel of a common Jewish heritage, not as the one decisive yardstick on which to base the propagation of Jesus as the Messiah, or the hierarchical structure of the church. The uniqueness of the Dead Sea Scrolls, as collections of Jewish writings, should not deflect our attention from the fact that other influences of equal strength existed which cannot be documented any more by original manuscripts, simply because such manuscripts have not survived. But again and again, we did see that Essenes, first Christians and other Jews had one root in common of which we still have a complete record: the books of what we call the Old Testament. For our understanding of the overriding Jewish element in early Christianity, those books still are and always will be more important than the scrolls or any other – unlikely – discoveries in the future.

Jews in Cairo continued to read the Damascus Document into the high Middle Ages and beyond – we followed the route of the scroll discovered in the Ben Ezra synagogue of Old Cairo, and we saw how people such as the Christian theologian Hippolytus in Rome, around AD 200, and the early medieval Jewish Karaite movement in the Middle East knew much more about Essene thinking than someone like Philo or Josephus who studied their teaching before AD 70. It means that Essene writings remained well read, perhaps even popular, as Jewish religious documents, long after the demise of the movement itself. We may even doubt whether the Cairo Jews were aware that the Damascus Document was 'Essene', or whether they assumed it was merely the expression of a particular unidentified, but attractive inner-Jewish school of thought; after all, the name 'Essenes' never occurs in any of the scrolls. And if some scholars suggest that certain statements about early Christian practice should be attributed to Essene influence, we may find the wish, rather than the fact, is father to the thought.[7]

Even those Essenes who did become Jewish Christians in the first decades after Easter did not alter the all-decisive, shared teaching of the *Torah*, and most importantly, of the historical Jesus himself. The traces of their influence, and of general Essene influence on early Christianity which we did detect in the chapters of this book, do not make Christianity an Essene offshoot. This should have become obvious enough. The extreme definition of the inviolable holiness of the sabbath, the ultra-orthodox legalism, certain types of asceticism and other aspects of Essene teaching remained alien to the first Christians.

In other words, the Jewishness of early Christianity cannot be grasped by focusing on the Essenes, nor even by studying the Dead Sea Scrolls as a whole, nor by contrasting the different strands incorporated in these sources with the pharisaic theology preserved in the Talmud, nor by changing track completely, looking at Hellenistic Judaism in the Holy Land and in the diaspora. Without the uniqueness of the person of Jesus the Messiah, in history and faith, Christianity would have been nothing more than the fleeting crest of a wave. Herein, in the person of Christ, lies the true challenge for all of us who are fascinated by the heritage of the Dead Sea Scrolls.

Notes

Introduction

1. The most useful analysis remains O. Betz and R. Riesner, *Jesus, Qumran and the Vatican: Clarifications*, London, 1994.

2. That is, comparing the style of handwriting of as many dated, or datable, manuscripts as possible to another manuscript which we want to date.

Chapter I

1. R. de Vaux, *Archaeology and the Dead Sea Scrolls: The Schweich Lectures 1959*, London, 1973, pp. vii–viii. De Vaux led the first archaeological campaigns at Qumran. In spite of recurrent criticism of his conclusions, the results of his findings have been validated by recent research. Useful surveys of the continuous debate about the origins of the Essenes, Qumran and the scrolls can be found in the varied contributions to a recent volume, F.H. Cryer/Th.L. Thompson (eds), *Qumran Between the Old and New Testaments* (Copenhagen International Seminar 6), Sheffield, 1998.

2. De Vaux, *Archaeology and the Dead Sea Scrolls*, p. 93; B. Pixner, 'Unravelling the Copper Scroll Code: A Study on the Topography of 3Q 15', *Revue Biblique* 11 (1983): 323–65; and others. On Secacah as Qumran, see also H. Eshel, 'A Note on Joshua 15:61–62 and the Identification of the City of Salt', *Israel Exploration Journal* 45 (1995): 37–40.

3. See below in this chapter, 'An interlude: celibacy or marriage?'

4. Confirmed by the Community Rule (also called the Manual of Discipline) 6, 18–23.

5. Quite literally, since the palm trees of En Feshkha next door were visible from the settlement.

6. See Chapter II.

7. Synesius of Cyrene, *Dion or Of Life After His Example* 3, 2.

8. Philo, *On Abraham* 14.

9. In the description of manuscripts, the Septuagint is abbreviated LXX, which is the Roman numeral for seventy and thus renders the meaning of the Latin word 'Septuaginta'. According to an old tradition, seventy (or seventy-two) men translated the Torah from Hebrew into Greek. The Letter of Aristeas, second century BC, is the most elaborate account of this tradition.

10. Philo, *Quod omnis probus liber sit* 75–79.

11. This insistence on the Essenes' communitarian lifestyle, which goes far beyond Pliny's text, should not be understood as a description of poverty. The community as such was probably quite wealthy, profiting by the donations of newcomers and others, and the list of hidden treasures in the Copper Scroll from Cave 3 may well be a reliable guide to their considerable property. Cf. also the Community Rule, 1QS 1:11–12, etc.

12. It may be said that there were no professional merchants at Qumran, but they certainly bought and sold, as Philo himself states a few sentences further down. The Essenes in the 'camps' outside Qumran certainly engaged in trade, and had both male and female servants (CD 11–13).

13. This and the following translation closely follow G. Vermes and M. Goodman (eds), *The Essenes According to the Classical Sources*, Sheffield, 1989, pp. 20–21, 26–31.

14. Philo, *Apologia pro Iudaeis* 11–18 (cf. Eusebius, *Praeparatio Evangelica* 8, 6–7) .

15. Many scholars have assumed that the so-called Testimonium Flavianum (*Antiquities* 18, 63–64) is an interpolation by later Christian scribes. Recent linguistic research has shown, however, that there are no solid philological reasons to assume that Josephus could not have written what he wrote about Jesus, if it is properly understood. Conversely, his account of the illegal killing of James in AD 62 (*Antiquities* 20, 200–3) is undisputed and has led a majority of classical historians to date the New Testament book of Acts, which ends before it reaches the year of James' death, to the period before AD 62.

16. Josephus, *Life* 10–11.

17. *Antiquities* 18, 20; *War* 2, 124.

18. CD 12:19–23; 14:3–6.

19. Cf. Philo, *De Vita Contemplativa* 1–2; *Quod omnis probus liber sit* 12.

20. The most daring hypothesis was suggested by B. Rocco, who thought that Clement of Rome, one of the first Christian overseers or 'bishops' of Rome and author of at least one important letter among the New Testament Apocrypha (1 Clement), was a convert from Essenism and one of the 'many [Essene] priests' who became Christians according to a recent interpretation of Acts 6:7. See B. Rocco, 'San Clemente Romano e Qumran', *Rivista Biblica* 20 (1972): 277–90. See also Chapter VII.

21. M. Broshi, 'The Archaeology of Qumran', in D. Dimant and U. Rappaport (eds), *The Dead Sea Scrolls*, Leiden, 1992, pp. 103–55. A German scholar, H. Stegemann, even thinks there were merely fifty to sixty Essenes at Qumran: *Die*

Essener: Qumran, Johannes der Täufer und Jesus, Freiburg, 1993, pp. 69–71.

22. Josephus, *War 2*, 120–25. The translation follows Vermes and Goodman, *The Essenes According to the Classical Sources*, pp. 38–39.

23. On the whole passage, cf. the Community Rule (Manual of Discipline) 5:13–14; 6:2–6; Rule of the Congregation 1QSa 2:11–22.

24. Hippolytus of Rome, *Refutation of All Heresies* 9, 21. The translation follows Vermes and Goodman, *The Essenes According to the Classical Sources*, pp. 64–67.

25. Hippolytus of Rome, *Refutation of All Heresies* 9.27. Josephus seemed to think the Essenes did not believe in a bodily resurrection, but in that of the soul: *War 2*, 154-55; *Antiquities* 18,18.

26. Murabba'at 45, 6. P. Benoit, J.T. Milik and R. de Vaux, *Les Grottes de Murabba'at, DJD II*, Oxford, 1961, pp. 163–64. The term *chasidim* is very rare in ancient Hebrew texts, but it occurs twice in the Qumran scroll 4Q 521, the so-called Messianic Apocalypse.

27. Roman arrowheads were found, but the date as such can be determined by the lack of Jewish coins after AD 68, followed by the sudden presence of Roman coins minted as from AD 67/68. See De Vaux, *Archaeology and the Dead Sea Scrolls*, pp. 36–44, particularly p. 41, on the problems connected with dating from coinage. The Roman coins were discovered in the archaeological level above the Jewish coins, which implies a chronological sequence of occupation. Some of the Roman coins came from the army mints at Caesarea and Dora, where the troops had been stationed in AD 67/68. Cf. F. Rohrhirsch, *Wissenschaftstheorie und Qumran: Die Geltungsbegründungen von Aussagen in der Biblischen Archaeologie am Beispiel von Chirbet Qumran und En Feschcha*, Freiburg/Göttingen, 1996, pp. 230–34.

28. *War 2*, 152–53.

29. The abbreviation CD means 'Cairo–Damascus' (although another explanation is the French 'Codex de Damase'), and refers to Salomon Schechter's discovery, in 1896/97 – exactly fifty years before the discovery of the first Qumran cave – of tenth- and eleventh-century manuscripts of this book in the *genizah* of the Ben Ezra Synagogue in Old Cairo, and to the land of 'Damascus', mentioned in the book as the place where the New Covenant was made. Some scholars have assumed 'Damascus' is merely symbolic, a cryptogram perhaps for Qumran or Babylon, but recent research into CD and the Copper Scroll leads to the conclusion that Qumran (Secacah) and Damascus (or Babylon) are indeed separate places. 'The land of Damascus' probably means the whole region of the Yarmuk, one of the main settlement areas of the Essenes together with Qumran and Jerusalem. Furthermore, people in the region of Damascus used an Aramaic dialect, Nabatean, which was 'exported' to Qumran. Among other such finds, the great library Cave 4 contained a Nabatean letter (4Q 343).

30. See also CD 10:21; 11:5–6; 12:19; 12:23; 13:20; 14:3; 14:9; 19:2.

31. *War 2*, 160.

32. As the preceding sentence says, 'The Sabbath is holy,' some scholars have assumed that the Jerusalem celibacy applies only to the sabbath. But this is clearly not the case. The statement about the sabbath is a matter-of-fact observation in a list of rules and regulations, unconnected to the preceding and the following sentences.

33. *War 5*, 145.

34. See B. Pixner, D. Chen and S. Margalit, 'Mount Zion: The Gate of the Essenes Re-excavated', *Zeitschrift des Deutschen Palästina-Vereins* 105 (1989): 85–95, with plates 8–16.

35. On the purifying baths, the latrines and the rituals linking them, see above all B. Pixner, *Wege des Messias und Stätten der Urkirche*, Giessen/Basel, 3rd ed., 1996, pp. 180–209.

36. *War 2*, 148–49.

37. 4Q 213a, no. 3–4, published by M. Stone and J.C. Greenfield, *Qumran Cave 4 XVII, DJD XXII*, Oxford, 1996, pp. 33–35, with plate II.

38. F.M. Cross and E. Eshel, 'Ostraca from Khirbet Qumran', *Israel Exploration Journal* 47 (1997): 17–30; Cross and Eshel, 'The "Yahad" (Community) Ostracon', in A. Roitman (ed.), *A Day at Qumran: The Dead Sea Sect and its Scrolls*, Jerusalem, 1997, pp. 38–40.

39. See, for example, the Community Rule (1QS).

40. See note 20 above, and Chapter VII.

41. The most vociferous advocate of the theory of foreign origins is Norman Golb. But the first scholar to suggest constructively that at least one identifiable group of Qumran texts – everything written in Greek – was imported is Emanuel Tov: 'Hebrew Biblical Manuscripts from the Judean Desert: Their Contribution to Textual Criticism', *Journal of Jewish Studies* 39 (1988): 10–25.

42. F.M. Cross, *The Ancient Library of Qumran and Modern Biblical Studies*, Grand Rapids, rev. ed., 1989, p. 57.

43. F.M. Cross, 'The Early History of the Qumran Community', in D. Freedman and J. Greenfield (eds), *New Directions in Biblical Archaeology*, Garden City, 1971, p. 77.

44. Cf. A. Rabinovich's note in *The Jerusalem Post*, international edition, week ending 7 February 1998, p. 4. I owe further information to the archaeologist and anthropologist Joe Zias of Jerusalem.

45. Pliny, *NH* 5, 73, writes *infra hos Engada*, which means that En Gedi was situated south of the Essene settlement, which is accurate if Qumran is meant, but could *theoretically* be understood as a description of En Gedi below the settlement of the Essenes, therefore referring to an Essene settlement somewhere above En Gedi itself.

46. At Qumran, fragments were found in Caves 4 and 11.

47. *War* 4, 402–4.

Chapter II

1. Philo, *De Vita Mosis II*, 25–44, particularly 37.

2. G. Mercati, *Note di letteratura biblica e cristiana antica*, Rome, 1901, pp. 28–60. Mercati rediscovered Origen's text in a ninth-century manuscript of the psalms preserved at the Bibliotheca Ambrosiana, Milan. He published the manuscript in 1958: *Codex Rescriptus Bybliothecae Ambrosianae O 39 sup. phototypice expressus et transcriptus*, Città del Vaticano, 1958. See also, for a brief comment and a plate, B. Metzger, *Manuscripts of the Greek Bible: An Introduction to Palaeography*, New York/Oxford, 1981, pp. 108–9 (plate 30). In other words, since 1901 every biblical scholar who had forgotten the reference about the Jericho cave in Eusebius's *Church History*, 6, 16, 1–4 could and should have been aware of Origen's own reference to a scroll cave near Jericho. For an assessment of the debate about the Mercati manuscript and Origen's philological knowledge, cf. E. Ulrich, 'Origen's Old Testament Text: The Transmission History of the Septuagint to the Third Century BC', in Ch. Kannengiesser/W.P. Peterson (eds), *Origen of Alexandria: His World and His Legacy*, Notre Dame, 1988, pp. 3–33; repr. in E. Ulrich, *The Dead Sea Scrolls and the Origins of the Bible*, Grand Rapids/Cambridge/Leiden, 1999, pp. 202–23.

3. Eusebius, *Church History* 6, 16, 1–4.

4. There is no evidence for a return of Essenes to the Qumran settlement and caves after AD 68, and one of the archaeological certainties about Qumran is the fact that the caves were not reused by anyone until their discovery in 1946/47. But this does not apply to the whole region. In fact, some Nahal Hever caves were used for the first time in c. AD 135, and the Khirbet Mird finds are fifth or sixth century AD and later – deposited by Christian settlers and monks.

5. O. Braun, 'Der Brief des Katholikos Timotheus I über biblische Studien des 9. Jahrhunderts', *Oriens Christianus* 1 (1901): 299–313; R.J. Bidawid, *Les Lettres du Patriarche Timothé*, Rome, 1956; T. Darmo, *Letters of Patriarch Timothy*, Trichur, 1982.

6. Among his examples is Matthew 2:23, 'He will be called a Nazarene,' which is not mentioned anywhere in the Old Testament. However, Matthew does not claim to give a *verbatim* prophecy; he refers to 'words' (plural) of 'the prophets' (again plural) and therefore merely provides the gist of prophetic teaching. Passages such as Isaiah 11:1, also Isaiah 4:2; 53:2; Jeremiah 23:5; 33:15; Zechariah 3:8; 6:12 and others may have come together. (Judges 13:5 must be excluded, since it is not a messianic prophecy and refers to a Nazorite, something Jesus never was.) Another of Timothy's examples is 1 Corinthians 2:9, 'As scripture says: "What no eye has seen and no ear has heard, what the mind of man cannot conceive, all that God has prepared for those who love him,"' which could indeed be a single quotation from a popular writing outside the Hebrew canon, the Apocalypse of Elijah (a lost work suggested by Origen), or the Ascension of Isaiah (where it occurs almost literally; but this book may be younger than 1 Corinthians), or a paraphrasing combination of Isaiah 64:3 and 65:16 with Jeremiah 3:16. From the time of Origen, scholars have suggested different solutions; and Timothy was quite entitled to look for the answer in a new supply of Hebrew scrolls.

7. This is the odd bit about this letter – why did Timothy write to fellow Christians nowhere near Jerusalem, rather than to someone in Jerusalem, whether Jew or Christian? Did he think the scrolls had been handed over to them? This would have been highly unlikely, given the story of their discovery, which involved an Arab and Jews (who would have had every reason to guard them), but no Christians.

8. *Tanakh* is the common Jewish name for the Hebrew Bible. It is an acronym composed of the initial letters of the names of the three sections of the Jewish Bible: *Torah, Nevi'im, Ketuvim* – the Law, the Prophets and the Writings.

9. Masoretes is a collective term for the Jewish philologists who began to edit the Hebrew text of the Bible on the basis of all available manuscripts, in the eighth century AD, adding – among other editorial measures – diacritical signs to establish the vocalization of the consonant text. There were different 'schools' in East and West; in the end, after centuries of fluctuation, the western Ben Asher family carried the day, not least thanks to the influence of Maimonides who had access to the Ben Asher *Aleppo Codex* and considered it authoritative.

10. See the facsimile edition by S. Löwinger, *Codex Cairensis of the Bible from the Karaite Synagogue at Abbasiya*, Jerusalem, 1971. For a commentary on the text and its tradition, see M.H. Goshen-Gottsein, *The Rise of the Tiberian Bible Text*, Cambridge, MA, 1963.

11. A leading Qumran scholar, Lawrence Shiffman, has suggested that the Essene Zadokites were in fact Sadducees. According to his theory, a group of originally Sadducean priests, led by the Teacher of Righteousness, developed into the group which left us the scrolls found at Qumran (see e.g. L.H. Shiffman, 'The Sadducean Origins of the Dead Sea Scroll Sect', in H. Shanks (ed.), *Understanding the Dead Sea Scrolls*, New York, 1992, pp. 35–49, 292–94). There is of course an etymological relationship between 'Zadokites' and 'Sadducees'. And there are similarities between the Letter of the Teacher of Righteousness, 4Q MMT, and Sadducean teaching as we know it from the later Mishnah (second century AD and later, e.g. Babylonian Talmud, Yadayim 4, 6–7). But certain agreements would have been normal among a multitude of Jewish movements. It does not make them identical. If the Sadducean priests did indeed derive their group name from Zadok, then the least one should say is this: they developed in a completely different direction from that of the orthodox wing which eventually reached the Dead Sea. None of the early, contemporary informers – Philo and Josephus – saw any identity or near-identity of Sadducees and Essenes, and Josephus in particular, who had first-hand experience, differentiates unequivocally between these movements. The Qumran tenets of a bodily resurrection and of the existence of a multitude of angels, for example, are diametrically opposed to mainline Sadducean theology. One might suggest, however, that the common heritage of Zadok was used strategically by the Qumranites: they intended to be the true 'Sadduceans', the true followers of the priesthood of Zadok. Occasional similarities, including – for example – the refusal of an oral law were also shared by Jesus who was most certainly never anywhere near the Sadducees in his theology (cf. e.g. Josephus, *Antiquities* 13, 297, with Mark 7:6–8, and 4Q MMT).

12. Cf. P. Kahle, 'The Age of the Scrolls', *Vetus Testamentum* 1 (1951): 38–48; E. Bammel, 'Höhlenmenschen', in E. Bammel, *Judaica: Kleine Schriften I*, Tübingen, 1986, pp. 95–106.

13. Cf. R. Gundry, *Matthew: A Commentary on His Handbook for a Mixed Church Under Persecution*, Grand Rapids, 2nd ed., 1994, pp. 4, 18.

14. Rabbi Hillel the Elder, who lived from c. 70 BC to c. AD 10 and was, according to some scholars, an inspirer (if not even a personal teacher) of Saul/Paul the Pharisee, once taught that no one is able to keep everything in the law, but that fifty-one per cent (the 'absolute majority', so to speak) would qualify a person for the kingdom, to enter the new eschatological world. (C.G. Montefiore and H. Loewe (eds), *A Rabbinic Anthology*, London, 1938, pp. 594–97, 664.) A contemporary of Hillel, Shammai (c. 50 BC to c. AD 30, like Jesus a builder by trade, who probably died in the same year as Jesus), preferred a much harsher yardstick: even ninety-nine per cent is not enough. But since both Hillel and Shammai were archetypal representatives of the oral law of the scribes and Pharisees, it may be doubted whether Jesus or the Zadokite Essenes would have had much time for them. Two of Shammai's sayings, however, come close to their own teachings: 'Study the Torah regularly,' and, 'Say little, but do much' (Babylonian Talmud, Avoth 1, 15).

15. These similarities are matched, as it were, by numerous differences between Jesus and the Teacher of Righteousness. For example, Jesus taught that the arrival of God's kingdom coincides with the revelation of salvation for all those who repent, accepting God's rule (Mark 1:14–15). The Teacher of Righteousness, on the other hand, saw the same eschatological event as a time of judgment and punishment (1Q pHab 2:6–7; 7:1–8).

16. S. Schechter, *Documents of Jewish Sectaries, vol. I: Fragments of a Zadokite Work*, Cambridge, 1910. A re-edition, including the material belonging to the Damascus Document from Caves 4, 5 and 6, was published eighty-two years later by Magen Broshi: *The Damascus Document Reconsidered*, Jerusalem, 1992.

17. For a detailed analysis, Aramaic text and (German) translation, see K. Beyer, *Die aramäischen Texte vom Toten Meer*, Göttingen, 1984, pp. 188–209. See also new material provided by M.E. Stone and J.C. Greenfield, 'The Prayer of Levi', *Journal of Biblical Literature* 112 (1993): 247–66.

Chapter III

1. In the Copper Scroll from Qumran Cave 3, the central cave in this wadi, called Cave Netef, is mentioned as a hiding place for treasures. In the fourth century, Christian hermits lived in the cave, most notably St Chariton, after whom it was later named.

2. M. Burrows, J.C. Trever and W.H. Burrows (eds), *The Dead Sea Scrolls of St Mark's Monastery*, vol. I, New Haven, 1950 (with the great Isaiah scroll, and the Habakkuk Commentary (i.e. the Habakkuk Pesher); followed in 1951 by vol. II with the Manual of Discipline (i.e. the Community Rule)).

3. 'Nahal' (Hebrew) and 'wadi' (Arabic) mean the same thing, a watercourse which is completely

dry for most of the year, but becomes a river, and occasionally a life-threatening torrent, in the rainy season. In Dead Sea archaeology, the choice between the two words is often determined by the nationality of the archaeologists or their masters; i.e. since Qumran was discovered under Jordanian rule, we call it Qumran and speak of Wadi Qumran, rather than of Secacah and the Nahal Secacah. As the Murabba'at finds were made under Jordanian rule, and by non-Jewish discoverers, Wadi Murabba'at is more common than Nahal Dagar, and Israeli scholars accept this state of play, not least because the manuscripts have all been given 'Mur.' numbers. The caves between Masada and En Gedi, however, and these two sites themselves, belonged to Israeli territory even before 1967 and were explored by Israeli archaeologists, often aided by the army who supplied military logistics and experienced mountaineers. Hence, here it is 'nahal' rather than 'wadi'.

4. The team was led by Lankester Harding, director of the Jordanian-run Antiquities Authority at the John-Rockefeller-Museum and Roland de Vaux of the French Dominican École Biblique, both based in East Jerusalem.

5. This date, 'the first Heshvan in the sixth year of Masada', appears to be based on the Jewish occupation of Masada, previously held by the Romans, in AD 66.

6. For the Aramaic text of all three documents, see Beyer, *Die aramäischen Texte vom Toten Meer*, pp. 306–9.

7. For the use of the Greek term, cf. Josephus, *Antiquities* 18, 156.

8. From this perspective, John's Gospel was a welcome deepening and broadening of the synoptic tradition, surplus to the legal niceties of the time.

9. Cassius Dio, *Roman History* 59, 14, 3.

10. See, e.g. Babylonian Talmud, Taan 18a.

11. P. Benoit, J.T. Milik and R. de Vaux (eds), *Discoveries in the Judean Desert II: Les Grottes de Murabba'at*, 2 vols (*textes et planches*), Oxford, 1961, p. 234 and plate 81.

12. C. Austin (ed.), *Comicorum Graecorum Fragmenta in Papyris Reperta*, Oxford, 1973, no. 360.

13. For the necessity to have such synagogue libraries with the scrolls of the Old Testament, see Acts 17:11; and, in detail, C.P. Thiede, *Ein Fisch für den römischen Kaiser. Juden, Griechen, Römer: Die Welt des Jesus Christus*, Munich, 1998.

14. Masada fragment 1039–200, Qumran fragments 4Q 400–7; 11Q 17. See C. Newsom

(ed.), *Songs of the Sabbath Sacrifice: A Critical Edition*, Atlanta, 1985.

15. For the texts and their analysis, see H.M. Cotton and J. Geiger (eds), *Masada II: The Latin and Greek Documents*, Jerusalem, 1989.

16. For the text, see Cotton and Geiger, *Masada II*, pp. 31–35, with plate 1.

17. Menander's comedy, *Thais*, is quoted in 1 Corinthians 15:33 (some scholars think Menander himself had originally taken it from Euripides' play *Aiolos*, fr. 1024); Aratus' natural-philosophical poem *Phainomena* 5 is quoted by Paul in his speech on the Areopagus, Acts 17:28; and a tragedy of Aeschylus, *Agamemnon* 1624, is quoted by the risen Christ, and requoted by Paul to Herod Agrippa and Festus at Caesarea Philippi, Acts 26:14 (the latter, about the kicking against the goads, was a popular line which occurred in similar form in another play by Aeschylus, *Prometheus* 325, and later in a work by the youngest of the three classical Greek tragedians, Euripides, *Bacchae* 795). Titus 1:12 quotes from Epimenides, *Peri Chresmon* (some scholars think Paul took it from Callimachus, *Eis Dia*, 8). For a discussion of classical quotations in the New Testament and their background, see Thiede, *Ein Fisch für den römischen Kaiser*, pp. 43–56, 224, 325–28, 358.

18. See Thiede, *Ein Fisch für den römischen Kaiser*, pp. 35–51, 323–27.

19. For further examples of Virgil quoted in papyri discovered at Roman military sites, see A.K. Bowman and J.D. Thomas (eds), *The Vindolanda Writing Tablets (Tabulae Vindolandenses II)*, London, 1994, p. 66.

20. See also, for example, the pioneering studies of S. Lieberman, *Greek in Jewish Palestine*, New York, 1942, and *Hellenism in Jewish Palestine*, New York, 1950, and the more recent publications of Martin Hengel, such as 'The Pre-Christian Paul', in J. Lieu, J. North and T. Rajak (eds), *The Jews Among Pagans and Christians*, London, 2nd ed., 1994, pp. 29–52.

21. Clement of Alexandria, *Stromateis* 1, 23; Pseudo-Eustathius, *Commentary on the Hexaemeron* (in *Patrologia Graeca* 18, 729D); Eusebius, *Praeparatio Evangelica* 9, 28–29 (including the reference to Alexander Polyhistor).

22. See, with further references, M.E. Stone (ed.), *Jewish Writings of the Second Temple Period*, Assen/Philadelphia, 1984, 125–30.

23. With one exception, νομος, of which, however, equivalent terms such as 'commandment' and 'to order' occur.

24. In Benoit, Milik and De Vaux, *Discoveries in the Judean Desert II (DJD II)*, vol. I, *textes*, pp. 275–77, and vol. II, *planches*, 103.

25. For an attempt at a partial reading, see C.P. Thiede and M. d'Ancona, *The Quest for the True Cross*, London, 2000, pp. 135–41.

26. See, for example, H.J.M. Milne, *Greek Shorthand Manuals: Syllabary and Commentary*, London, 1934; H. Boge, *Griechische Tachygraphie und Tironische Noten: Ein Handbuch der antiken Schnellschrift*, Berlin, 1973; H. Boge, *Die Entzifferung griechischer Tachygraphie auf Papyri und Wachstafeln, mit Bemerkungen zu den Giessener tachgraphischen Fragmenten sowie zur Geschichte der Tachygraphie und zur Frage der Priorität ihrer Erfindung*, Giessen, 1976; J.C. Teitler, *Notarii and exceptores*, Amsterdam, 1985; D. Ganz, 'On the History of the Tironian Notes', in P.F. Ganz (ed.), *Tironische Noten*, Wiesbaden, 1990, pp. 35–51; C.P. Thiede, 'Schrift VII: Tachygraphie/Kurzschrift', in *Das Grosse Bibellexikon*, Wuppertal/Giessen, 2nd ed., 1990, pp. 1401–3; C.P. Thiede, 'Shorthand Writing and the New Testament', in C.P. Thiede, *Rekindling the Word: In Search of Gospel Truth*, Leominster, 1995, pp. 80–83.

27. Bowman and Thomas, *The Vindolanda Writing Tablets (Tabulae Vindolandenses II)*, p. 72.

28. For a detailed discussion, see Thiede and d'Ancona, *The Quest for the True Cross*, pp. 123–34.

29. Thiede and d'Ancona, *The Quest for the True Cross*, pp. 135–41.

30. E.g. E.J. Goodspeed, *Matthew, Apostle and Evangelist*, Philadelphia, 1959, pp. 16–17; R.H. Gundry, *The Use of the Old Testament in St Matthew's Gospel*, Leiden, 1967, pp. 182–84; C.P. Thiede and M. d'Ancona, *The Jesus Papyrus*, London, 1996, pp. 158–60; for Greek shorthand among Jewish Christians in Rome, in the mid-first century, see B. Orchard and H. Riley, *The Order of the Synoptics*, Macon, 1987, pp. 269–73.

31. The case for Tertius as a shorthand expert is argued by E.R. Richards, *The Secretary in the Letters of Paul*, Tübingen, 1991, pp. 169–72.

32. E.g. Justin Martyr (at the time of the revolt a young man, from Shechem/Nablus), *Apology* 1, 31; Eusebius, *Church History* 4, 8, 4.

33. Babylonian Talmud, Aboda zara 4, 5.

34. For the first evaluation of the new finds, see B. Lifshitz, 'Greek Documents from the Cave of Horrors', *Israel Exploration Journal* 12 (1962): 201–7.

35. The first complete edition with the Bedouin finds of the early 1950s and the Israeli discovery of 1961 is D. Barthélemy (ed.), *Les dévanciers d'Aquila: Première publication intégrale du texte des fragments du dodécaprophéton trouvés dans le désert de Juda, précédée d'une étude sur les traductions et récensions grecques de la Bible réalisées au premier siècle de notre ère sous l'influence du rabbinat palestinien*, Leiden, 1963.

36. The oldest existing evidence for palaeo-Hebrew dates from the sixteenth century BC. See W.F. Albright, 'The Early Alphabetic Inscriptions from Sinai and their Decipherment', *Bulletin of the American Schools of Oriental Research* 110 (1948): 6–22; cf. W.F. Albright, *Palestinian Inscriptions*, Princeton, 3rd ed., 1969.

37. In Psalm 15:3, the half sentence, 'who has no malice on his tongue', is missing.

38. See Y. Yadin, *The Finds from the Bar-Kokhba Period in the Cave of Letters*; N. Lewis, Y. Yadin and J.C. Greenfield (eds), *The Documents from the Bar Kokhba Period in the Cave of the Letters: The Greek Papyri*, Jerusalem, 1989.

39. H. Dessau, *Inscriptiones Latinae Selectae, (ILS)*, Berlin, 1892–1916, No. 2683.

40. Cf. also K. Rosen, 'Jesu Geburtsdatum, der Census des Quirinius und eine jüdische Steuererklaerung aus dem Jahr 127 nC.', *Jahrbuch für Antike und Christentum* 38 (1995): 5–15. For the edition of (most of) the Babata texts, see N. Lewis (ed.), *Judean Desert Studies: The Documents from the Bar Kokhba Period in the Cave of Letters*, Jerusalem, 1989. Cf. also J. Starcky, 'Un contrat nabatéen sur papyrus', *Revue Biblique* 61 (1954): 161–81: the first publication of an (unrecognized) Babata archive document found by Bedouins years before the official Israeli excavation under Yigael Yadin.

41. Joseph was a builder or craftsman (the Greek word *tektôn*, Matthew 13:55; Mark 6:3, means 'building worker/artificer/craftsman' rather than 'carpenter' in the narrow sense of someone working with wood; cf. in the Greek Old Testament 1 Samuel 13:19; 2 Samuel 5:11; Isaiah 44:12–17; Hosea 13:2; cf. also our modern word 'architect', the 'arch-*tektôn*' or 'chief-builder'). He would have gone where the work was, and Sepphoris was being rebuilt as the magnificent capital of Galilee precisely at the time of his move. Nazareth, some three miles away, was one of the nearest settlements.

Chapter IV

1. S. Goranson, 'Qumran: A Hub of Scribal Activity', *Biblical Archaeology Review* 20/5 (1994): 36–39.

2. The winter villa theory was championed by Pauline Donceel-Voute and Robert Donceel. See e.g. P. Donceel-Voute and R. Donceel, 'The Archaeology of Chirbet Qumran', in M.O. Wise, N. Golb, J.J. Collins and D.G. Pardee (eds), *Methods of Investigation of the Dead Sea Scrolls and the Chirbet Qumran Site: Present Realities and Future Prospects*, New York, 1994, pp. 51–72. The same volume also contains one of Norman Golb's published theories of a (Jewish) military installation:

'Chirbet Qumran and the Manuscript Finds of the Judean Wilderness', pp. 51–72.

3. See M. Broshi and H. Eshel, 'How and Where Did the Qumranites Live?', paper delivered at the Utah Conference on the Dead Sea Scrolls, 1996, used in: Roitman, *A Day at Qumran*, pp. 24–26, 59, 69. Cf. R. Price, *The Stones Cry Out: What Archaeology Can Reveal About the Truth of the Bible*, Eugene, 1997, pp. 288–94.

4. A. Schick, O. Betz and F.M. Cross, *Jesus und die Schriftrollen von Qumran*, Berneck, 1996, p. 209.

5. See also R. Reich, 'A Note on the Function of Room 30 (the "*Scriptorium*") at Khirbet Qumran', *Journal of Jewish Studies* 46 (1995): 157–60. Reich concludes that there is no convincing alternative to the writing table suggestion first made by R. de Vaux. The peculiar shape of the tables, narrowing towards the base, would have helped the scribe to assume a comfortable squatting position on the lower bench, crossing his knees and resting them against the base. For evidence of ancient Jews writing on tables – contrary to usual practice before late antiquity – cf. S. Krauss, *Talmudische Archaeologie*, vol. III, Leipzig, 1912, p. 158.

6. On this aspect of the Qumran library system, see below.

7. A preliminary report has just been published: J. Gunneweg/M. Balla, 'How Neutron Activation Analysis can assist research into the provenance of the pottery at Qumran', in D. Goodblatt, A. Pinnick, D. R. Schwartz (eds.), *Historical Perspectives: From the Hasmoneans to Bar Kokhba in Light of the Dead Sea Scrolls*, Leiden 2001, 179-185.

8. Other techniques have been used to study the specific local technologies of pottery production, such as Dispersive X-Ray Fluorescence and Petrography.

9. And confirmed in a conversation with the author in Jerusalem, in August 1999.

10. The jar was restored from its fragments at the John-Rockefeller-Museum, Jerusalem, for the exhibition 'Dalla Terra alle Genti – La diffusione del cristianesimo nei primi secoli', Rimini, 1996, for which the author of this book acted as director of the Comitato scientifico. See C.P. Thiede, 'Giara iscritta', in A. Donati (ed.), *Dalla Terra alle Genti – La diffusione del cristianesimo nei primi secoli*, Milano, 1996, p. 323, with a photo of the reconstructed jar.

11. If the *wahw* is understood as a *holam*, it must be vocalized as an open 'o' (e.g. like the 'o' in English 'lore'). An alternative would be the vocalization as *shuruq*, to be pronounced like an 'oo', as in 'flute'. Ideally, the two pronunciations can be distinguished by a dot above (*holam*) or in the middle of the letter (*shuruq*). But there is, of course, no dot on this early first-century jar.

12. J.A. Fitzmyer, 'A Qumran Fragment of Mark?', *America* 126 (26 June 1972): 649. Since the jar was broken and the fragments were therefore not actually found *in it*, some sceptics have doubted that they ever were inside. It is a bit like doubting the yolk was in the broken egg.

13. For pictures, see e.g. *The Illustrated Bible Dictionary*, Leicester, 1986, vol. I, p. 558, and vol. III, pp. 1409, 1469, 1648.

14. Josephus, *War* 3, 233. It may be identical to the 'Rumah' mentioned in the annals of Tiglath-Pileser III; cf. also 2 Kings 23:36. The spelling of Josephus is Greek and therefore inconclusive; the Hebrew of 2 Kings 23:36 is not identical with that on the jar: instead of the *aleph* on the jar, the Galilean (?) place name is written with a final *heh*.

15. H. Stegemann, *Die Essener, Qumran, Johannes der Täufer und Jesus: Ein Sachbuch*, Freiburg/Basel/ Wien, 4th ed., 1994, pp. 59–63.

16. De Vaux, *Archaeology and the Dead Sea Scrolls*, pp. 10–11.

17. For example, a six-month and a twelve-month exclusion are mentioned in a fragment associated with the Community Rule, 4Q 265 fr. 1, I, 13 and II, 9–10; a period of two years is mentioned in the Community Rule 1QS VII, 17–25.

18. See the Community Rule 1QS VI, 6–9.

19. O. Gillie, 'Scroll Fragment Challenges Basic Tenet of Christianity', *The Independent*, 1 September 1992, quoting from an interview with the Qumran scholar, Geza Vermes.

20. I.H. Marshall, *The Gospel of Luke: A Commentary on the Greek Text*, Grand Rapids/Exeter, 1978, p. 67.

21. A reliable 'scroll catalogue' is included in G. Vermes, *The Complete Dead Sea Scrolls in English*, London, 4th ed., 1995, pp. 602–19.

22. Fragments of Aramaic Enoch in Caves 1, 2, 4 and 6 are among the most important Qumran discoveries; they have opened up new avenues of Qumran research (see e.g. G. Boccaccini, *Beyond the Essene Hypothesis: The Parting of the Ways Between Qumran and Enochic Judaism*, Grand Rapids/ Cambridge, 1998). The Enoch writings are not originally Essene, but belonged to the popular, commonly known non-biblical Jewish theology of the time. References and quotes in the New Testament are further evidence for the popularity of Enoch. See, for example, Jude 13–16; 1 Peter 3:19 and Mark 12:25. The latter passage is striking. Jesus answers the Sadducees in the dispute about the bodily resurrection of the dead and says, 'For when they rise from the dead, they neither marry nor are given in marriage, but are like angels in heaven.' In the Greek text, the introductory *gar*, 'for/since', implies a

reference to a well-known teaching. And the source is Enoch 15:6 with 51:4.

23. But see a Prayer of Manasseh in the manner of a psalm, 4Q 381.

24. The five small fragments from Cave 8, the one unidentified papyrus from Cave 9 and the *ostracon* from Cave 10 are inconclusive.

Chapter V

1. E-mail to the author, 14 April 1999. Charlesworth's assessment may sound provocative, but it comes from a scholar who spends much of his time chasing unknown scroll fragments still owned by private collectors. When someone like him mentions such a figure, it cannot be dismissed as a wild guess. Tantalizingly, we shall have to wait and see if a fragment of Esther turns up, not in another cave at Qumran, but in a safe somewhere in France or California. But even without it, the case for Esther among the Dead Sea Scrolls, and in orthodox Jewish thought at the time of the Essenes, is strong enough.

2. Megillah 7a; Yadaim 3, 5.

3. His title and name, Rabbi Moses Ben Maimon, were abbreviated RMBM and vocalized 'Rambam'.

4. Cf. W. Anderson, *Introduction and Exegesis of Esther*, Nashville, 1954, p. 830.

5. Megillah 7a.

6. A recent proponent of the 'missing elements' is J.D. Levenson, *Esther: A Commentary*, London, 1997. See, however, among others, R. Gordis, 'Studies in the Esther Narrative', *Journal of Biblical Literature* 95 (1976): 43–58; R. Gordis, 'Religion, Wisdom and History in the Book of Esther – A New Solution', *Journal of Biblical Literature* 100 (1981): 359–88; A.D. Cohen, 'Hu ha-Goral: The Religious Significance of Esther', *Judaism* 23 (1974): 87–94.

7. Outside the book of Esther, this feast is first recorded in 2 Maccabees 15:36, where it is called 'the Day of Mordecai'.

8. Pirqe Avoth 3:1 – 4:22 offers the most concentrated and powerful passage.

9. Cf. R.H.H. Donin, *To Be a Jew: A Guide to Jewish Observance in Contemporary Life*, New York, 1991, p. 303; S. Bamberger (ed.), *Siddur S'fat Emet*, Basel, 1992, p. 310.

10. *Antiquities* 11, 227; translated after R. Marcus (ed.), *Josephus, Jewish Antiquities, Books IX–XI*, Cambridge/London, 1978, pp. 424–25.

11. S. Goldman, 'Esther. Introduction and Commentary', in A. Cohen (ed.), *The Five Megilloth: Hebrew Text and English Translation with Introduction and Commentary*, London, 11th ed., 1974, p. 194.

12. In 4:14, the Greek text is inconclusive, as 'from another place' is rendered by the classical Greek composite adverb *allothen*, quite literally 'from another place'.

13. Cf. C.P. Thiede, *Small is Beautiful: The Wholeness of Fragments in Ancient and Modern Experience*, Beer-Sheva (CGS Lecture Series No. 1), 1998, pp. 13–16.

14. See e.g. Genesis 33:20; Deuteronomy 12:11; 1 Samuel (1 Kings) 12:17; 1 Kings (3 Kings) 17:21; Job 5:8; Psalm 13:4; 17:6; 98:6; 114:4; 117:5; Isaiah 55:6.

15. In the canonical Greek text of Esther, God/*theos* occurs in 2:20; 6:1; 6:13. A later version, the so-called A-Text, has further references to God in its canonical main text: 4:14; 4:16; 7:2. For a full discussion of Greek Esther, see K.H. Jobes, *The Alpha-Text of Esther: Its Character and Relationship to the Masoretic Text*, Atlanta, 1996; E. Tov, *The Text-Critical Use of the Septuagint in Biblical Research*, Jerusalem, 2nd rev. enl. ed., 1997.

16. See pp. 127–30.

17. J.T. Milik, 'Les modèles araméens du livre d'Esther dans la grotte 4 de Qumrân', *Revue de Qumrân* 15 (1992): 321–406; Beyer, *Die aramäischen Texte vom Toten Meer*, pp. 113–17. James Charlesworth calls the fragments a 'Commentary on Esther', a category which indicates 'that we cannot claim that Esther was not important to the Qumranites and was thus not in their collection', e-mail to the author, 14 April 1999. Cf. Vermes, *The Complete Dead Sea Scrolls in English*, pp. 578–79, who thinks Milik discovered 'an Aramaic *model* of Esther at Qumran'. Cf. also S. Talmon, 'Was the Book of Esther Known at Qumran?', *Dead Sea Discoveries* 2 (1995): 249–67.

18. D.L. Sayers, 'A Vote of Thanks to Cyrus', in D.L. Sayers, *Unpopular Opinions*, London, 2nd ed., 1951, pp. 23–58, here pp. 23–24. Cf. C.P. Thiede 'A Critic of the Critics: Dorothy L. Sayers and New Testament Research', in Thiede, *Rekindling the Word*, pp. 113–26.

19. Cf. Beyer, *Die aramäischen Texte vom Toten Meer*, pp. 113–17.

Chapter VI

1. The inverse fragment on clay, 7Q 19, must have come from a manuscript. It is only natural to assume it was a papyrus.

2. 4Q 120 (Leviticus in Greek) and 4Q 127 (Greek fragments of an Exodus commentary or paraphrase) in P.W. Skehan, E. Ulrich and J.E. Sanderson (eds), *Qumran Cave 4, IV: Palaeo-Hebrew and Greek Biblical Manuscripts*, Oxford, 1992. Further papyri in Cave 4, all in Hebrew

or Aramaic and mainly unpublished, are: 4Q 223–24 (from the Book of Jubilees); 4Q 252–54 (a commentary on Genesis); 4Q 255 (a rule); 4Q 272–73 (fragments of the Damascus Document); 4Q 302 (a praise of God); 4Q 310 (an unknown Aramaic text); 4Q 311 (an unknown Hebrew text); 4Q 331–33 (an unknown historical work); 4Q 347 (a deed in Aramaic); 4Q 361 (some 'doodles'); 4Q 382 (a paraphrase of the books of Kings); 4Q 384 (a text based on Jeremiah); 4Q 391 (a text based on Ezekiel); 4Q 398 (a fragment of the Letter of the Teacher of Righteousness, the Miqsat Ma'ase ha-Torah); 4Q 478 (a text on festivals); 4Q 482–83 (probably from the Book of Jubilees); 4Q 489 (an Aramaic apocalypse); 4Q 499 (fragments of hymns and prayers); 4Q 500 (a benediction); 4Q 502 (a marriage ritual); 4Q 503 (daily prayers); 4Q 512 (a ritual of purification); 4Q 512–20 (undeciphered papyrus fragments); 4Q 559 (a biblical chronology).

3. They have been identified as fragments from Daniel, Samuel/Kings, a benediction and a hymn. A single, unidentified scrap of papyrus was found in Cave 9.

4. Two famous and undoubtedly pre-Christian exceptions are the Papyrus Rylands Greek 458, from the mid-second century BC, with fragmentary passages from Deuteronomy, and the voluminous Papyrus Fouad 266, from the late second century BC, consisting of fragments from Genesis and from two scrolls of Deuteronomy. Both are papyri.

5. Most books on the Dead Sea Scrolls still ignore the issue. It is as though the early studies have failed to make their mark. The first to try was H.M. Orlinsky, 'Qumran and the Present State of Old Testament Text Studies: The Septuagint Text', *Journal of Biblical Literature* 78 (1959): 26–33. It was not until 1981 when the first serious attempt at a detailed evaluation was made: Tov, *The Text-Critical Use of the Septuagint in Biblical Research*; this was followed by E. Ulrich, 'The Greek Manuscripts of the Pentateuch from Qumran, Including Newly Identified Fragments of Deuteronomy (4Q LXXDeut)', in A. Pietersma and C. Cox (eds), *De Septuaginta: Studies in Honour of John William Wevers on His Sixty-Fifth Birthday*, Mississauga, 1984, pp. 71–82. Patrick W. Skehan's preliminary editions of 4Q LXXLev[a] (1957) and 4Q LXXNum (1977) did not inaugurate a debate about the importance of the discoveries, nor did John Wevers' reference to them in his Göttingen Septuagint editions of Leviticus and Numbers (*Leviticus. Septuaginta: Vetus Testamentum Graecum II.2*, Göttingen, 1986; *Numeri. Septuaginta: Vetus Testamentum Graecum III.1*, Göttingen, 1982). Eugene Ulrich evaluated the state of affairs in 1992: E. Ulrich, 'The Septuagint Manuscripts from Qumran: A Reappraisal of Their Value', in G.J. Brooke and B. Lindars (eds), *Septuagint, Scrolls and Cognate Writings*, Atlanta, 1992, pp. 49–80. Ulrich's essays on the Greek text of the Old Testament are collected in Part 2, 'The Scrolls, the Septuagint and the Old Latin', in E. Ulrich, *The Dead Sea Scrolls and the Origins of the Bible*, pp. 165–289. Another outstanding recent study is M. Müller, *The First Bible of the Church: A Plea for the Septuagint*, Sheffield, 1996.

6. The Cave 7 papyri were published by M. Baillet, J.T. Milik and R. de Vaux (eds), *Les 'Petites Grottes' de Qumran (DJD III)*, 2 vols, Oxford, 1962.

7. *Iota, alpha, omega*: pap4Q LXXLev[b]/4Q 120, fr. 20, line 4.

8. See the analysis by Ulrich, 'The Septuagint Manuscripts from Qumran', in Brooke and Lindars,*Septuagint, Scrolls and Cognate Writings*, pp. 49–80.

9. Ulrich, 'The Septuagint Manuscripts from Qumran', p. 74

10. There may be text-critical reasons for the divergence. But the decisive point is simply that Stephen's speech correctly reflects a reliable Greek text which is corroborated by a pre-Christian Hebrew manuscript discovered at Qumran.

11. E. Tov, 'The Contribution of the Qumran Scrolls to the Understanding of the LXX', in Brooke and B. Lindars, *Septuagint, Scrolls and Cognate Writings*, pp. 11–47, here 18–19. Tov explains that the Hebrew Bible texts at Qumran cannot be identified as the precise textual model used by the Septuagint translators: 'The Hebrew scrolls from which the LXX was translated, mainly in Egypt, have *not* been found in Qumran, and neither should one look for them in Palestine. Since many, if not most of the biblical texts of the third and second centuries BC were unique, there is but one place where they should be sought, namely in Egypt itself, even though ultimately they were imported from Palestine' (pp. 42–43).

12. The Samaritan Pentateuch is an edition of the five books of the Torah which came into being during the second century BC at the latest. It was the indirect result of a split within Judaism, when the Samaritans – known to New Testament readers not least because of Jesus' parable of 'the good Samaritan', Luke 10:25–37, and his encounter with the Samaritan woman, John 4:7–30 – separated from Jerusalem and the Temple, to build an independent centre with a temple on Mount Gerizim. As they preserved the Torah in their own, distinctive Hebrew writing which did not go through the stages leading

to the mainstream Hebrew 'Masorah', many scholars regard it as an important witness to the state of the Hebrew text at the time when the Septuagint was translated. No less than 6,000 variants over against the text of the Masoretes have been counted, most of them details of orthography (that is, the spelling of words). But, in a number of cases, the vocabulary and the structure have changed, and quite often, such details are corroborated by Qumran discoveries. This, in any case, would imply that the Samaritan text was widespread and widely read prior to the destruction of Jerusalem in AD 70. Scholars mention at least three cases where the New Testament agrees with the Septuagint against the standard Hebrew text, but in a manner which makes it very likely that the Septuagint itself was based on a text preserved by the Samaritan Pentateuch: see Acts 7:4 and 7:32, and Hebrews 9:3–5.

13. That is, the translation of the Hebrew and Greek Bible, including the New Testament, into Latin, commonly (*vulgata*) distributed and received.

14. M. Baillet, 'Les manuscrits de la grotte 7 de Qumrân et le Nouveau Testament', *Biblica* 53 (1972): 508–16, here p. 516; M. Baillet, 'Les manuscrits de la grotte 7 de Qumrân et le Nouveau Testament, *Suite*', *Biblica* 54 (1973): 348–49.

15. J. O'Callaghan, *Los papiros griegos de la Cueva 7 de Qumrân*, Madrid, 1974, pp. 89–91.

16. To be precise, there were three such fragments in Cave 7: fragment 1, with the thirty-five letters on six lines, has two more letters, *sigma* and *pi*, σπ, on the other side, the *verso*. It seems both sides once belonged to different papyrus documents, as did the tiny fragments 2 and 3 of 7Q 19. Fr. 2 has four illegible letters, perhaps *iota* and *epsilon*, ιε, twice, above each other; fr. 3 has the word (or part of a word) τον, and, on the other side, an *alpha*, α. See Baillet, Milik and De Vaux, *Les 'Petites Grottes' de Qumrân, DJD III*, pp. 145–46 and Planche XXX.

17. O'Callaghan, *Los papiros griegos de la Cueva 7 de Qumrân*, pp. 89–91.

18. 'Les quelques mots que l'on peut saisir font penser à un texte de caractère théologique', Baillet, Milik and De Vaux, *Les 'Petites Grottes' de Qumrân, DJD III*, pp. 145–46.

19. See C.P. Thiede, 'Das unbeachtete Qumran-Fragment 7Q 19 und die Herkunft der Höhle 7', *Aegyptus* 74 (1994): 123–28, with particular reference to the writings of Philo, e.g. *De Abrahamo* 61; *Quis Rerum Divinarum Heres* 106; 159; *De Fuga et Inventione* 4; *De Specialibus Legibus* I, 214, II, 104,

134; *De Congressu Quaerendae Eruditionis Gratia* 34, 90; *De Optificio Mundi* 77; *De Decalogo* 8, 37.

20. See *Contra Apionem* 2, 45. An exception to this 'rule' may be Philo's *De Abrahamo* 236, and his *De Vita Mosis* II, 40, where there is no 'holy' before the 'writings' (or after them, for that matter). In the first passage, however, Philo does not talk about the Bible, but refers to a common 'wisdom of the world'. And in the second passage, he discusses the usage of Greek and Chaldean literature in translation.

21. See H.J. Leon, *The Jews of Ancient Rome*, Peabody, rev. ed., 1995, pp. 135–37.

22. Now lost, although it was suggested that the tiny scrap 7Q 9 could contain parts of Romans 5:11–12. But while it is true that the few letters on 7Q 9 match the passage in Romans without alterations, there are too few of them to be certain that it could not be a completely different text. See O'Callaghan, *Los papiros griegos de la cueva 7 de Qumrân*, pp. 73–74.

23. J. O'Callaghan, '¿Papiros neotestamentarios en la cueva 7 de Qumrân?', *Biblica* 53 (1972): 91–100; O'Callaghan, 'Notas sobre 7Q tomadas en el "Rockefeller Museum" de Jerusalén', *Biblica* 53 (1972): 517–33.

24. This includes Luke. The widespread theory that he was a non-Jew is highly improbable and was based on extremely weak sources: in the early fifth century, Jerome invented Luke's pedigree as a proselyte from paganism who became a Jew before he converted to the Christian faith (*Quaestiones hebraicae in Genesim*). Jerome and those who think he was a kind of Godfearer apparently misunderstand Colossians 4:11–14. No source older than Jerome calls Luke a (former) Gentile or a proselyte. This is a remarkable fact, as he would otherwise have been the great exception, living proof, as it were, that the Gentile mission had 'caught' an outstanding historical and literary mind, the only non-Jew among the authors of the New Testament writings. The silence of the early sources on this point seems to indicate that he was neither a Gentile nor a proselyte, but a Jew like all the others. See further E.E. Ellis, *The Gospel of Luke*, London, 1966, pp. 52–53; cf. A. Deissmann, *Light from the Ancient East*, Grand Rapids, 1927, pp. 437–38.

25. Stephen and his circle belonged to these 'Hellenists' (see Acts 6:1–12, 54–60). The description, reiterated by Luke, may not imply that they did not know any Hebrew at all – but Greek was certainly their home language. If Stephen had remained an (exclusively) Greek-speaking Jew, it would follow that he gave his great speech in Greek. And this in turn would

imply that his opponents were fluent enough to understand him and react as they did. Historically, such a scene is absolutely plausible in the Jerusalem of the AD 30s.

26. See e.g. D. Webster, *The Concept of Mission in the Old Testament*, London, 1973; and in detail, with valuable source material, P. Borgen, *Early Christianity and Hellenistic Judaism*, Edinburgh, 1996, pp. 45–69. A negative position is presented by M. Goodman, 'Jewish Proselytizing in the First Century', in Lieu, North and Rajak, *The Jews Among Pagans and Christians in the Roman Empire*, pp. 53–78.

27. On 3 January 1999, with Prof. Shemaryahu Talmon, one of the editors of the Dead Sea Scrolls and former president of the Hebrew University of Jerusalem, Prof. James Charlesworth of Princeton University, editor of the Dead Sea Scrolls Pseudepigrapha, Bargil Pixner, the excavator of the Essene Gate on Mount Zion, Prof. Joan M. Vernet of Cremisan College, Bethlehem, a Cave 7 specialist, the church historian Prof. Nicola Bux of Bari University, and the author of this book.

28. This was his relationship with Jesus according to Paul's letter to the Galatians 1:19, and Josephus, *Antiquities* 20, 200–1.

29. It was put like this, unchallenged, by Joan Vernet at the Jerusalem panel discussion mentioned above. And no one doubted that the texts concerned, those Jewish-Christian writings later collected as the New Testament, could have been written and dispatched before AD 68. As far as Mark's Gospel is concerned a date around, or prior to, AD 68 has become the majority consensus in recent years, with some scholars opting for dates up to (or down to) AD 40. Even 1 Timothy has occasionally been given dates earlier than AD 68, irrespective of the question of authorship – a recent development engendered not least by J.A.T. Robinson's courageous and mould-breaking monograph, *Redating the New Testament*, London, 1976.

Chapter VII

1. As for 1 Timothy, the fashionable tendency to doubt Pauline authorship and pre-AD 70 dates was decisively challenged by J. Jeremias, 'Zur Datierung der Pastoralbriefe', *Zeitschrift für die neutestamentliche Wissenschaft (ZNW)* 52 (1961): 101–4; followed by more recent authors such as S. de Lestapis, *L'Énigme des Pastorales de St Paul*, Paris, 1976; B. Reicke, 'Chronologie der Pastoralbriefe', *Theologische Literaturzeitung* 101 (1976): 81–94; J. van Bruggen, *Die Geschichtliche Einordnung der Pastoralbriefe*, Wuppertal, 1981; G.D. Fee with his commentary *1 and 2 Timothy, Titus*, San Francisco, 1984; and M. Prior, *Paul the Letter-Writer and the Second Letter to Timothy*, Sheffield, 1989, pp. 13–59. Studies in English in the same vein also include the aforementioned monograph by J.A.T. Robinson, *Redating the New Testament*, pp. 67–85 and D. Guthrie, *New Testament Introduction*, Leicester, 4th ed., 1990, pp. 607–55. The dates attributed to 1 Timothy vary between AD 58 and 61.

2. P. Grelot, 'Notes sur les propositions du Pr. Carsten Peter Thiede', *Revue Biblique* 102 (1995): 589–91, here p. 591. Grelot calls those who follow the reasoning of O'Callaghan and myself 'journalistes qui ignorent toutes les données du problème et qui sont prêts à accepter n'importe quoi en raison de cette ignorance'.

3. Cotton and Geiger, *Masada II*, pp. 31–34.

4. The infrared photo has been reproduced repeatedly; it can best be studied in O'Callaghan, *Los papiros griegos de la cueva 7 de Qumrân*, lamina IV. The text was first edited by O'Callaghan in his paper '¿1 Tim. 3, 16; 4, 1.3 en 7Q 4?'.

5. Also called 'paragraphus', after the horizontal bar underneath the first word or syllable in such a line, which is not visible here, of course, since the beginning of the line has not survived.

6. See e.g. F. Voelker, *Papyrorum Graecarum syntaxis specimen*, Bonn, 1900, p. 36; E. Mayser, *Grammatik der griechischen Papyri aus der Ptolomaerzeit I/1*, Leipzig, 1906, p. 207; L. Rademacher, *Neutestamentliche Grammatik. Das Griechisch des Neuen Testaments im Zusammenhang mit der Volkssprache*, Tübingen, 2nd ed., 1925, p. 47. José O'Callaghan thought of a further possibility: ρητων (*rêtôn*) instead of ρητως (*rêtôs*) can also be understood as a true textual variant. The word as we have it here, the adverb ρητως, is extremely rare. There is not a single instance in the Greek Old Testament, the Septuagint. And it occurs only once in the New Testament, in the standard text of 1 Timothy, where it means 'expressly'. Ρητως, however, occurs twice in the Greek Bible (Exodus 9:4 and 22:8) and elsewhere in Greek literature. As a nominalized adjective it means, according to the standard Greek lexicon, something 'that can be spoken or enunciated, communicable in words' (H.G. Liddell, R. Scott and H.S. Jones, *A Greek-English Lexicon*, with a rev. supplement, Oxford, 1996, p. 1570). If the scribe of 7Q 4 thought of this much more familiar word when the text was dictated to him or when he copied it from another manuscript, his sentence *to de pneuma ton rhêtôn* would mean 'The Spirit of what can be spoken', 'the Spirit of words', 'the Spirit which speaks', meaning of course the Spirit from which words come, the Spirit behind words. As this passage in 1 Timothy is about the prophetic

word of the Holy Spirit, it is a perfectly sensible conjecture. But the simple spelling shift from *sigma* to *nu* remains of course the easier solution.

7. In his reconstruction of the *missing* part of this line, O'Callaghan wrote πλανης, whereas the standard Greek text has πλανοις, but this is not a variant of 7Q 4 in the strict technical sense, since the alternative form can be found in other manuscripts of this verse as well: P, Ψ and several minuscules (i.e. later manuscripts written in a small, running hand), etc. He did it, of course, because he wanted to remain as close as possible to the average number of letters per line in the 7Q papyri.

8. Between vo]μιστεον and υπαρχειν, the four-word sequence η κλτεον ωστε θεους is missing.

9. S.R. Pickering (ed.), 'P. Macquarie Inv. 360 (+ P.Mil. Vogl. Inv. 1221): Acta Apostolorum 2.30–37, 2.46 – 3.2', *Zeitschrift für Papyrologie und Epigraphik (ZPE)* (1986): 76–78, with plates I b, c. The papyrus P91 omits other words, as well: εσμεν in Acts 2:32 and και after οτι in Acts 2:36. A similar case can be found in the oldest payprus of John's Gospel, the famous P52 at the John Rylands University Library, Manchester: in John 18:37, the second *eis touto*, 'for this', is missing. P52 is the only manuscript without these words. And yet, their omission is not even noted in the apparatus of Nestle-Aland's standard edition of the Greek New Testament, let alone taken seriously as a text-critical problem – although it is one of the many pieces of circumstantial evidence for the unrhetorical, sparse style of the oldest gospel papyri. Cf. C.P. Thiede, *The Oldest Gospel Manuscript? The Qumran Fragment 7Q 5 and its Significance for New Testament Studies*, Exeter/ Carlisle, 1992, pp. 17–19.

10. G.-W. Nebe, '7Q 4 Möglichkeit und Grenze einer Identifikation', *Revue de Qumran* 13 (1988): 629–33.

11. See the analysis in Thiede, *The Earliest Gospel Manuscript?*, pp. 48–52, and C.P. Thiede, 'Papyrologische Anfragen an 7Q 5 im Umfeld antiker Handschriften', in B. Mayer (ed.), *Christen und Christliches in Qumran?*, Regensburg, 1992, pp. 57–72, here 59–64.

12. E.A. Muro, 'The Greek Fragments of Enoch from Qumran Cave 7 (7Q 4, 7Q 8, & 7Q 12 = 7Q en gr = Enoch 103:3–4, 7–8)', *Revue de Qumran* 70 (1997): 307–11.

13. É. Puech, 'Notes sur les fragments grecs du manuscrit 7Q 4 = 1 Hénoch 103 et 105', *Revue Biblique* 103 (1996): 592–600; É. Puech, 'Sept fragments grecs de la Lettre d'Hénoch (1 Hén 100, 103 et 105) dans la grotte 7 de Qumrân (= 7Q he>ngr)', *Revue de Qumran* 70 (1997): 313–23.

14. It was argued by Nebe that the New Testament already quotes Enoch in Greek; he refers to Beyer, *Die aramäischen Texte vom Toten Meer*, pp. 249–50. The one unequivocal Enoch quotation in the New Testament occurs in Jude's letter, verses 14–15. But it is quite unlikely that Jude quoted a Greek version of Enoch. The whole style of the quotation as indeed the style of the whole letter presupposes the knowledge of a Hebrew/Aramaic text, by the author and by his readers.

15. C. Bonner (ed.), *The Last Chapters of Enoch in Greek*, London, 1937.

16. He qualifies this by remembering that C.H. Roberts had suggested Zechariah 8:8, Isaiah 1:29f., Psalm 18:14f., Daniel 2:43 and Ecclesiastes 6:3 for 7Q 8, and that G.D. Fee had thought of Numbers 22:38. With such a tiny and unprofitable scrap as 7Q 8, consisting of seven letters, three of them damaged, on just four lines, almost anything can be done. O'Callaghan himself, without giving it any weight, had briefly considered James 1:23–24, as an afterthought to the identifications of 7Q 4 (1 Timothy) and 7Q 5 (Mark), frankly explaining his approach: 'The motivation to see if in any of the smallest papyri of any 7Q any NT text could be identified was exclusively the desire to verify whether any other *possible* fragment of the Greek NT might be found in the same cave. Obviously I never considered it opportune to base my theory on the most insignificant fragments of 7Q' ('The Identifications of 7Q', *Aegyptus* 56 (1976): 287–94, here p. 289).

17. As the first editors noted and described correctly in 1962, followed by O'Callaghan in 1972.

18. Puech, 'Notes sur les fragments grecs du manuscrit'; Puech, 'Sept fragments grecs de la Lettre d'Hénoch'. This was refuted in the same year: C.P. Thiede, *Jésus selon Matthieu. La nouvelle datation du papyrus Magdalen d'Oxford et l'origine des Évangiles. Examen et discussion des dernières objections scientifiques*, Paris, 1996, 102–4.

19. See note 16 above, on José O'Callaghan's own attitude to his reference to the letter of James.

20. Let us remember the archaeological observation that no objects were deposited in the Qumran caves after AD 68, nor after the departure of the Romans in c. AD 115. In fact, if – for whatever inconceivable reason – Christians had gone to the Qumran caves after AD 115, to deposit their writings, it would have been codices, not scrolls – the Christian codex was introduced at the end of the first century at the very latest, probably before AD 66 (see Thiede, *Rekindling the Word* and *Ein Fisch für den römischen Kaiser*, pp. 195–206). But all manuscripts discovered at Qumran are (fragments of) scrolls.

21. Puech, 'Sept fragments grecs de la Lettre d'Hénoch', p. 322.

22. O. Montevecchi, *La Papirologia*, Milan, 2nd enl. ed., 1988.

23. O. Montevecchi, review of A. Passoni dell'Acqua, *Il Testo del Nuevo Testamento*, Torino, 1994, *Aegyptus* 74 (1994): 206–7; cf. Passoni dell'Acqua herself, pp. 33–37.

24. That is, the early Greek writing found on clay tablets of the second millennium BC. H. Koskenniemi, 'Uutta tietoa evankeliumien syntyajoista', *Sanansaattaja* 23 (1996): 4.

25. Mazar concludes: 'The picture which is beginning to emerge is that of an early Church with a strong evangelical commitment and an enterprising spirit during the years immediately following Jesus' life on earth,' quoted in *Jerusalem Christian Review* 10/3 (1999): 6.

26. G. Vermes, *An Introduction to the Complete Dead Sea Scrolls*, London, 4th rev. ed., 1999, p. 9.

27. See also the differentiation expressed in the title of my *The Earliest Gospel Manuscript? The Qumran Fragment 7Q 5 and its Significance for New Testament Studies*.

28. Vermes, *An Introduction to the Complete Dead Sea Scrolls*, p. 172.

29. Thiede, *The Earliest Gospel Manuscript?*; J. O'Callaghan, *Los primeros testimonios del Nuevo Testamento: Papirologia neotestamentaria*, Madrid, 1995, pp. 95–145. (This book contains a probability calculus of all letters and readings suggested for 7Q 5 between 1962 and 1995 and the suggested identifications based on them, by the university mathematician Albert Dou: 'El cálculo de probabilidades y las posibles identificaciones de 7Q 5', pp. 116–39; Dou concludes that the likelihood of 7Q 5 not being Mark 6:52–53 is 1:900,000,000,000); Thiede and d'Ancona, *The Jesus Papyrus*, pp. 49–69; J.M. Vernet, 'Si riafferma il papiro 7Q 5 come Mc 6, 52–53?', *Rivista Biblica* 46 (1998): 44–60.

30. Vernet, 'Si riafferma il papiro 7Q 5 come Mc 6, 52–53?', p. 60.

31. 'Il reste maintenant à identifier sereinement 7Q 5 pour lever toute doute équivoque de la présence de manuscrits évangéliques dans une grotte de Qumrân.' Puech, 'Sept fragments grecs de la Lettre d'Hénoch', p. 322. There is, of course, a history of rival attempts, but since not even the latest opponents of the Markan identification of 7Q 5 take them seriously, this is not the place to discuss them all once more. The last word, methodologically speaking, belongs to the German epistemologist, New Testament scholar and archaeologist, Ferdinand Rohrhirsch, who rejected one such attempt by Victoria Spottorno. Apart from her apparent lack of papyrological expertise and her ensuing errors of judgment, the most obvious shortcomings of her and her predecessors' suggestions are strictly methodological: F. Rohrhirsch, 'Zur Relevanz wissenschaftstheoretischer Implikationen in der Diskussion um das Qumranfragment 7Q 5 und zu einem neuen Identifizierungsvorschlag von 7Q 5 mit Zacharias 7, 4–5', *Theologie und Glaube* 85 (1995): 80–95. The *conditio sine qua non* simply is: 'As soon as a textual suggestion manages with fewer auxiliary hypotheses than the Marcan identification, this new textual suggestion deserves to be preferred' (p. 85). (The auxiliary hypotheses in 7Q 5 = Mark 6:52–53 are the variant spelling from δ to τ, and the non-inclusion of επι την γην (*epi tên gên*).) Rohrhirsch notes that none of the fewer than twenty alternative suggestions meets this basic criterion. Having analysed Spottorno's own suggestion, the last one so far, he concludes that Zechariah 7:4–5 should be ruled out, not least because it poses far more textual and palaeographical problems than Mark 6:52–53, and that the Marcan identification is 'demonstrated as rationally justified' (p. 95). Cf. also F. Rohrhirsch, *Markus in Qumran? Eine Auseinandersetzung mit den Argumenten für und gegen das Fragment 7Q 5 mit Hilfe des methodischen Fallibilismusprinzips*, Wuppertal, 1990; and 'Kleine Fragmente im Lichte des Popperschen Fallibilismusprinzips. Ein Vergleich zwischen 7Q 5 und P73 unter dem Aspekt der recto-verso Beschriftung', in Mayer, *Christen und Christliches in Qumran?*, pp. 73–82. Spottorno herself regards anything and anyone disagreeing with her own position as 'anti-scientific, anti-academic' (V. Spottorno, 'Can Methodological Limits Be Set in the Debate on the Identification of 7Q 5?', *Dead Sea Discoveries* 6, 1 (1999): 66–77, here p. 68), and prefers to ignore Rohrhirsch completely. Instead, her target is an internet interview(!) with José O'Callaghan. Having decided to pursue her approach of inventing impossible letters and text-critical variants, an error which Rohrhirsch had demonstrated to her conclusively, she creates a new system of coordinates for the dating of the papyrus, so she can rule out a date of about AD 50, and underlines her bias by claiming there is no 'objective support' for Mark 6:52–53. It is as though decades of scholarship had passed her by without as much as a whiff of contact. Her major support is a review by J.K. Elliott who exclaims, 'it is universally recognized that they [the Dead Sea Scrolls] tell us absolutely nothing about the origins of the NT gospels!' (p. 71). One likes to think, tongue in cheek, that Elliot must indeed live in a different

universe if he can publish such a palpably wrong statement, ending it even with the flourish of an exclamation mark. Spottorno does not strengthen her position when she repeats her Zechariah hypothesis, which had already been refuted by Rohrhirsch. Finally, impressed by Puech's Enoch attempts in 7Q 4 which, as we saw above, do not make sense, she thinks of Enoch 15:9d–10 for 7Q 5. To achieve this, she has to invent an *omicron*, o, in line 2, after what she thinks is an *iota*, ι, (instead of the proven *nu*, ν), realizes the impossibility herself and substitutes an equally impossible *alpha*, α, for it; she has to insist on a non-existent *pi*, π, instead of the evident *tau*, τ, in line 3, and to turn the final *sigma*, σ, of line 4 into a *theta*, θ. In line 5, the clear rounded trace left of the first letter, read as a *theta* in the Markan identification, suddenly becomes a *kappa*, κ – unfortunately for her, there is no Greek alphabet in which the right-hand part of a K can look like the right-hand part of a *theta* or any other letter with a right-hand curvature. Again she realizes her own mistake and substitutes the correct *theta*. She also reads an *iota*, ι, instead of an *eta*, η (which even the first editors had recognized), at the beginning of line 3. That, of course, is the end of that, but Spottorno herself has to admit that she goes on to reconstruct a Greek text of 'Enoch' with two omissions, the substitution of one word, taken from a different context, for a word which should be there, and by deleting a word which should be there and putting a word not documented in the Greek Apocrypha in its place. Finally, she has to ignore the clear and undisputed gap, the 'spatium'/ 'paragraphus', before the και in line 3. Her 'Enoch' continues uninterrupted, but since everyone who has ever looked at 7Q 5 – proponents and opponents of Mark alike – agrees that there is this gap before the και at the beginning of a new sentence/paragraph, this fact alone rules out her theory. In other words, she creates far more problems than she pretends to have solved, and certainly many more than those posed (but solvable) by the Markan identification. And if one does wonder, once again, why some authors are so desperate to get rid of Mark at Qumran, Spottorno is at least frank. She still believes the Cave 7 fragments are likely to have 'come from the milieu of Qumran' – which is a position commonly abandoned for all Greek scrolls at Qumran since Emanuel Tov's 'Hebrew Biblical Manuscripts from the Judean Desert', here p. 19. On the basis of her false assumption, she then thinks all Greek texts found at Qumran must belong to 'the Septuagint and the Book of Enoch, or related Greek literature'. Needless to say, in her world-view, the term 'related Greek literature' does not include the texts of Greek-writing Jews such as Mark and Paul. Unaware of recent scholarship, she still believes Greek Enoch 'fits in better with the society and cultural milieu of Qumran' (p. 77) and apparently thinks this is an argument against the documents of eschatological, messianic Jews who happened to believe in Jesus of Nazareth as the prophesied Messiah.

32. Under the α in line 2, the η and the ω in line 3, the first ν and the σ in line 4 and the θ, ε and σ in line 5.

33. The fragment 'peut provenir de quelques généalogie', Baillet, Milik and De Vaux, *Les 'Petites Grottes' de Qumrân (DJD III), Textes*, p. 144. The editors add that 'le déchiffrement et les notes sont dues au R.P. Boismard'.

34. H. Hunger, '7Q 5: Markus 6, 52–53 oder?', in Mayer, *Christen und Christliches in Qumran?*, pp. 33–39, with twenty-two photos. The microscopal analysis at the forensic department of the Israel National Police, Jerusalem, was published as an appendix to the same volume; C.P. Thiede, 'Bericht über die kriminaltechnische Untersuchung des Fragments 7Q 5 in Jerusalem', pp. 239–45, with four photos. Amazingly, some opponents of the Markan identification still managed to ignore the unequivocal evidence or to manipulate it by creating wrong super-impositions. The most puzzling recent case is R. Riesner, *Essener und Urgemeinde in Jerusalem: Neue Funde und Quellen*, Giessen/Basel, 2nd. enl. ed., 1998, p. 131. Riesner claims he 'cannot see' a left top beginning of a diagonal stroke on the photo from the Jerusalem analysis. A similar approach was attempted by R.H. Gundry, 'No *Nu* in Line 2 of 7Q 5: A Final Disidentification of 7Q 5 with Mark 6:52–53', in *Journal of Biblical Literature* 117 (1999): 698–707. Ignoring all of Hunger's details, he relies on Stephen Pfenn who – according to Gundry – had looked at 7Q 5 under a microscope in 1995. Pfenn's reliability as a judge of manuscripts was recently called into question, however, when he was the only Qumran scholar to support the spurious 'Angel Scroll' (see below). Against Riesner and Gundry, Hunger's analysis remains intact, corroborated by a microscopal analysis which was witnessed by unbiased forensic specialists at a laboratory of the national police in Jerusalem who could (one would think) not really be accused of being pro-Markan propagandists. Riesner and Gundry defend the old error of the first editors and suggest an *omega*, ω, followed by an *iota adscript*, followed by remnants of an *alpha*, α, which, they claim – against the evidence of the original and the photographs – are not broken off but drawn as the beginning of a new letter. Since there is a complete *alpha* in the following line, it is obvious enough to the trained Greek papyrologist that

there is not even the widest margin of tolerance which could turn the remaining ink into anything resembling a capital *alpha*. Boismard and the first editors of 7Q 5 in 1962 may be excused, since they were not really interested in an identification (or the refusal of one) and simply offered some guesswork. But today, with infrared photographs, electronic microscope print-outs and first-rate enlargements at our disposal (and, needless to say, the opportunity of checking them against the original, which the author of this book did on several occasions), to insist on an *alpha* suggests hidden agendas. We should have left this stage behind us. Riesner places his curious aside in a book which otherwise is full of valuable information on the Essenes and the first Christians in Jerusalem; it is by far the most useful book on this subject. There is no such saving grace in the case of another recent article, written by a theology student about to conclude his diploma dissertation: S. Enste, 'Qumran-Fragment 7Q 5 ist nicht Markus 6, 52–53', *Zeitschrift für Papyrologie und Epigraphik (ZPE)* 126 (1999): 189–93. In order to achieve his rejection of an N, and his preference for I + A, he has to resort to a wide range of operations on the photographic evidence, in one case even inventing measurements and manipulating the known scientific descriptions of the technical procedure applied in an electronic microscopal analysis. The errors and distortions of this paper will, of course, be corrected in a forthcoming issue of *ZPE*. Papyrology apart, the opponents of the Markan identification may still be unaware of the paradigm shift in Judeo-Christian studies which has made the theological offensive against a papyrus of Mark at Qumran quite unnecessary; but they cannot be excused for ever. A correct reconstruction of the N in line 2 is available on plate 8 in Thiede and d'Ancona, *The Jesus Papyrus*.

35. Colour photographs of both stones in A. Millard, *Discoveries from the Time of Jesus*, Oxford, 1990, p. 83.

36. This hard fact has proved so embarrassing to opponents of the Markan identification of 7Q 5 that they called its existence and discovery 'an accident' – a new category of 'scholarly' criteria which would put an end to some ninety per cent of all archaeological excavations (H.-U. Rosenbaum, 'Cave 7Q! Gegen die erneute Inanspruchnahme des Qumran-Fragments 7Q 5 als Bruchstück der Ältesten Evangelien-Handschrift', *Biblische Zeitschrift* 31 (1987): 189–205, here p. 200); or even went to the extremes of denying its existence (Enste, 'Qumran-Fragment 7Q 5 ist nicht Markus 6, 52–53', here p. 189). For a circumspect analysis of the inscription, see P. Segal, 'The Penalty of the Warning Inscription from the Temple of

Jerusalem', *Israel Exploration Journal* 39 (1989): 79–84.

37. Liddell and Scott, *Greek–English Lexicon*, p. 451.

38. F.T. Gignac, *Grammar of the Greek Papyri of the Roman and Byzantine Periods, I, Phonology*, Milan, 1976, pp. 80–83. The text dated AD 42 has τικης (*tikês*) for δικης (*dikês*). Numerous biblical papyri have the δ to τ shift, among them the P66, the oldest papyrus of John's Gospel, and the two oldest papyri of Luke's Gospel, P4 and P75. Cf. J. O'Callaghan, 'El cambio δ > τ en los papiros biblicos', *Biblica* 54 (1973): 415–16.

39. To my knowledge, the first scholar who noted that the words επι την γην (*epi tên gên*) are not omitted in 7Q 5, but are a later scribe's or editor's erroneous insertion copied by the post-AD 70 textual tradition, was the Qumran specialist James Charlesworth, Princeton University (letter to the author, 21 October 1991). Elsewhere in the same gospel, in Mark 5:21, the second oldest papyrus (after 7Q 5), P45, does not have *eis to perán*, 'to the other side' in a sentence beginning *kai diaperásantos*. Even one of the most committed opponents of the Markan identification, M.-É. Boismard, admitted recently and reluctantly, but twice, that 'one may suppose the existence of a short text which omits the words *epi tên gên*, and 'that it is of course not impossible that the original text of Mark 6:53 did not include the words *epi tên gên*' (M.-É. Boismard, 'À propos de 7Q 5 et Mc 6, 52–53', *Revue Biblique* 102 (1995): 585–88, here p. 587). For a reply to Boismard and the essays by Puech and Grelot published in the same volume, see C.P. Thiede, '7Q 5 et P64. Les deux papyrus les plus anciens des Évangiles. Une réponse à la critique', in Thiede, *Jésus selon Matthieu*, pp. 101–18.

40. See C.P. Thiede, 'On the Development of Scroll and Codex in the Early Church', in *Rekindling the Word*, pp. 84–92; Thiede and d'Ancona, *The Jesus Papyrus*, pp. 66–70.

41. See e.g. in the 80s of the first century, the successful PR efforts of the Roman poet Martial. Cf. Thiede and d'Ancona, *The Jesus Papyrus*, pp. 122–25; C.P. Thiede, *Jesus – Life or Legend?*, Oxford, 2nd enl. ed., 1997, pp. 67–84.

42. See, among others, R.L. Rubinstein, *My Brother Paul*, New York, 1972, p. 115; M. Hengel, 'Das früheste Christentum als eine jüdische messianische und universalistische Bewegung', *Theologische Beiträge* 28 (1997): 197–210, here pp. 201–3.

Chapter VIII

1. M. Kalman, 'Scroll names Jesus as sect member. Fact or fake? A mystery scroll is found by a Bedouin tribesman in the late 1960s and

taken to a dealer in Amman, sparking an international scramble by academics', *The Times*, 7 November 1999, p. 25.

2. N.C. Gross, 'The Mystery of the Angel Scroll. Find of the Century or Elaborate Hoax?', *The Jerusalem Report*, 11 October 1999, pp. 40–44.

3. Its place at the end of the New Testament is not chronological; according to Klaus Berger of Heidelberg University and other scholars, Revelation was written in AD 69 at the latest. (See K. Berger, *Theologiegeschichte des Urchristentums*, Tübingen/Basel, 1994, pp. 569–71; cf. also, among others, J. Sweet, *Revelation*, London, 1979, pp. 21–27; Robinson, *Redating the New Testament*, pp. 221–53.

4. Midrash r. Par. 81 on Genesis 35:1. This plays on the Hebrew word for truth, *Emet*, describing God, which begins with an *aleph* and ends with a *tau*. For details on the (independent) use of *alpha* and *omega* in the Greek magical papyri, etc., see D. Aune, *Revelation*, Dallas, 1997, p. 57.

5. For a detailed portrayal of such concepts in antiquity, see C.P. Thiede, 'A Pagan Reader of 2 Peter: Cosmic Conflagration in 2 Peter 3 and the Octavius of Minucius Felix', *Journal for the Study of the New Testament* 26 (1986): 79–96.

6. Recent research into the social structure of Galilee at the time of the disciples has shown that people like Simon Peter, his brother Andrew and the two brothers John and James with their father Zebedee were multilingual entrepreneurs. Like all male Jews at the time, they had access to an education in Hebrew scripture, reading, writing and an advanced techique of learning by heart. A mastery of the Bible, and of Hebrew, Aramaic and Greek were not exceptional, but normal. When members of the Sanhedrin regard Peter and the others as 'unschooled, ordinary men' (Acts 4:13), this merely means they had not received the 'college' education of the Sadducees and Pharisees and were therefore not seen as qualified interpreters of the Bible.

7. This is not the place to discuss the authorship and date of 2 Peter. Suffice it to say there are valid reasons to accept, with S. Bénétreau, Ch. Bigg, M. Green, D. Guthrie, P.H.R. van Houwelingen, S.J. Kistenmaker and others, that the arguments in favour of Petrine authorship (and thus for a date before his death in c. AD 67) outweigh those traditionally put forward in favour of pseudonymous origins at the end of the first or even towards the middle of the second century.

8. One realizes that it is a particularly weak argument against Petrine authorship and a pre-AD 67 date of this letter to pretend that such teaching

about a delayed 'parousia' betrays the second or third generation of Christians. On the contrary, the first 'fathers' in the faith (2 Peter 3:4) had died as martyrs in AD 35 (Stephen), AD 41 (James the son of Zebedee) and in AD 62 (James, the brother of the Lord), and Christ had not returned. High time to remind people of Psalm 90 and its corollaries. At the end of the first century, let alone in the mid-second century, such admonition would have come pointlessly late.

9. R. Bauckham, in his commentary *Jude, 2 Peter*, Waco, 1983, pp. 306–9, tries to argue that 2 Peter could have borrowed the thought from a Jewish apocalypse, but he fails to convince: all the examples of rabbinic and other Jewish writings which he manages to provide are indirect and later than 2 Peter (as Bauckham himself has to acknowledge); and this remains the case even if the letter were not written in Peter's lifetime.

10. J. Finegan, *The Archaeology of the New Testament: The Life of Jesus and the Beginning of the Early Church*, Princeton, rev ed., 1992, p. 16, with a photo of the Byzantine church on p. 17.

11. Cf. Josephus, *War* 2, 128; 140–150. Essene self-immersion is prefigured in 2 Kings 5:10–14.

12. E.g. W. Nauck, *Die Tradition und der Charakter des ersten Johannesbriefes*, Tübingen, 1957, pp. 167–73; A.T. Lincoln, *Ephesians*, Dallas, 1990, p. 327; R. Riesner, 'Das Jerusalemer Essener-Viertel und die Urgemeinde', *Aufstieg und Niedergang der Römischen Welt (ANRW)*, Teil II: Principat, Band 26, 2, Berlin/New York, 1995, pp. 1775–922, here p. 1882.

13. The inner circle of the 'three' (Peter, John and James) is no counter-argument. Several times, a fourth disciple is added to their number (Andrew); Peter was not of priestly descent (John and James may have been, according to some scholars), which is, however, a prerequisite for the Essene 'three'; and finally, the inner circle of three (or four) disciples came from within the group of twelve, whereas the three Essene priests are added to the twelve councillors.

14. Cf. Hebrews 9:15–28!

15. It is difficult to see why these statements should not be authentic. They do not conflict with the general mood of messianic expectancy at the time, and the messianic self-description of Jesus is a prerequisite, if seen within its historical context. The action taken against Jesus by some leading members of the Sanhedrin, and Pilate's execution order with the (mocking?) indictment 'King of the Jews' depend on the outspoken, but refuted messianic terminology used by Jesus and his entourage.

16. And it is a passage like this which militates against all attempts at treating 2 Peter as a non-Petrine, pseudonymous or 'pseudepigraphic' concoction of post-apostolic times.

17. Cf. the Temple Scroll (11Q 19–21) and the *pesher* Nahum 4Q pNah I, 6–8, in Y. Yadin's interpretation: Y. Yadin, *The Temple Scroll: The Hidden Law of the Dead Sea Sect*, London, 1985. See also M. Hengel, *Crucifixion in the Ancient World and the Folly of the Message of the Cross*, London, 1977. For the image of the 'tree' and the cross, see Galatians 3:1–14, with the conclusion in verses 13–14: 'Christ redeemed us from the curse of the law by becoming a curse for us – for it is written, "Cursed is everyone who hangs on a tree" – in order that in Christ Jesus the blessing of Abraham might come to the Gentiles, so that we might receive the promise of the Spirit through faith.' Cf. T. Elgvin, 'The Messiah who was Cursed on the Tree', *Themelios* 22/3 (1997): 14–21. Cf. also J. Tabory, 'The Crucifixion of the Paschal Lamb', *The Jewish Quarterly Review* 86 (1996): 395–406.

18. 'Crucifixion Before Christ', *Time*, 6 February 1956.

19. When the matter reached Europe, five Qumran scholars, R. de Vaux, J.T. Milik, P. Skehan, J. Starcky and J. Strugnell wrote a 'Letter concerning certain broadcast statements by Mr John Allegro', which was published in *The Times*, 16 March 1956, p. 11.

20. Subsection 'A Key to the Caves', above.

21. Translation from the Aramaic after Vermes, *The Complete Dead Sea Scrolls in English*, p. 577; and M. Wise, M. Abegg, Jr, and E. Cook, *The Dead Sea Scrolls: A New Translation*, London, 1996, pp. 269–70. It adequately renders an original text which presents a negative image of the 'Son of God' character. There are, however, attempts to interpret him positively; see recently J.J. Collins, *The Scepter and the Star: The Messiahs and the Dead Sea Scrolls and Other Ancient Literature*, New York, 1995; J.D.G. Dunn, '"Son of God" as "Son of Man" in the Dead Sea Scrolls? A Response to John Collins on 4Q 246', in S.E. Porter and C.A. Evans (eds), *The Scrolls and the Scriptures: Qumran Fifty Years After*, Sheffield, 1997, pp. 198–210.

22. Cf. the lucid exegesis by O. Betz, 'Kontakte zwischen Christen und Essenern', in Mayer, *Christen und Christliches in Qumran?*, pp. 157–75, here pp. 172–73.

23. A. Sussman and R. Peled (eds), *Scrolls from the Dead Sea*, Washington, 1993; latest edition, in German, *Qumran: Die Schriftrollen vom Toten Meer*, St Gallen, 1999, pp. 80–83; all editions mention only two publications: J. Tabor, 'A Pierced or

Piercing Messiah? The Verdict Is Still Out', *Biblical Archaeology Review* 18 (1992): 58–59; G. Vermes, 'The Oxford Forum for Qumran Research: Seminar on the Rule of War from Cave 4 (4Q 285)', *Journal of Jewish Studies* 43 (1992): 85–90.

24. 'Precisely because the cross of Christ, God's anointed, stands at the centre of the gospel, such a Qumran text could destroy the character and divine power of the "word of the cross".' Betz and Riesner, *Jesus, Qumran and the Vatican: Clarifications*, p. 84.

25. Pixner, *Wege des Messias und Stätten der Urkirche*, pp. 333–34, 367–69, 386–87, with references to publications by H. Braun, G.W. Buchanan, Y. Yadin. Pixner and these authors suggest the letter to the Hebrews was addressed to such converted Essene priests.

26. See also Josephus, *Antiquities* 18, 16; *War* 2, 165.

27. For the imprisonment and execution of the Baptist on Machaerus, see *Antiquities* 18, 116–119.

28. *Against All Heresies* 9, 27.

29. The link is even more obvious in the Greek (Septuagint) version of this psalm. A similar case, in our context, is 2 Samuel 7:11–14. Nathan receives a prophecy for David from God. The Hebrew text says, 'When your days are fulfilled and you lie down with your ancestors, I will raise up your offspring [or "seed"] after you... your son... and I shall make his royal throne secure for ever.' It is not immediately obvious, and no contemporary reader of the Hebrew text would have seen it automatically, that 'raise up' implies a bodily resurrection. But the pre-Christian Greek text of the Septuagint, known to many Jews and indeed to the first Christians themselves, makes that point quite unequivocally: the Greek word used here, *anestêsô*, is the word employed for the act of resurrection. The translators had paved the way for a resurrection faith which involved God's own son, in the line of David, raised by God as his seed. Psalms 2 and 89 resume this theme, and the Qumran fragment 4Q 174 – a florilegium of scripture quotations on the last days – combines them as messianic prophecies.

30. Individual rabbis were later associated with resurrection miracles: Rabbi Chanina resurrects his own wife at home (Ketubboth 62b); Rabbi Jochanan raises Raw Kahana from the tomb (Bawa kamma 117a/b).

31. G.D. Fee, *The First Epistle to the Corinthians*, Grand Rapids, 1987, p. 724.

32. J.E. Zias, 'Qumran, the Essene Cemeteries and the Question of Celibacy – An Anthropological Re-evaluation', Abstract in K. McMichael, K.L.

Collins and S.H. Jackson (comp.), *Abstracts of the Annual Meeting of the American Academy of Religion (AAR) and the Society of Biblical Literature (SBL)*, Boston, 1999, p. 271. The author of this book is grateful to Joseph Zias for additional information received in Jerusalem, 7 December 1999. Zias' full paper will be published in 2000.

33. See B. Capper, 'The Palestinian Cultural Context of Earliest Christian Community of Goods', in R. Bauckham (ed.), *The Book of Acts in its First-Century Setting: Vol. 4, Palestinian Setting*, Grand Rapids/Carlisle, 1995, pp. 323–56, here pp. 338–39.

34. Josephus, *War* 2, 143.

35. And see, for the archaeological and historical evidence in the context of immediate contacts in Jerusalem, the excellent summary by Capper, 'The Palestinian Cultural Context of Earliest Christian Community of Goods', pp. 341–50; and Capper, 'In der Hand des Ananias. Erwägungen zu 1QS VI, 20 und der urchristlichen Gütergemeinschaft', *Revue de Qumran* 12 (1986): 223–36; Pixner, 'Archaeologische Betrachtungen zum Jerusalemer Essener-Viertel und zur Urgemeinde', in Mayer, *Christen und Christliches in Qumran?*, pp. 89–113, with eight plates; Riesner, 'Das Jerusalemer Essenerviertel und die Urgemeinde', pp. 1775–922.

36. See pp. 217–18.

37. For a recent survey of comparative studies, see F. Garcia Martinez and J. Trebolle Barrera, *The People of the Dead Sea Scrolls*, Leiden, 1995, pp. 191–232.

38. See, above all, the Damascus Document CD 13:7–12. Soon after the publication of the Damascus Document from the Cairo *genizah*, J. Jeremias was the first scholar to realize the close links between the *mebaqqer* and the early Christian overseer or 'bishop': J. Jeremias, *Jerusalem zur Zeit Jesu, II*, Göttingen, 1929, p. 133.

39. Hengel, 'Jakobus der Herrenbruder der erste "Papst"?', pp. 72–104. Cf. also R.A. Campbell, *The Elders: Seniority Within Earliest Christianity*, Edinburgh, 1994; C. Marcheselli-Casale, 'Tracce del mebaqqer nell'episkopos del Nuovo Testamento?', in R. Penna (ed.), *Qumran e le origini cristiane*, Bologna, 1997, pp. 177–210.

40. Cf. J. Dupont, '"Je rebâtirai la cabane de David qui est tombée" (Cac 15.16 = Am 9.11)', in Grässer and O. Merk, *Glaube und Eschatologie*, pp. 19–32.

41. For a balanced assessment of James' action, see F.F. Bruce, *The Epistle to the Galatians: A Commentary on the Greek Text*, Exeter, 1982, pp. 130–33; cf. C.P. Thiede, *Simon Peter: From Galilee to Rome*, Exeter, 1986, Grand Rapids, 2nd rev. ed.,

1988, pp. 165–67, 250. It seems obvious enough that Peter did not 'betray' the Gentiles when he discontinued the meals he shared with them; he, as much as Barnabas, would have explained to them that an apostle could not eat with only one group in the wider community, and that it was the Jews, not the Gentiles, who had been neglected.

42. *Against Marcion* 1, 20.

43. See, among others, D.J. Moo, *The Letter of James*, Leicester/Grand Rapids, 1985; L.T. Johnson, *The Letter of James*, New York, 1995; T.C. Penner, *The Epistle of James and Eschatology*, Sheffield, 1996.

44. Penner, *The Epistle of James and Eschatology*, has shown the closeness of James 3 and Part 4 of the Comunity Scroll. The style and approach of James are independent, but the way he takes up the same themes is noticeable and cannot be wholly accidental. This is not the book to discuss Robert Eisenman's creative rewriting of the earliest sources about James, who, in his latest monograph on the subject (*James the Brother of Jesus: Recovering the True History of Early Christianity*, London, 1997) is presented as a hero of all Jews (bar the pro-Roman faction who helped to kill Jesus and later killed his brother James), and as a justified enemy of evil Paul. Eisenman accumulates a stupendous amount of impossible theories (e.g. the famous Letter of the Teacher of Righteousness, 4Q MMT, which in reality is second century BC, is a 'Jamesian' letter written to an ostensibly Judaized 'Arab' monarch in Northern Syria (p. 296), or perhaps rather 'the actual letter sent down' at the end of the 'Jerusalem Council', Acts 15:23–29 (p. 520)). Eisenman, himself a Jew, is driven by a love for what he calls 'Jamesian Christianity', uniting Judaism, Christianity, and even Islam, against the errors of the Pauline church (conversation in Rome, 14 December 1999).

45. Cf. C. Spicq, 'L'Épître aux Hébreux: Apollos, Jean-Baptiste, les Hellénistes et Qumrân', *Revue de Qumran* 1 (1958/59): 365–90; J. Maier and K. Schubert, *Die Qumran-Essener*, München/Basel, 1982, p. 130; R. Riesner, 'Jesus, the Primitive Community and the Essene Quarter of Jerusalem', in J. Charlesworth (ed.), *Jesus and the Dead Sea Scrolls*, New York, 1992, pp. 198–234; Pixner, *Wege des Messias und Stätten der Urkirche*, pp. 333–34; Thiede, *Ein Fisch für den römischen Kaiser*, pp. 169–71.

46. For an analysis of this and other pieces of circumstantial evidence, see S.E. Johnson, 'The Dead Sea Manual of Discipline and the Jerusalem Church of Acts', *Zeitschrift für alttestamentliche Wissenschaft* 66 (1954): 106–20; see also H. Braun, *Qumran und das Neue Testament*

I, Tübingen, 1966, p. 153 (bibliography); Pixner, *Wege des Messias und Stätten der Urkirche*, pp. 219–22.

47. See A. Roitman, with a contribution by M. Albani, U. Glessmer and G. Grasshoff, 'From Dawn to Dusk Among the Qumran Sectarians', in Roitman, *A Day at Qumran*, pp. 19–59, here pp. 19–22.

48. A possibility first suggested by A. Jaubert, 'Le calendrier des Jubilées et la Secte de Qumrân', *Vetus Testamentum* 3 (1953): 250–64, and E. Ruckstuhl, *Jesus im Horizont der Evangelien*, Stuttgart, 1988, pp. 101–84; cf. a recent survey of the debate for and against this theory in Riesner, 'Das Jerusalemer Essener-Viertel und die Urgemeinde', pp. 1775–922, here pp. 1886–87.

49. See C.-H. Hunzinger, 'Neues Licht auf Lc 2:14 *anthropoi eudokias*', *Zeitschrift für die neutestamentliche Wissenschaft* 44 (1952/53): 85–90; J.A. Fitzmyer, 'Peace Upon Earth Among Men of His Good Will (Luke 2:14)', in Fitzmyer, *Essays on the Semitic Background of the New Testament*, London, 1971, pp. 101–4.

Epilogue

1. See e.g. G.H. Bearman and S.I. Spiro, 'Archaeological Applications of Advanced Imaging Techniques', *Biblical Archaeologist* 59 (1996): 56–66.

2. M. Morgenstern, E. Quimron and D. Sinan, 'The Hitherto Unpublished Columns of the Genesis Apocryphon', *Abr-Nahrain* 33 (1995): 30–52.

3. Cf. C.P. Thiede and G. Masuch, 'Confocal Laser Scanning and the Dead Sea Scrolls', in G. Marquis et al. (eds), *The Dead Sea Scrolls Fifty Years After Their Discovery*, Jerusalem, 2000, with seven plates (in print). Our work at the IAA has been facilitated thanks to the patient cooperation of the Head of Artifacts Conservation and Reconstruction, Pnina Shor, and her colleagues.

4. P. Palau inv. 163.

5. P. Masada 721 a, inv. no. 1039–210. See, for both cases, C.P. Thiede and G. Masuch, 'Neue mikroskopische Verfahren zum Lesen und zur Schadensbestimmung von Papyrushandschriften', in B. Kramer et al. (eds), *Akten des 21: Internationalen Papyrologenkongresses 1995*, vol. 2, Stuttgart/Leipzig, 1997, pp. 1102–12, with six colour plates.

6. See J. Magnin, 'Notes sur l'Ébionisme [V]', *Proche-Orient chrétien* 28 (1978): 220–48; R. Riesner, 'Einleitung', in A. Schlatter, *Die Geschichte der ersten Christenheit*, Stuttgart, 6th ed., 1983, VI (with bibliography).

7. See, for example, W. Rordorf's suggestion that the incompatibility of the Roman military oath of allegiance with the divine sacrament of baptism, as stated by Tertullian (*De idololatria* 19, 2 – Tertullian here coins the phrase, 'Non potest una anima duobus deberi, Deo et Caesari,' 'One soul cannot serve two lords, God and Caesar'; cf. Matthew 6:24; 22:21; Luke 16:13) – may have an Essene background: W. Rordorf, 'Tertullians Beurteilung des Soldatenstandes', *Vigiliae Christianae* 23 (1969): 105–41, here pp. 134–36.

Index

References to sites, names and quotations in the Notes are not included.